T0301308

Regulating Transport in Europe

Regulating Transport in Europe

Edited by

Matthias Finger

College of Management of Technology, ÉPFL – École Polytechnique Fédérale de Lausanne, Switzerland

Torben Holvad

Transport Studies Unit, University of Oxford, UK

Edward Elgar
Cheltenham, UK • Northampton, MA, USA

Published by
Edward Elgar Publishing Limited
The Lypiatts
15 Lansdown Road
Cheltenham
Glos GL50 2JA
UK

Edward Elgar Publishing, Inc.
William Pratt House
9 Dewey Court
Northampton
Massachusetts 01060
USA

A catalogue record for this book
is available from the British Library

Library of Congress Control Number: 2013932956

This book is available electronically in the ElgarOnline.com Economics Subject Collection, E-ISBN 978 1 78100 483 8

ISBN 978 1 78100 482 1

Typeset by Servis Filmsetting Ltd, Stockport, Cheshire
Printed and bound in Great Britain by T.J. International Ltd, Padstow

Contents

Contributors

Monika Bak is Habilitatus Doctor in Economics and Associate Professor at the University of Gdansk, Poland. She specializes in the area of economic transformation in Central and Eastern Europe. She also has expertise in transport systems integration and assessment of policy measures towards transport sustainability. She has been involved in European Union (EU) funded projects (4th to 7th Framework Programmes) and projects for the European Commission, and was a research advisor to the High Level Group on Road Freight Transport (established by the European Commission, DG MOVE) in 2011–12. She is an independent expert on European research and innovation.

Jan Burnewicz is Professor of Economics and head of the Chair of Comparative Research of Transport Systems at the University of Gdansk, Poland. His most important books are: *Innovative Perspective of Transport and Logistics*, *Costs and Charges in Transport*, *EU Road Transport Sector* and *Analytical Transport Economics*. He has been involved in EU funded projects, the 4th to 7th Framework Programmes (e.g. SCENES, SPECTRUM, GRACE, INTERCONNECT) and projects for the European Commission (e.g. ASSESS, IMPACT, TREMOVE). He is a consultant for the Polish Ministry of Transport and the Ministry of Regional Development.

Javier Campos is Associate Professor of Industrial Organization at the University of Las Palmas, Spain. He studied at the London School of Economics and the Bank of Spain. He has worked for the World Bank, where he gained field experience on transport regulatory policies. His current research areas include the empirical and theoretical analysis of competition and regulation in infrastructure sectors, in which he has published several books and papers.

Matthias Finger holds a PhD in Political Science and a PhD in Adult Education from the University of Geneva, Switzerland. He has been an Assistant Professor at Syracuse University, New York, USA, an Associate Professor at Columbia University, New York, USA, and a Full Professor of Management of Public Enterprises at the Swiss Federal Institute of Public Administration. Since 2002, he has held the Chair of Management of Network Industries at the École Polytechnique Fédérale de Lausanne

(ÉPFL), Switzerland. Since 2010 he has also been a part-time Professor at the European University Institute in Florence, Italy, where he directs the Florence School of Regulation's Transport Area. His main research interest is on the liberalization, re-regulation, and governance of infrastructures in the transport, energy, and communications sectors. He is the co-editor-in-chief of the journal *Competition and Regulation in Network Industries.*

Torben Holvad is Economic Adviser at the European Railway Agency, France; senior research associate at the Transport Studies Unit, University of Oxford, UK; a research associate at the École Polytechnique Fédérale de Lausanne (ÉPFL), Switzerland; and External Associate Professor at the Department of Transport, Danish Technical University, Denmark. He obtained his Economics degrees from Copenhagen University, Denmark (MSc) and the European University Institute in Florence, Italy (MA and PhD).

Rosário Macário is Professor of Transportation at the Department of Civil Engineering, Architecture and Georresources at Instituto Superior Técnico (IST) Lisbon Technical University, Portugal. As a partner and board member at TIS.PT (Consultores em Transportes, Inovação e Sistemas s.a) she has much experience in the coordination of international research and also in conducting national studies with a specific focus on transport policy and planning and exploitation of transport systems. Rosário Macário is Vice-President of the Scientific Council of WCTRS, the World Conference on Transportation Research Society, and co-founder of PANAMSTR, the Panamerican Society for Research in Transportation.

Chris Nash is Research Professor at the Institute for Transport Studies (ITS), University of Leeds, UK, where he specializes in research on rail policy and transport infrastructure charges. Recent work includes contributing to the EVES-rail project on vertical separation in railways for the CER (Community of European Railway and Infrastructure Companies). He has acted as advisor to many bodies, including the European Commission High Level Group on Transport Infrastructure Charging, the European Union Committee of the House of Lords, the Transport Committee of the House of Commons and the Railways Group of the European Conference of Ministers of Transport (ECMT).

Adolf K.Y. Ng is an Associate Professor in the Department of Supply Chain Management, I.H. Asper School of Business, University of Manitoba, Canada. He obtained his DPhil from the University of Oxford, UK. Core research interests include transport geography and regional development; port governance and management; maritime security; climate change and adaptation planning in transport infrastructure. He has more than 100 publications in leading journals, books, conference proceedings and professional publications. He is frequently invited by intergovernmental organizations to offer expert advice in port and transport development, such as the United Nations Conference on Trade and Development (UNCTAD), the United Nations Economic Commission for Europe (UNECE) and the European Commission (EC). Currently, he is also a Council Member of the International Association of Maritime Economists.

Tilman Erich Platz works for MARLO Consultants, a consultancy specialized in transport and logistics. He received his Diploma in Business Administration from the University of Mannheim, Germany, and his PhD from the Radboud University Nijmegen, the Netherlands. He worked for the German research association for intermodal transport SGKV, and was Director of Studies at the University of Cooperative Education in Bad Hersfeld, Germany.

Kees Ruijgrok is Professor in Transport and Logistics Management at the Tilburg Institute of Advanced Studies (TIAS) of Tilburg University, the Netherlands. Between 1986 and 2008 he headed TNO (Dutch Organization for Applied Scientific Research) research groups performing logistics research, and he has held other strategic positions at TNO during his career. He now acts as a strategic advisor, associated to TNO.

Sergi Saurí is Assistant Professor of Transportation at Universitat Politècnica de Catalunya (UPC) BarcelonaTech, Spain and Project Manager at the Centre for Innovation in Transportation (CENIT) at UPC. His research centres on maritime transportation and transport economy. He received his PhD and Bachelor's degree in Civil Engineering from UPC and his Bachelor's degree in Economics from the University of Barcelona, Spain. He is the author of several publications.

Mateu Turró holds the Chair of Transport and Spatial Development at the Universitat Politècnica de Catalunya (UPC) in Barcelona, Spain. He is Honorary Director of the European Investment Bank, where he worked between 1988 and 2009. He has authored numerous publications, including *Going Trans-European: Planning and Financing Transport Networks for Europe* (Pergamon, Elsevier, 1999) and *RAILPAG, Rail Project Evaluation Guidelines* (EIB, European Commission, 2005).

Didier van de Velde is researcher in public transport institutions at the Faculty of Technology, Policy and Management of Delft University of

Technology, the Netherlands. He is also director of inno-V consultancy, Amsterdam, the Netherlands, advising authorities at local, national and international level. He is an expert on institutional reforms in the public passenger transport and railway sector.

Walter Vassallo is an economist with expertise in European policy. He has experience in developing and managing projects in the area of transport, environment, innovation and smart city related issues. He has been involved in some 30 EU-funded projects. He mentors entrepreneurs and public authorities in policy and strategy development, acquiring new private and public business as well as increasing their visibility and portfolio on the EU scene. He is the author of several publications, a frequent speaker at international conferences and a member of the WG Smart City University Bocconi, Italy.

Preface

This book is about transport regulation and regulatory policy, covering the different transport modes, and focuses mainly on Europe. It gathers together state-of-the-art description and analysis, written by the respective experts of the different transport modes.

We believe that regulation and regulatory policy, not only in transport but in all infrastructure, though often dominated by lawyers and economists, requires a truly transdisciplinary approach, including engineering and political science. It also requires a deep understanding of both theory and practice. This book thus reflects our commitment to such a comprehensive and relevant treatment of a crucial issue of our times: transport, in Europe and beyond.

This book is the first such output of the Florence School of Regulation, Transport Area. The Transport Area, launched in 2010, is the latest addition to the Florence School of Regulation, complementing the Energy Area (launched 2004) and the Telecommunications and Media Area (launched 2009). Even though regulation and regulatory policy is often seen as being in conflict with the regulated firms, the Florence School operates with the assumption that both only reflect the two faces of the same coin: neither without firms, nor without regulation, will there be functioning transport markets, both in Europe and elsewhere. This book perfectly illustrates our philosophy and comprehensive approach to the problems at hand.

Matthias Finger and Torben Holvad

1. Setting the scene: background and overview of regulatory reform in the transport sector

Matthias Finger and Torben Holvad

1.1 BACKGROUND

This book concerns the regulation of transport within a European context, covering air, rail, road passenger and freight, urban public transport, inland waterways, short sea shipping and intermodal transport. All these sectors have experienced substantial changes over the last three decades and this book aims to present the main such changes and their impacts. Over this period, and since the publication of the first European Commission (EC) Transport White Paper in 1992 (European Commission, 1992), important reforms of the transport sectors have been introduced in individual member states and supported by various EC initiatives, including implementation of several Directives and a number of Green and White Papers, most recently in 2011 (European Commission, 2011). Even though this has not been an objective of the Commission, there have been changes in ownership structures moving away from significant state intervention towards more autonomous entities and even private sector involvement for both transport infrastructure and operations. Some progress has also been achieved in terms of competition for transport operations, facilitated amongst others through third-party access rights to the markets. As for infrastructure, the situation with respect to competition has remained more stable with either monopolies or competition for the market (tendering), where relevant taking into account the inherent natural monopoly characteristics for infrastructure provision. It should be mentioned that all sectors and all countries in the European Union (EU) have experienced liberalization,[1] although its degree varies among sectors and countries. This difference is partly caused by different starting points, with some sectors or countries already characterized by relative high levels of liberalisation, while others were only taking the very first steps.

In this book the regulatory evolution of the transport sector over the past

three decades will be analysed in order to highlight not only the main regulatory changes but also the processes leading to those changes, as well as
their implications. Its specific focus is on the performance-related effects,
where 'performance' should be understood broadly as covering a range of
dimensions including economic, social, environmental, operational and
technical (Finger et al., 2011). The book will also provide timely policy
recommendations, including possible European future policy initiatives.

Each of the following chapters is dedicated to a specific sector within
European transportation in order to provide a detailed account of its main
changes. This introductory chapter serves to define the broader context of
the policy and regulatory changes that have taken place in Europe over
the past three decades. We will start out with a more theoretical discussion about regulation in the transport sector, its rationales and the various
forms it has taken over time (section 1.2). We will then provide information on the transport sector in Europe as a backdrop to understanding its
evolution (section 1.3). In a third step, we will present an overview of the
main policy and regulatory policy reforms in the broad European transport sector, covering all the transport modes (section 1.4). Finally, we will
try to derive the main implications of these initiatives for European transport in general, and the different transport modes in particular (section
1.5). A look into the future will conclude this introductory chapter (section
1.6).

1.2 UNDERSTANDING OF REGULATION AND ITS SIGNIFICANCE FOR TRANSPORT

In this section, we will briefly discuss the importance and exact functions
of regulation in the various transportation sectors. We will first define
the concepts of 'regulation' and 'regulatory policy', discuss regulatory
practice and then examine how these concepts play out in the different
transportation sectors.

1.2.1 What is 'Regulation' and 'Regulatory Policy'?

The concept of 'regulation' is used differently in different political and
administrative environments. While in the United States the term 'regulation' is basically used for any government intervention, the use of the
concept in the European context is much more restrictive. Here the
concept of regulation pertains to a particular form of state intervention,
namely the intervention by means of independent (national) regulatory
authorities, that is, bodies that have been especially created in the context

of the liberalization of the network industries since the 1980s. Indeed, liberalization – and subsequent market creation – in the network industries is by definition imperfect, owing to the fact that in these industries some monopolies or monopolistic bottlenecks remain. To create and sustain competition in this context requires particular agencies, so-called independent sector-specific regulators. These bodies are independent from the firms they regulate, as well as from the political authorities once they have been created. Their main role is to create and sustain markets, to avoid market dominance and abuse, and to make sure that political intervention into the sector – for example by way of subsidies (state aid) for public service obligations – does not distort the market. As such, independent regulatory authorities are new entities that have no precedent in the traditional politico-administrative system, and most closely resemble judicial bodies. Such regulators can today be found in most network industries – in the energy, communications and transportation sectors – where markets are by definition imperfect. This is especially the case in the industrialized countries, most notably in Europe.

Consequently, 'regulatory policy' is a form of institutional policy (as opposed to a substantive policy), whose aim it is to define the regulation and corresponding regulatory institutions (i.e., the rules) of the various network industry sectors. Regulatory policies, at least in the European context, take the form of various Directives that define the de- and the re-regulation of the different sectors, such as electricity, gas, telecommunications, postal services, air transport and rail transport. Generally, as part of such regulatory policies and as a step within this process, independent regulatory authorities (see above) are being set up. The remits and the powers of these regulatory authorities are again the subject of such regulatory policies.

In other words, in the European context regulation, regulatory policies and regulatory authorities are very precisely defined. They are thus different from general policies and forms of government intervention by way of command and control activities of the administration. In this book, we will be using the terms 'regulation' and 'regulatory policies' in this more restrictive and more technical sense, and we will mainly be focusing on regulation and regulatory policies from this perspective.

1.2.2 Regulatory Practice

Quite logically, regulatory practice follows this narrow definition. By 'regulatory practice' we mean the intervention of independent regulatory authorities into imperfect markets in the network industries. Of course, regulatory practice is defined and confined by regulatory policy, that is, by the remits and the powers given to the regulators by the policy-makers. Nevertheless, over the past 20 years, regulators in all the network industries have generally managed to extend their remits and their powers: from regulating market creation and market sustenance, they have managed increasingly also to become in charge of regulating public services (so-called universal service obligations), that is, regulating political objectives as opposed to correcting market imperfections. Also, increasingly, regulatory practice has evolved into technical areas, notably in matters of interoperability, interconnection, congestion management and system management. Today, sector-specific regulation goes far beyond the initially planned regulation of (imperfect) markets. It has also come into conflict with competition regulation, which at a more general level also focuses on correcting market imperfections. Finally, regulation and regulators are increasingly being criticized for venturing into policy-making, not directly by way of their regulatory practices, but more indirectly by way of influencing policy-makers because of their technical expertise.

1.2.3   Regulation in Transport

Regulation in the transport sector is a prevalent and increasingly important phenomenon owing to the imperfect markets in many of the transport modes. In this section, we will briefly highlight the main aspects that are generally regulated, at least from a theoretical point of view, and discuss to which transport modes such regulation applies.

Generally, (sector-specific) regulation is most prevalent in those sectors where there is a monopolistic infrastructure, the competitive usage of which has to be regulated. This is typically the case of air transport, where the usage of the airspace is highly regulated, mostly for safety reasons. Similarly, this is the case for the railway infrastructure (tracks, signals, perhaps stations), the access to which by competitive users also has to be regulated, even though so-called 'access competition' turns out to be of minor importance. This type of regulation is also possible for inland waterways, even though it is not yet practiced. By analogy, the regulation of the access to a monopolistic infrastructure can also be found in road passenger and freight transport. However, such regulation is generally not (yet) done by sector-specific regulators and remains in the hands of the traditional public administration which, however, defines and enforces the rules for accessing and using such road infrastructures.

In railways, as in urban (and regional) public transport, competition increasingly takes the form of competitive tendering (or franchising), whereby concessions (i.e., temporarily limited monopolies) are put out for tendering. Such tendering is generally also regulated, even though not always by way of sector-specific regulators, and sometimes only by contract and court action.

Besides monopolistic infrastructures, transport is also characterized by numerous so-called monopolistic bottlenecks; the access to and usage of these also increasingly has to be regulated. Such monopolistic bottlenecks typically are airports where ground-handling services, maintenance and airport slots are progressively being regulated. Similarly, one more and more speaks of regulating the access to so-called 'rail-related services' in the railway sector. Such considerations can also be applied to ports and corresponding regulation.

Competition among operators using the monopolistic infrastructures – such as competition between airlines, train operating companies, trucking firms and shipping firms – is generally not explicitly regulated, at least not by sector-specific regulators. Normally, such regulation falls under the remit of competition regulatory authorities, even though the border between the remit of competition regulators and sector-specific regulators is often not very clear.

In all these transport modes – for example, rail, air, road, maritime, urban – other aspects are often regulated as well, as mentioned above. Such regulation generally pertains to technical matters, namely standards, in the areas of interoperability and interconnection and often also safety. This is particularly the case for air and rail transport, but also for maritime transport. Other areas to be regulated pertain to environmental matters (emissions, pollution, etc.), which is clearly observable in the road passenger and freight sector. Finally, one can also observe growing regulation in matters of public service obligations and consumer protection, such as in the case of air and rail passenger rights.

As for intermodal transport, regulation, as we will see in this book, is still in its infancy. Indeed, regulation is still mainly focused on the various transport modes, where it seeks to optimize the functioning of the internal transport market, as well as to protect the consumers within this mode of transport. An area to be developed therefore clearly pertains to the regulation of intermodality, though both theory and literature remain very scarce in this respect.

1.3 EUROPEAN TRANSPORTATION IN 1980 AND 2010

In this section we will take a look at the different transport sectors in Europe. Firstly, we will identify key features of the different transport sectors in order to identify similarities and differences. This will include the distinctions between passenger and freight, as well as between inter-urban and urban transport. Secondly, we will set out how each transport sector was organized in 1980. Thirdly, the corresponding picture for 2010 will be outlined. This will highlight the main evolution of European transport over the past 30 years and the different position of each sector. On this basis the following section will then go into more detail regarding the regulatory policies over this period with the focus on explaining the key elements.

1.3.1   Transport Sectoral Characteristics

The different transport sectors share one fundamental characteristic. They are all network industries, possessing a number of common properties (Glachant, 2002), albeit with variable importance across transport sectors, notably: economies of scale and scope; externalities in production and consumption; and being perceived as providing services of general interest. These characteristics create significant regulatory challenges, as discussed in section 1.2. As noted in Finger et al. (2011), network industries can be characterized as 'very complex, technical, economic and political systems in which the interplay of technology and institutions has a significant impact on performance'. This characterization highlights again the regulatory challenges involved, although the transport sectors may vary in terms of complexity (e.g. road freight and particular inland waterways are less complex than aviation or railway transport). Overall, the supply of transport can be divided into three levels which are valid for all transport sectors (Quinet and Vickerman, 2004, p. 169):

- the infrastructure level (e.g. roads, railways, airports and ports);
- the infostructure level concerning information technology (IT) and information systems to utilize the available infrastructure (e.g. signalling systems for railways, air traffic control, urban traffic management);
- the service level (e.g. coach services, road haulage services, rail services, flights, short sea shipping).

A key regulatory consideration concerns the extent to which the supply of transport should then be undertaken within a vertical and/or horizontal integrated system (the former would refer to integration between the three levels, while the latter would involve integration within a given level). This would be dependent on (among other factors) the patterns regarding economies of scale and scope which may not be identical for all three levels, and the different transport sectors also vary in this aspect. Furthermore, there may be considerations regarding whether coordination of the supply of transport is best handled through organization (calling for vertical and/or horizontal integration) or the market (following vertical and/or horizontal separation). The choice would then reflect the importance of transaction costs compared to competitive pressure.

The differences between transport sectors in terms of industry structure and the regulatory framework can be considered by taking into account several factors including: (1) level of entry and exit costs (sunk costs); (2) extent of economies of scale and scope; (3) importance of services of general interest; (4) externalities (with particular reference to elements such as environment, congestion and accidents).

The level of entry and exit costs are key determinants of the industry structure, by influencing the extent to which entry of new companies takes place as well as the competitive pressure that companies already in the market face from potential entrants (as put forward in the contestable market theory, Baumol et al., 1982). Examples of transport sectors with predominantly low entry and exit costs would be road freight and inland waterway transport (although particular problems are present with respect to small-sized companies within the latter sector, which may face relatively high sunk costs). As a result both sectors are also characterized by a relatively large number of enterprises. On the other hand, entry into the railway sector or aviation is relatively costly: in both cases new operators will need relevant licences and certificates as well as either acquiring or leasing relevant assets (rolling stock and planes, respectively). Road passenger transport and urban public transport probably represent intermediate cases as far as entry cost for individual routes are concerned, but these costs may be more substantial when considering entry for an entire network. As for short sea shipping, there could also be substantial (sunk) costs linked to terminals, intermodal arrangements and information systems, apart from the costs relating to vessels. The position regarding intermodal transport depends on the category of operations. In the case of centrally controlled intermodal operations,[2] entry costs could be substantial, while for independently functioning intermodal operations,[3] the sector is relatively open to new entrants.

Consideration of economies of scale and scope relates to optimal industry structure in terms of the number of firms and the range of services supplied. In particular, there would be strong economies of scale in those industries characterized by relatively large fixed costs, whereas economies of scope would be dependent on the existence of synergies in the production or supply of two or more outputs, linked to indivisible fixed costs. With significant economies of scale and scope there would be a tendency towards natural monopoly. Available evidence points towards strong economies of scale with respect to infrastructure, but the same is not necessarily the case for transport services. The literature on estimates regarding economies of scale and scope is rather substantial, encompassing a range of findings where the variations are linked to output specification and functional forms. Complicating factors in the case of transport are the geographical dimension of the network structure and its multi-product character, making the output specification complex in terms of parameters to be considered. Below, a few examples of this work are given, though without being exhaustive. Quinet and Vickerman (2004) mention that for rail (looking at infrastructure and services together) there are significant economies of scale (although not as substantial as previous estimates). Road haulage has limited (if any) scale economies (a similar case is likely for inland waterways), while air transport is viewed as an intermediate case. Recent studies of urban public transport have also indicated the existence of scale and scope economies (e.g. Farsi et al., 2007), while Di Giacomo and Ottoz (2010) reach the same result for intercity bus operations.

Defining services of general interest imply that these may be underprovided by the market where the relevant (state) authority can guarantee their provision through public service obligations (PSOs) which may include financial compensation to the service provider. In the transport sector PSOs are principally specified in the passenger domain rather than in the freight domain. In particular, there are PSOs in place for passenger operations of all main modes, notably railways, urban public transport, interurban road passenger transport, air and passenger ferry operations. It also appears that public service obligations are more likely for urban, suburban or regional contexts as compared to long-distance inter-urban services. A key feature of PSOs is that these can ensure that non-profitable services not provided by the market on its own initiative will still be provided. In these cases entry and exit to the market for these types of services would not otherwise take place, and private sector involvement is only through some form of contractual arrangement between the authority and the operator.

Externalities (notably, external costs) have relevance for all transport sectors, albeit that given the variation in external costs between forms of transport there would be differences in terms of the extent of regulation. In particular, the regulatory focus is likely to be on road-based transportation and aviation due to their relatively high contribution to external costs (CE Delft et al., 2008).

1.3.2 European Transportation in 1980

At the outset it should be mentioned that in 1980 there were obviously significant differences between those countries in Europe belonging to

COMECON (Council for Mutual Economic Assistance) and the other European countries in terms of general economic, political and social frameworks. Essentially, for the former countries there were varying degrees of planned economy, while the latter countries were organized as market or mixed economies with different features. Revisiting 1980 in terms of the regulatory frameworks for transport will focus on the situation in the countries with a market or mixed economy, whereas the regulatory issues linked to transportation in the COMECON countries mainly reflected the general features of a planned economy and were similar to other sectors.

Overall, in the countries with a market or mixed economy, network industries including the different transportation sectors were in 1980 often subject to strong (national) government influence and regulation, limited competition and market orientation, and a significant role as national champions. Indeed, most network industries including transport had since the late 1960s typically been organized in accordance with the following parameters (Thatcher, 2006):

- ownership: public;
- supply: monopoly;
- allocation of regulatory powers: governments;
- rules governing supply: few formal rules, except those of the general public sector;
- relations between governments and suppliers: close;
- norms in objectives of suppliers: public service; fiscal and political aims of governments; long technological and economic development.

Even though it is possible to consider this as the typical model, there were sectoral and country differences in 1980 (and earlier) reflecting specific characteristics and contexts. Below, a quick review of the different transport sectors in Europe in 1980 will be given in terms of regulatory framework. For each of these sectors more details will be given in the following chapters, especially concerning the regulatory evolution and its implications.

Aviation

The aviation industry in Europe in the early 1980s was still subject to significant national control and influence. This included control or approval of fares, flying frequencies, airport access conditions and capacity rules for airlines. National flag carriers (largely in public ownership) dominated the intra-European airline market with entry on routes being determined through bilateral agreements between national governments, effectively eliminating any competition between carriers. Airports were publicly owned, as was air traffic control.

Railways
Prior to the onset of the reform process in the early 1990s the railway sector in Europe was predominantly organized in monolithic public-owned companies (such as NS, ÖBB, SNCB and FS) responsible for almost all passenger and freight transport services along with other ancillary services and management, development and maintenance of the railway infrastructure. Third-party access (TPA) possibilities were largely not available in practice. Often the railways were subject to substantial political influence, and independent regulation was non-existent.

Road freight
Road freight was one of the most heavily regulated sectors in the Organisation for Economic Co-operation and Development (OECD) area until the late 1970s, despite it being in principle a competitive industry (having low entry costs and limited scope for economies of scope and scale, and with the road network publicly available and free of charge). Regulation notably concerned entry into the industry, licensing for entry onto certain routes, limitations on cabotage rights and approval of freight rates. The sector at that point in time already had significant involvement by private sector companies.

Road passenger
In 1980 regular coach services were largely regulated and in public ownership, with few exceptions (notably Great Britain where deregulation had been introduced that year). Coach transportation was often seen as a threat to rail, such that in a number of countries (e.g. France and Germany) regulation restricted coach services to those which complemented railways without being in direct competition.

Urban public transport
For urban public transport (covering buses, trams, light rail, urban heavy rail and metro), the industry in 1980 was largely monopolized. As such, the 'classic' model of regulated, publicly owned monopolies remained the dominant organizational form across Europe. This includes the case where the transport services were provided by an in-house operator being part of the (local) authority as well as the case where the operator was a publicly owned company not being a part of the authority. There are also

examples of private companies playing a role in urban public transport (largely bus services) either as subcontractors or operating services under exclusive rights on selected routes or networks (e.g. in the context of the so-called 'French model').

Inland waterways

In the case of inland waterways in 1980 it is necessary to distinguish between two contexts: (1) the Rhine navigation area where there had already been a liberal market regime for about 120 years; (2) other navigation areas where the regulatory situation used to be different and was far from deregulated, with different national regulatory regimes. In the latter context there were restrictions on market access for foreign shipping companies including cabotage prohibition on canals in France, Germany and the Netherlands. Also there were examples of fixed tariffs (e.g. in Germany), and a system of chartering by rotation (*tour de rôle*) was applied to allocate shipments to transport operators and ships. The inland waterway sector already had significant private sector involvement with reference to the shipping companies.

Short sea shipping

European short sea shipping was in 1980 subject to various national regulations (e.g. complex administrative procedures) and restrictions on cabotage within the sector due to protectionism. In this way short sea shipping services within the EU maritime area could not be provided freely. The role of ports, including access to their services, was important. This context contributed to preventing short sea shipping from utilizing its full potential in Europe (despite a number of inherent advantages compared to other regions such as its extensive coastlines). As a whole, there was relative little attention given to short sea shipping from a European perspective.

Intermodal transport

The development of intermodal transport commenced during the 1950s with the introduction of container-based freight transport (in shipping). However, even in 1980 intermodal freight transportation faced numerous obstacles due to the lack of integration between different modes of transport. This was partly a reflection of a unimodal focus by transport sector companies and authorities alike, and partly a result of regulatory policies in place limiting access rights within modes, thereby also limiting transportation between modes (intermodality).

1.3.3 European Transportation in 2010

Below, the same transport sectors will be reviewed as of 2010, after the previous decades of transformation and regulatory evolution.

Aviation
In contrast to the situation in 1980 there is today, in principle, a single European market for airlines with no limitations regarding routes, capacities, flying frequencies and fares. This was achieved in 1997 following three so-called 'deregulation packages' of EC legislative measures whereby all nationally imposed restrictions for flying within Europe were removed. In particular, a carrier with a valid permit from an EU member state has the right to enter on all intra-European routes provided at least 50 per cent of the carrier is owned by EU member states and/or nationals of EU member states. As a result there has been significant entry to the market, especially coming from new low-cost airlines, e.g. Ryanair and Easyjet. On many routes there are two or more carriers operating in direct competition. On the other hand, for the majority of routes in Europe there is still only one operator present due to, among other factors, the concentration of (tourist-related) traffic flows on certain routes and residual barriers to entry. The flag carriers have responded to the competitive pressure in various ways, including the establishment of strategic alliances along with restructuring initiatives, as well as whole or partial privatization. However, there remain difficulties for competition in this sector for several reasons, including differential interpretation and implementation in member states of the European legislative measures, and national regulatory authorities retaining powers. Also the role of airports is important in this context, especially in terms of airport access for carriers on fully non-discriminatory terms. Indeed, the pace of change regarding airports has been slower compared to the changes to airlines in terms of both management and governance, and airport competition. Indeed most airports remain in public ownership. Similar considerations are valid for air traffic control.

Railways
This sector has gone through significant changes over the past two decades, mostly driven through EC legislative initiatives starting in 1991 (Directive 91/440) as well as measures in certain countries going beyond the EC requirements (notably in Great Britain and Sweden). Although most railway companies are still in public ownership, initiatives for restructuring and unbundling of the incumbents have changed the sector. Today a range of new players responsible for certain aspects of railway activities are emerging (e.g. infrastructure managers or capacity-allocating

bodies), along with increased use of outsourcing of non-core activities (e.g. maintenance of rolling stock). In many countries complete separation of infrastructure and operations has taken place, with separate companies established, although this is not uniform. In a number of cases there are also separate companies responsible for passenger and freight, respectively. Since 2007 the entire rail freight market in Europe has been open and significant entry has taken place, albeit with country variation. More limited access rights for the passenger market have been prescribed by EC legislation (so far only for international passenger services) although some countries have already opened the domestic market resulting in entry in these cases (mostly competition for the market rather than competition in the market). Also at authority level there are new players in the form of independent regulators (with respect to market and safety) although in this field too there are variations regarding the specifics. As a key aim is to create a single European railway area, the sector faces particular challenges due to a variety of technical and operational differences between the EU countries.

Road freight
Today, the sector looks very different compared to 1980. Road haulage is now one of the most liberalized sectors in Europe. This has been achieved through introduction of uniform rules for access to the profession and access rights to the (international) markets (bilateral international transport,[4] cross-trade[5] and cabotage[6]). As for bilateral international transport and cross-trade, access is based on a community licence which is issued by the relevant national authority to the haulier and valid across Europe (previously called community authorization) on the basis of fulfilling qualitative criteria (such as being of good repute in terms of no conviction for any infringement of national rules in certain fields, for example commercial law, road traffic, trafficking in human beings or drugs, as well being able to meet its financial obligations). It should be noted that cabotage is not fully open yet. The existing provisions allow for each haulier to perform up to three cabotage operations within a seven-day period (these operations may be in the same member state or in different ones). Further liberalization of the cabotage market is currently being considered by the Commission with proposals expected during 2013.

Efforts have been made to ensure fair competition in Europe with regard to fiscal (e.g. vehicle taxation and road infrastructure charges), social (e.g. working time and driver attestation) and technical (e.g. weight and dimensions of vehicles) aspects in order not to put road haulage companies from particular countries at a disadvantage. However, differences between EU countries in these areas remain, partly due to different enforcement practices (e.g. concerning rest periods). Further regulatory harmonization and coordination between the national authorities may therefore be required in order to ensure fair competition. The sector is still characterized by a relatively large number of enterprises of variable size (though typical small): there are nearly 600 000 road haulage companies in the EU-27 with an average of five employees (although larger companies have grown in importance).

Road passenger

Although inter-urban road passenger transport (coach) has experienced major changes over the past two to three decades, in the main this has primarily been due to specific national initiatives rather than driven by the EC. European legislation has however enabled the liberalization of the international coach market including the possibility for operators to undertake cabotage services (albeit with restrictions, as these should be in the course of a regular international service). It should be noted that cabotage has rather limited importance in the European coach transport market as a whole, with a few exceptions (notably Greece and Sweden). As a result of the limited European legislative involvement there is today significant variation among the EU member states regarding the regulatory environment for road passenger transport operations. In some countries the coach market has been fully liberalized (e.g. Great Britain and Sweden), facilitating on-road competition between operators. Other countries (e.g. Spain) are using a concession tendering model where the competition between operators is for the market and not in the market. In certain countries liberalization is only starting, where directly awarded concessions are still used and restrictions on competition with existing services are in place. Indeed France and Germany prohibit road passenger services that compete with rail (although changes in both countries may be under way in the near future). As a whole there is today a larger involvement of the private sector in operating services, sometimes even including the planning and network design stage, although this involvement varies significantly across the EU member states with publicly owned operators remaining important in some countries.

Urban public transport

Significant changes have occurred regarding the organization and provision of urban public transport over the past two decades although the regulatory evolution has been less driven by EC legislation and more based on national and regional initiatives compared to other transport sectors (notably air, rail, road freight). This has resulted in great variety across Europe in the organizational forms and their evolution. Today, in-house operations still exist but the relation between operator and authority has in many cases been reshaped, with emphasis on corporatization, contractualization and clearer identification of roles and responsibilities for the different parties. Increasingly, there is also use of contracting by the authority based on competitive tendering (notably route contracting[7] or network contracting,[8] although various intermediate forms also exist), typically combined with some form of exclusive rights for the duration of the contract. This has allowed increased private sector involvement in urban public transport services provision by being awarded contracts, although publicly owned operators may not necessarily be excluded from participating. More extended reliance on the market is also present today, with particular reference to bus transport in Great Britain outside London since 1986, where private companies are free to provide any services they wish while the authority contracts for additional non-profitable services. In this case additional regulation has subsequently been introduced in order to ensure that the market is functioning appropriate (e.g. quality partnerships and service coordination). The example from Great Britain is the best known, although in Eastern Europe there are also cases of minibus services being provided within a free market framework.

Inland waterways
This sector is today fully liberalized (including full cabotage rights) across Europe, such that the dual system of free markets (Rhine Navigation Area and international shipping on the Danube) and regulated ones (largely elsewhere) has disappeared. This was achieved by 2000 following EC legislation from the late 1980s and early 1990s. The rota system (see above) has been terminated such that companies requiring inland waterway transportation have free choice of carrier. Also the system of fixed tariffs used in Germany and elsewhere has been abolished with prices now being negotiated freely. However, despite the liberalization significant problems remain that hamper the functioning of the market. These relate among others to the existence of administrative and regulatory barriers linked to harmonization gaps (e.g. regarding insurance of vessels, ship certification and mutual recognition of boat masters' certificates). In part these problems may be linked to multiple stakeholders with a role in the harmonization (notably UNECE,[9] the European Commission, the Rhine and the Danube Commissions[10] as well as national governments). Particular regulatory challenges for inland waterways have concerned the significant overcapacity exacerbated by the presence of independent bargemen with limited incentive to reduce capacity; EC initiatives regarding capacity regulation (including scrapping schemes and old-for-new programmes) were active until 2003 but are presently dormant.

Short sea shipping
Today this sector is clearly in focus from a European perspective, being seen as critical to contribute towards a more sustainable transport system, as illustrated in the latest EC Transport White Paper from 2011 (European Commission, 2011) and the inclusion of so-called Motorways of the Sea projects within the Trans-European Transport Network (TEN-T) in 2004. The market for maritime services has been liberalized throughout Europe since the mid-2000s following EC legislation from 1986, 1988 and 1992. This includes full cabotage rights such that complete domestic connections can be provided by companies registered in other EU member states. This has strengthened the competitive position of short sea shipping multimodal-based transportation with respect to mainly unimodal road transportation. However, significant factors are still preventing short sea shipping from being able to compete effectively with road transport. A key factor is linked to the competitive environment regarding ports, where EC initiatives have been less successful in introducing liberalization measures, for example addressing terminal operator monopolies on cargo handling. Renewed EC effort regarding ports is foreseen for 2013. Available information suggests that the port handling costs can be substantial relative to the total costs of multimodal transportation, with short sea shipping highlighting the importance of measures to enhance port efficiency. As for port ownership, the typical form is the so-called landlord port where the (public) port authority acts as landlord and port operations are undertaken by private companies. There are also examples of ports with a clearer publicly owned orientation (e.g. so-called tool ports), while fully privatized ports are the exception (Great Britain).

Intermodal transport
Today, intermodal transport has a stronger position in the freight transport market, being seen as an alternative to road-only-based solutions. Public policy proposals at national and European levels are including initiatives to support the development of this form of transportation. Furthermore, the regulatory measures adopted for specific modes have contributed to facilitate intermodal transport solutions (e.g. the gradual opening of the rail freight market in Europe would also assist in strengthening intermodal alternatives). However, there is also evidence that intermodal transport has not increased as much as was expected initially. In part this is a reflection of delays in implementing proposed policy measures. Intermodal transport faces particular challenges compared to other transport sectors in terms of coordination at industry and authority levels. This also raises key regulatory issues in terms of promoting cooperation between the different stakeholders (e.g. the various transport

operators that could participate in intermodal transport) within a competitive environment.

1.4 BACKGROUND TO REGULATORY REFORM FOR THE EUROPEAN TRANSPORT SECTOR

The different segments of the transport sector – air, railways, road, urban public transport, inland waterways and short sea shipping – have experienced significant liberalization processes over the past 30 years. Liberalization has generally been accompanied by re-regulation, leading among other things to the creation of sector-specific regulatory authorities, whose main role is to open up and sustain markets for the benefit of users and customers. This process of simultaneous liberalization and re-regulation has been particularly active in Europe, promoted as it is by the European Commission.

In this section we will provide an overview of the regulatory policies that have shaped the different transport sectors over the past three decades. Firstly, we will take a look at the origins of the initiatives in the mid-1980s for the European transport sector. Secondly, it will be highlighted that these regulatory policies are not unique in terms of the transport sector in comparison to other network industries in Europe, nor in terms of space (as transport regulatory reforms have occurred in other parts of the world as well). Thirdly, the key elements in the regulatory policies for European transport will be set out, identifying the common elements as well as the main sectoral specifics.

1.4.1 Key Origins of the Regulatory Policies

From a European perspective one of the main starting points for this regulatory reform process was taken in 1985 when the Court of Justice concluded that inland transport of goods and passengers should be open to all Community firms. Further impetus emerged in the same year from the Commission's White Paper on the completion of the internal market which contributed to a more rapid development of the Common Transport Policy (CTP). Subsequently, the Commission published in December 1992 the first White Paper on transport setting out further directions for the CTP 'from a policy which has aimed essentially at the completion of the internal market through the elimination of artificial regulatory barriers to the provision of services, towards a more comprehensive policy designed to ensure the proper functioning of the Community's transport systems' (European Commission, 1992). The 1992 White Paper highlights the principle that transport undertakings should be able to take full advantage of the internal market within a framework where safety requirements, technical specifications and professional standards are harmonized. The CTP was put forward in order to address transport efficiency, social cohesion and environmental considerations.

1.4.2   Transport as Compared to Other Network Industries in Europe

The regulatory reform initiatives of the different transport sectors are mirrored in other network industries in Europe including information networks (post, telephone) and utility networks (electricity, gas, water). Although there are specifics for each industry and country, there are a number of common elements for many network industries, notably: separation of infrastructure and downstream services; access to the infrastructure; interconnection of networks; phasing of the reform; safeguarding of the public interest; and the need for regulation. The overall theme of the network industry reforms was liberalization, often addressing the (public) monopolies playing a key role in these industries and moving from separate national markets towards European markets (Finger and Künneke, 2011).

It should be noted that the reform objectives varied between the different network industries. In certain cases, the objective was to increase consumer welfare, notably by way of introducing competition. In other cases, such as railways, the aim was to reduce the losses incurred by the incumbent state-owned operator and thus to relieve the state budget, together with rebalancing the modes.

A key impetus to the start of the reform process for all network industries was the European Court's judgment on British Telecom from 1985 (confirming an earlier decision from the European Commission from 1982). The 1985 European Court judgment determined that British Telecom should no longer be allowed to forbid the high-speed forwarding of telex messages between foreign countries by private message-forwarding agencies in Great Britain (Knieps, 2010). This judgment had particular importance for considerations regarding entry into the markets for network industries. In practice, the process of liberalization and removal of entry barriers took much longer (more than two decades) and is not yet completed across all network industries. Another key legal decision of the European Court of Justice (ECJ) was the so-called Nouvelles Frontiéres[11] case where the ECJ confirmed that the competition rules of the EC Treaty applied to air transport. Knieps (2010) highlights that legal decisions from the European Court and national High Courts have played a significant role in other aspects of regulatory reform of network industries:

- Proper identification of market failure (judgment of the European Court: the Bronner case from 1998).[12] In particular, this case related to the conditions under which network access regulation is needed and the identification of essential facilities.
- Competitive framework for network infrastructure capacities (judgment of the British High Court: the Guernsey Transport Board Case from 1999).[13] The legal decision is directly relevant to airport slot allocation approaches and grandfather rights, which is relevant to other network industries characterized by scarce capacity.
- The role of negotiated access versus regulated access (judgment of the German Federal Court of Justice: Juridification of the Associations' Agreement Electricity II plus from 2005).[14] This judgment is linked to the issue of monopolistic bottlenecks for network infrastructures such that negotiated access may not succeed or result in abuse of a dominant position.
- Cost-based access regulation versus incentive regulation (judgment of the European Court: the Arcor case from 2008).[15] The case highlighted important considerations in access charging for network industries in order to ensure efficient use of infrastructure where it is necessary to take into account the perspective of the owners and users of infrastructure.

1.4.3 European Context as Compared to Regulatory Reforms Elsewhere

The regulatory reforms in Europe of the transport sectors have been accompanied by initiatives elsewhere in the world on a similar theme in terms of liberalization and increased private participation. In Table 1.1 we briefly look at three transport sectors (rail, road, aviation) in three countries (the United States, Japan and Australia). The table provides an overview of the selected sectors and countries.

1.4.4 Overview of Regulatory Reform Elements

Reform elements of the transport sectors in Europe have a number of common elements which will be considered in the following. However, it should be noted that there are obvious sectoral differences regarding the specific approaches adopted. The typical headings for the reforms include:

- Liberalization.
- Ownership transformation.
- Unbundling.
- Independent regulation.

Table 1.1 Regulatory reform in selected countries outside Europe

	US	Japan	Australia
Rail	Staggers Rail Act of 1980 provided for deregulation of rail freight while retaining a reasonable regulatory framework to prevent abuse of dominant position.	The 1986 Japan National Railways Reform Law provided for the JNR privatization. Six private regional passenger companies (the JRs) and a nationwide freight carrier (JR Freight) were established.	Rail access provisions in 1995 under the Trade Practices Act. Regulatory reform has mainly aimed at harmonization of regulatory regimes and at standardization of key infrastructure.
Road freight	The Motor Carrier Act of 1980 removed or eased a number of restrictions and regulations giving more commercial freedom to the trucking companies regarding rates, goods carried and routes used.	Motor-truck Transport Business Law enacted in 1991 that relaxed entry and pricing regulations. Certain safeguard clauses were retained (e.g. regarding entry under excessive supply and prices significantly different from costs).	Interstate economic regulation phased out in 1954 following Privy Council judging. Intrastate economic regulation continued until the early 1980s. Regulatory effort in the 1990s shifted towards ensuring a uniform regulatory framework.
Aviation	Airline Deregulation Act of 1978 phased out the Government's control of fares, routes and market entry while retaining safety regulation.	A more gradual approach to deregulation has been adopted starting in 1986. The following year Japanese Airlines (main carrier) was privatized.	Interstate domestic aviation industry deregulated through the Airline Agreement (Termination) Act of 1990 ending its Two Airlines Policy.

- From unimodal focus to multimodal consideration including integration and co-modality.
- Transport governance: from national-oriented contexts to a European dimension.

Below, each of these will be outlined with a focus on liberalization and ownership transformation.

Liberalization

A common step of the regulatory reforms introduced across the different transport sectors in Europe has involved liberalization in terms of (gradually) opening up the market for competition (e.g. through permitting companies to enter and exit the market) and establishing an entry-friendly regulatory regime. The main rationale for liberalization is the possible advantages from competition in terms of improved efficiency in production and enhanced consumer choice, which would then result in increased economic welfare. A detailed analysis of the complexities arising in relation to liberalization processes aimed at introducing competition into regulated industries is provided in Armstrong and Sappington (2006), taking an economic perspective. In the following, some of the main issues will be outlined before an overview of the liberalization steps in the different sectors will be summarized.

From the outset consideration should be given to two critical questions: (1) Is competition feasible?; (2) Is competition desirable? There are four possible combinations (as put forward in UNESCAP, 2001); see Figure 1.1. The problem linked to network industries such as transport is the

		Is competition desirable?	
		Yes	No
Is competition feasible?	Yes	Usual case	'Cream-skimming'
	No	Entry deterrence	Severe natural monopoly

Source: UNESCAP (2001).

Figure 1.1   The desirability and feasibility of competition

possibility that one or both of the two questions would be answered negatively. The traditional view of network industries was that these represented natural monopolies. As a background to the liberalization process
this perception was replaced with one highlighting that only parts of the
network industries would have natural monopoly characteristics. The
regulatory challenges would then be to address the cases of either entry
deterrence (where the incumbent prevent entry even when competition
would be desirable) or the case where cream-skimming by new entrants is
possible but may not be desirable.

Armstrong and Sappington (2006) mention the possibility that even in
the case of significant economies of scale (which would indicate natural
monopoly) competitive pressure could be facilitated through competition
for the market (rather than competition in the market) where potential
companies bid for the regulated monopoly. Apart from this distinction
it should also be noted that liberalization could take place either under
vertical separation or under vertical integration. The former would ensure
that the incumbent cannot abuse any network (infrastructure-related)
advantages (entry deterrence) while there is the risk of loss of economies
of scope. On the other hand, economies of scope would not be lost if liberalization is combined with vertical integration, although would require
appropriate regulatory arrangements to ensure non-discriminatory third-
party access rights.

The different transport sectors have experienced liberalization processes
during the past two decades with variation regarding the specific elements,
including scope and timing (and also influenced by the mix of European
and national initiatives). In aviation, a single market for carriers in Europe
has been achieved although limitations remain with respect to PSO routes
as well as access to airports. The main elements of the liberalization were
completed in 1997. For railways the liberalization process started later
and with reduced scope. Complete market opening was achieved in the
rail freight market, while rail passenger liberalization only commenced (at
European level) in 2010 with respect to international services (although
some countries have also embarked on liberalization for domestic services). The road freight sector has seen substantial progress regarding
liberalization, although cabotage is not yet fully open and harmonization
issues remain to ensure a level playing field. Inter-urban road passenger
transport (mainly coach) is more mixed in terms of liberalization being
determined mainly by national initiatives rather than European direction
(with the exception of international road passenger services). Overall,
there is however some tendency towards frameworks facilitating entry
to the market (eventually through concessions). Urban public transport
is perhaps showing even more variation with respect to liberalization,

although the use of competitive tendering is increasingly used by urban transport authorities to select operators and other entities concerned. Inland waterway transport was atypical compared to the other transport sectors with having both deregulated and regulated markets before the liberalization process. The dual system ended in 2000 when a liberalized system was established (although harmonization problems and barriers to entry remain). For short sea shipping a single maritime area with, in principle, full access rights (including cabotage) have been established, with remaining problems being linked to port access. Intermodal transport is a reflection of the liberalization processes being undertaken for short sea shipping, road and rail freight as well as additional elements.

Ownership transformation
Reform initiatives have involved various ownership changes in the transport sector including privatization[16] (e.g. transfer of a publicly owned transport company to the private sector), although a change in ownership covers a spectrum of possible options. In particular, ownership changes could in principle cover any movement between the following options: (1) government department; (2) government agency; (3) public sector company; (4) mixed ownership; (5) private stock exchange listed; (6) private manager owned (Hartley et al., 1991). One remark about one of these categories, mixed ownership, is appropriate. The category is in the interface between public and private ownership and includes a variety of different organizational forms such as not-for-profit organizations and private sector companies heavily dependent upon public sector orders or financing. Details about the other categories are available in Hartley et al. (1991). Although this list broadens the concept of ownership change it may be possible to identify further subcategories covering intermediate ownership forms that better reflect specific cases. These categories would be relevant for both infrastructure and operations.

The theoretical case for ownership change away from structures permitting direct political intervention and control towards more independent organizations and even transfer to the private sector have been set out in numerous studies (e.g. Vickers and Yarrow, 1988). In particular, the rationale for privatization is linked to arguments regarding the incentives for higher efficiency in the private sector due to competitive pressure (if potential competitors are be present or could enter) or shareholding monitoring of managerial performance. More independent (public) organizations could create the possibility for more commercial and efficient use of resources rather than this being determined by political agendas in accordance with 'new public management' (Pollitt and Bouckaert, 2011) and 'public choice theories' (Mueller, 2003).

*Table 1.2   Changes in ownership for transport sectors in Europe
            (infrastructure)*

	Organizational form 1980	Organizational form 2010
Airports	Government agency	Public sector company
		Mixed ownership
Air traffic control	Government agency	Government department
	Government department	Public sector company
Railway infrastructure	Government department	Public sector company
Road infrastructure	Government department	Government department
		Government agency
Inland navigation	Government agency	Government agency
Seaports	Public sector company	Mixed ownership

*Table 1.3   Changes in ownership for transport sectors in Europe
            (operations)*

	Organizational form 1980	Organizational form 2010
Air transport	Public sector company	Mixed ownership
		Private stock exchange listed
Rail transport	Government department/ agency	Public sector company
		Mixed ownership
Road freight	Private manager owned	Private manager owned
Road passenger	Public sector company	Mixed ownership
		Private stock exchange listed
Urban public transport	Government department/ agency	Public sector company
		Mixed ownership
Inland waterways	Private manager owner	Private manager owned
Short sea shipping	Mixed ownership	Private stock exchange listed

Overall, the main movements as a result of regulatory reform initiatives have been away from those organizational forms with significant political intervention towards organizational forms with more autonomy and managerial discretion (e.g. from government department to public sector company; or from public sector company to private stock exchange listed company). Obviously, there are a few specific examples of movements in the opposite direction (e.g. from Estonia where the national railway company, EVR, was privatized in 2001 only to be renationalized in 2006). Tables 1.2 and 1.3 outline the ownership changes for the different transport sectors (comparing 2010 and 1980), distinguishing between infrastructure and operations. Obviously, this comparison highlights main changes on a European scale whereas there could be examples of countries not fully in accordance with this. Steps regarding ownership changes (in particular transfer from public to private ownership) have not been part of any requirements in EU legislative measures on regulatory reform of transport (Clifton et al., 2003). As such, the ownership changes have been the result of country-specific initiatives.

Unbundling

The principle of unbundling involves the separation of the non-competitive parts of a network industry (those exhibiting natural monopoly characteristics), typically the network infrastructure, from the competitive ones (production of services). Although the focus is usually on separation of infrastructure and operations, other elements may also be concerned (e.g. passenger and freight activities; PSO passenger services and commercial services; operations and planning/regulatory functions). The rationale for unbundling is linked to ensure a level playing field for competition. In particular, access to network infrastructure may not be non-discriminatory in case it is part of the incumbent. Unbundling is mainly considered in the context of railways, although it is also relevant for other transport sectors. For example, in the case of inland waterway transport companies from Western Europe were concerned about competition from vertically integrated (in public ownership) companies from Eastern Europe prior to the EU enlargement. Another example would be the case of vertical integration in aviation (e.g. between an airline and an airport), although preferential treatment of a country's flag carrier by the main airport would be sufficient to distort the market.

Independent regulation

The liberalization of the different transport sectors requires appropriate regulatory authorities to be in place in order to ensure the functioning of the market and prevent abuses of market power. In this context this involves assigning sufficient legal powers for the regulatory authority (e.g. regarding enforcement), as well as budget and human resources at a level allowing the authority to fulfil its responsibilities. There are arguments for ensuring the independence of regulators, with particular reference to government as well as the industry stakeholders. This would permit a regulatory institution to pursue general interest policies. On the other hand independence may increase the risk of regulatory capture and reduce accountability. Den Hertog (2010) provides an analysis of key considerations regarding the institutional design of regulatory authorities. As for regulatory authorities in the different transport sectors, practice varies and there are also country variations (as outlined in section 1.2).

From unimodal focus to multimodal consideration including integration and co-modality

During the regulatory evolution of the past 20 years there has been a shift away from the traditional unimodal focus towards an emphasis on multi-modality and integration of the different parts of the transport systems. For example, the recent EC Transport White Paper from 2011 high-lights the importance of a multimodal approach as part of the strategic policies: 'The objective for the next decade is to create a genuine Single European Transport Area by eliminating all residual barriers between modes and national systems, easing the process of integration and facilitating the emergence of multinational and multimodal operators' (European Commission, 2011, p. 10). Also, the European Commission introduced in 2006 the concept of co-modality: 'the efficient use of differ-ent modes on their own and in combination, will result in an optimal and sustainable utilisation of resources' (European Commission, 2006, p. 4). From a regulatory perspective there are clear challenges regarding how to facilitate integration within and between modes while maintaining a competitive environment and without resulting in increased transaction costs.

Transport governance: from national-oriented contexts to a European dimension

Prior to the start of the reform process the different transport sectors in Europe were largely organized and regulated at national level (with a few exceptions such as the role of the International Civil Aviation Organization, ICAO; recommendations on technical rules; and interna-tional agreements and rules in the railway sector). For most transport sectors there is now a much stronger European dimension linked to supporting the internal market of the EU and facilitating the free move-ment of goods, services and persons. This European dimension is clearly the case for aviation, railways, road freight, inland waterways, short sea shipping and intermodal transport. The two sectors with so far only a limited European governance role are inter-urban road passenger trans-port (mainly coach services) and urban public transport. For inter-urban road passenger transport, European measures have however opened the international coach market; while for urban public transport the main EC legislative focus has been on public service contracts and public procure-ment rules as well as harmonization of technical standards and dissemina-tion of best practice. Certain regulatory gaps are not closed completely for the other sectors, for example regarding nodal points: airports and ports. In all these sectors national authorities are in place, thereby sharing the governance with the EC.

1.5 IMPLICATIONS OF THE REGULATORY REFORMS

The reforms will lead to changes in the structure and governance of the transport sector. More importantly there will in turn be implications for the performance of the transport sector, covering a range of different dimensions as set out in Figure 1.2.

Examples of indicators per category are:

- Economic: price evolution in the sector, subsidies (e.g. subsidies per passenger-kilometre for railways), and production costs (e.g. costs per vehicle-kilometre for bus transportation).
- Social: consumer satisfaction, accessibility, affordability, quality of service.
- Operational: reliability, use of the network (e.g. average load factor in aviation), congestion.
- Technical: availability, losses, delivered service per capita.
- Environmental: greenhouse gas (GHG) emissions per passenger-kilometre for buses and coaches.

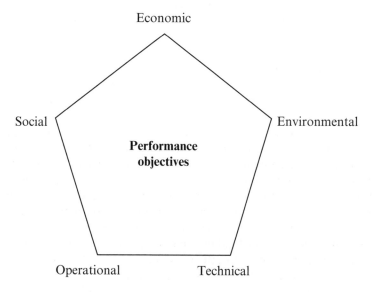

Source: Finger et al. (2011).

Figure 1.2 Performance categories

The regulatory reform initiatives are intrinsically linked to these performance dimensions against which the success of the regulatory change can be judged. Obviously, the weights given to different performance aspects vary across the transport sectors and between different countries in accordance with the originally stated objectives for the regulatory changes. Although such an evaluation is difficult in practice to undertake due to measurement problems and lack of harmonized data sets on a pan-European basis, it is an essential activity in order to ensure efficient and effective regulatory frameworks (or at least improved arrangements compared to the original situation). Over the past 10–15 years a number of studies covering the different sectors have been undertaken. For example, Blöndal and Pilat (1997) examined the performance implications of regulatory reform in air and road freight transport; Martin et al. (2005) looked at air transport and railways; while Copenhagen Economics (2005) analysed air, rail and urban transport. Overall, most of these studies have concerned economic performance impacts, whereas less attention has been given to environmental and social issues. It is outside the scope of this chapter to give an overview of the different studies undertaken. Instead we will provide a quick overview of how the reforms appear to have worked in practice, mainly considering economic aspects and, where possible, considering other aspects as well. The assessment is not intended to be exhaustive but rather a reflection on available indications.

1.5.1 Air Transport

Although there are still obstacles facing airlines within the European aviation market the liberalization was largely completed by 1997. The results have been substantial regarding competition, especially the emergence of low-cost carriers. This has also contributed towards providing customers with more choice in the range of services and fares available. Indeed, there is evidence of higher productivity, substantial reduction in costs and lower prices. There are also concerns linked to the business performance of (some) airlines, indicating that further adjustment in the industry structure may commence. Furthermore, obstacles linked to member states' implementation of the relevant EC Directives and airport access may limit the impact on performance of the reform measures.

1.5.2 Railways

Overall, rail liberalization has only recently (2007) been completed for rail freight at a European level and only started for passenger transport in 2010 with respect to international services. Therefore, it is perhaps too early to consider the possible implications for performance. Although access rights have been provided there remain important barriers to entry in different countries, thereby possibly limiting the extent of competitive entry. However, significant entry has occurred in the freight market, especially since 2007. More recently, there are also examples of entry in the passenger market, apart from entry relating to competition for the market. Indicative information points towards positive effects of market opening on productivity and prices for rail freight. Similar indications are not available for the passenger market as yet. However, evidence from countries that have gone further than EC provisions regarding the tendering of passenger services suggest typically (though not uniformly) the possibility for cost savings. Railways in many Eastern European countries face significant financial difficulties due to competition from other modes and limited PSO funding.

1.5.3   Road Freight

The main elements of the liberalization of road freight were completed in the 1990s (although cabotage is not fully open yet). As such there has been sufficient time available to enable more robust assessment of the implications for performance. Available evidence points towards improved efficiency and productivity leading to reduced prices for final customers. Transport volume has increased since 1990 and the transport market has changed, with a higher degree of internalization along with an increased role for companies from Eastern Europe. On the other hand important problems have also emerged, notably with respect to environmental costs linked to increased road transportation.

1.5.4   Inter-urban Road Passenger (Coach)

The coach market shows considerable diversity in terms of the evolution of organizational forms: some countries have chosen to liberalize and deregulate their coach markets during the past two decades, while others have introduced (tendered) concession regimes, and yet others have not changed the organizational form. These initiatives seem to have positive implications for performance, for example in terms of changes in fares and services provided. This sector is largely commercial, in contrast to many other forms of passenger transport. A concern in relation to liberalization of this market is the risk of market dominance by one or a few companies due to the possibility for economies of scale with respect to the network.

1.5.5 Urban Public Transport

The organization of urban public transport has evolved significantly over the past two decades, with increased use of contracting and competition in various forms. In this way there is substantial diversity in the frameworks for urban public transport between countries and even between cities. This has also opened the possibility for increased private sector participation. Available evidence suggests that increased competition or contracting can have important positive implications for performance. In particular, most empirical studies indicate that forms of competition in this transport sector can result in reduced costs and improved productivity. On the other hand the available evidence is less clear-cut with respect to implications for ridership and service quality. An important issue is that the studies undertaken to date do not allow for identifying more specifically what type of organizational form is optimal as long as it stimulates competitive pressure.

1.5.6 Inland Waterways

For this sector the main element of the liberalization process has been the gradual market opening of the traditional part of the sector concerning small and single undertakings, in contrast to the already competitive context of the main waterway corridors, notably the River Rhine. As part of this process measures have been introduced to facilitate the modernization of this segment in order to enable the undertakings to be competitive within an open market. Increased attention has been paid to this transport sector in order to establish (intermodal) alternatives to road-based transportation. An important regulatory challenge specific to this sector is the problems linked to overcapacity.

1.5.7 Short Sea Shipping

Liberalization of short sea shipping was largely completed by the mid-2000s following a start in 1986 (although during the 1990s cabotage was already possible between and within most EU member states). In parallel there is increased political support towards the development of short sea shipping in order to facilitate a rebalancing of modes away from road. Political support has been directed to the so-called Motorways of the Sea (MoS) initiative within the TEN-T, facilitating maritime services between ports in Europe. However, despite this context the outcome in terms of modal shift from road towards short sea shipping has been lower than expected. One of the main explanations for this is related to port performance. Available information suggests that the port handling cost represents a substantial share of multimodal transportation.

1.5.8 Intermodal Transport

Intermodal transport has in the last 15–20 years received increased attention at EU and national levels as well as at industry level. Furthermore, the liberalization process of other transport sectors – notably road, rail, short sea shipping and inland waterways – during the past two decades also facilitates intermodal transport. However, the growth of this market is lower than expected and remains relatively limited in terms of share of total freight transportation (measured in tonne-kilometres). This indicates that there still exist obstacles with respect to this transport sector. These obstacles include items linked to infrastructure (e.g. lack of coherent network of modes and nodal points), operations (e.g. diversity of loading units in use) and inconsistent regulations and practices between modes.

1.6   FUTURE PERSPECTIVES

After some 30 years of regulatory reform of the transport sector, observers of this process have become increasingly critical of liberalization, arguing that liberalization has not delivered fully on its promises and that new challenges are emerging in the infrastructures, requiring novel approaches to regulation. The most prominent of these challenges pertain to investments infrastructure systems' coherence, including interoperability, public services and public service obligations; and more generally to responsiveness of infrastructure operators to public policy objectives.

1.6.1 Investment

The question of whether liberalization of the network industries in transport and beyond (e.g., energy and even telecommunications) is capable of generating the investment needed for their development, or even for their maintenance, is raised. This question is especially relevant when it comes to the infrastructures per se, that is, the rail tracks, the roads, the ports, the airports, the terminals (as well as the electricity grids and the fibre optic cables). These infrastructures are of course the very foundations on the basis of which services can be offered. The profitability of such services, in turn, depends on the state of development of these infrastructures, as well as their quality. But service providers often have no incentives to invest or even to maintain such infrastructures, owing to their short-term interest, competitive pressure and the possibility to externalize the related costs. Of course, these questions have to be answered for each transport mode separately, but generally imply some sort of regulatory intervention so as to make sure that liberalization does not jeopardize investment into the infrastructures.

1.6.2   Infrastructure Systems' Coherence

Ultimately this is a question of coherence of the infrastructure systems; indeed, railway transport operators cannot thrive without tracks, and track operators cannot exist without transport operators using them and paying for them (in part), for example. If transport is subsidized, which it often is, the question then is where these subsidies should go to – infrastructure or transport – so as to produce the optimal performance (in economic, technical, environmental and other terms). This again requires a certain coherence in the approach of the infrastructures. Yet, once infrastructure systems are fragmented, not least as a result of liberalization, such coherence often comes from regulators and corresponding policies. Even if this may not be desirable, it appears nevertheless that liberalization leads to seeing transport and other infrastructure coherence more and more as a regulatory – that is, technocratic – task. This is even more the case if one starts to look at intermodal coordination, and regulation.

1.6.3   Public Services and Public Service Obligations

Liberalization leads to cost consciousness which in turn leads to identifying these transport services which do not cover their costs. Many such services nevertheless need to be provided for public policy reasons (at least as long as the public authorities are capable of paying for them). This in turn raises questions of efficiency of the provision of such services, questions of cross-subsidies and of market-distorting state aid. More broadly, and as seen above, this also raises the question of system coherence, as it may in some cases be overall more efficient to invest in the infrastructures (e.g., tracks, air traffic control) than to subsidize certain transport services.

1.6.4   Responsiveness of Infrastructure Operators to Public Policy Objectives

Finally, one may raise the even more general question of what transport and other infrastructures are ultimately for. Liberalization of network industries let one believe that infrastructure services are goals in themselves and should only be offered if there is a demand to pay for them. This, in our view, is too simplistic a view, and tends to forget that transport and other infrastructures serve other purposes as well. We think here in particular of the purposes of creating the conditions for a country or a region to thrive both economically and socially. Such considerations are even more relevant in times of ecological challenges (e.g., the policy objective of transferring road transport to rail and shipping) and economic crisis (e.g., the political need to offer low-cost mobility options to citizens). In this sense, transport and other infrastructure operators must remain open, more than ever, to evolving public policy objectives.

NOTES

1. Liberalization is understood as 'The opening up of competition, for example, through allowing firms freedom to enter and leave a market' in accordance with UNESCAP (2001). This definition is in line with Jaag and Trinkner (2009) who utilize the following definition: 'liberalization is a change of market access regulations towards a more entry-friendly regime'.
2. Centrally controlled intermodal operations involve a central management controlling the different elements of the transportation, whether by ship, truck or rail (achieved through ownership, leasing or contracting).
3. Independently functioning intermodal operations involves multimodal transportation but there is no central management element. This form requires coordination through networking.
4. Bilateral international transport is where either the loading or unloading activity takes place in the country where the vehicle is registered.
5. Cross-trade is where loading and unloading take place in two different countries, neither of which is the country where the vehicle is registered.
6. Cabotage is where loading and unloading take place in the same country, which is not however the country where the vehicle is registered.
7. Contracting out route by route, or groups of routes, of the services planned by the transport authority (Scandinavian model) typically with gross-cost contracts.
8. Network contracting usually involves tendering all services within an area or network (also referred to as the 'French model'). Typically, net-cost contracts are used (operators bearing both production and revenue risks).
9. UNECE is the United Nations Economic Commission for Europe.
10. The Central Commission for the Navigation of the Rhine (CCNR) was created in 1815 to ensure the freedom of navigation on the Rhine. The Danube Commission is an international intergovernmental organization established by the Convention regarding the regime of navigation on the Danube signed in Belgrade on 18 August 1948.
11. Ministere Public v Lucas Asjes ('Nouvelles Frontiéres') (Joined Cases 209-213/84) [1986] ECR 1425.
12. The Bronner case concerned whether the refusal of a media undertaking from Austria to include a rival daily newspaper in its delivery scheme represented an abuse of a dominant position.
13. From a general perspective the Guernsey Transport Board case concerned whether secondary trading of airport slots including side payments would be consistent with the Council Regulation of 1993 on common rules for the allocation of slots at Community airports (Council Regulation (EEC) No. 95/93 of 18 January 1993).
14. The case concerned a dispute between a provider of electricity and the local electricity

network with specific reference to whether the access fees for network access represented abuse of dominant position.

15. The dispute concerned whether the rates for unbundled access to the local loop for Arcor were set too high by Deutsche Telekom and in essence this related to the determination of the cost basis.

16. The United Nations Economic and Social Commission for Asia and the Pacific (UNESCAP, 2001) puts forward the following definition of privatization: 'The transfer of ownership and control of public or state assets, firms or services to private investors'.

REFERENCES

Armstrong, M. and D.E.M. Sappington (2006), 'Regulation, competition and liberalization', *Journal of Economic Literature*, **44** (2), 325–366.

Baumol, W.J., J.C. Panzar and R.D. Willig (1982), *Contestable Markets and the Theory of Industry Structure*, New York: Harcourt Brace Jovanovich.

Blöndal, S. and D. Pilat (1997), 'The economic benefits of regulatory reform', *OECD Economic Studies*, No. 28, 1997/I, Paris: OECD.

CE Delft et al. (2008), 'Handbook on estimation of external costs in the transport sector', produced within the study Internalisation Measures and Policies for All External Cost of Transport (IMPACT) for DG MOVE, European Commission, available at http://ec.europa.eu/transport/themes/sustainable/doc/2008_costs_handbook.pdf.

Clifton, J., F. Comin and D. Diaz-Fuentes (2003), *Privatisation in the European Union: Public Enterprises and Integration*, Dordrecht, Netherlands and Boston, MA, USA: Kluwer Academic Publishers.

Copenhagen Economics (2005), 'Market opening in network industries, final report to DG Internal Market', European Commission, available at www.copenhageneconomics.com/Website/Publications/Transport.aspx.

Den Hertog, J. (2010), 'Review of economic theories of regulation', Tjalling C. Koopmans Research Institute Discussion Paper Series, No. 10-18, Utrecht School of Economics, Utrecht University.

Di Giacomo, M. and E. Ottoz (2010), 'The relevance of scale and scope economies in the provision of urban and intercity bus transport', *Journal of Transport Economics and Policy*, **44** (2), 161–187.

European Commission (1992), 'The future development of the Common Transport Policy', EC Transport White Paper, COM (92) 494 final, Brussels.

European Commission (2006), 'Keep Europe moving – sustainable mobility for our continent, mid-term review of the European Commission's 2001 Transport White Paper', Communication from the Commission to the Council and the European Parliament, COM (2006) 314, Brussels.

European Commission (2011), 'Roadmap to a Single European Transport Area – towards a competitive and resource efficient transport system', EC Transport White Paper, COM(2011) 144 final, Brussels.

Farsi, M., A. Fetz and M. Filippini (2007), 'Economies of scale and scope in local public transportation', *Journal of Transport Economics and Policy*, **41** (3), 345–361.

Finger, M., N. Crettenand, M. Laperrouza and C. Duthaler (2011), 'Critical system-relevant functions and performance in network industries', working paper presented at the Florence School of Regulation Workshop on Performance in Network Industries, October.

Finger, M. and R. Künneke (eds) (2011), *International Handbook of Network Industries: The Liberalization of Infrastucture*, Cheltenham, UK and Northampton, MA, USA: Edward Elgar Publishing.

Glachant, J.-M. (2002), 'Why regulate deregulated network industries?', *Journal of Network Industries*, **3** (3), 297–312.

Hartley, R., D. Parker and S. Martin (1991), 'Organisational status, ownership and productivity', *Fiscal Studies*, **12** (2), 46–60.

Jaag, C. and U. Trinkner (2009), 'A general framework for regulation and liberalization in network industries', Swiss Economics Working Paper 0016, Zürich.

Knieps, Günter (2010), 'Regulatory reforms of European network industries and the courts', University of Freiburg, Institute for Transport Economics and Regional Policy Discussion Paper Series, No. 129.

Martin, R., M. Roma and I. Vansteenkiste (2005), 'Regulatory reforms in selected EU network industries', European Central Bank Occasional Paper Series, No. 28 / April.

Mueller, D.C. (2003), *Public Choice III*, Cambridge: Cambridge University Press.

Pollitt, C. and G. Bouckaert (2011), *Public Management Reform: A Comparative Analysis – New Public Management, Governance, and the Neo-Weberian State*, Oxford: Oxford University Press,

Quinet, E. and R. Vickerman (2004), *Principles of Transport Economics*, Cheltenham, UK and Northampton, MA, USA: Edward Elgar Publishing.

Thatcher, M. (2006), 'Europe and the reform of national regulatory institutions: a comparison of Britain, France and Germany', paper for Council of European Studies Conference, 15th Conference, Chicago, IL, 29 March–1 April.

UNESCAP (2001), *The Economic Regulation of Transport Infrastructure Facilities and Services Principles and Issues*, United Nations Economic and Social Commission for Asia and the Pacific Publication, New York: United Nations.

Vickers, J. and G. Yarrow (1988), *Privatisation: An Economic Analysis*, Cambridge, MA: MIT Press.

2. Air transport

Javier Campos

2.1 INTRODUCTION

Like the process of designing, building, and operating an aircraft, the development of a European air transport policy during the last 20 years has proven to be a challenging task. As will be shown in this chapter, setting the objectives, assembling all of the pieces together and making the machinery work in an efficient and smooth way has required the harmonized action of many manufacturers. Despite their efforts, under unfavourable weather conditions, the resulting flight has not always produced a pleasant experience.

In fact, the first decade of the twenty-first century has been a particularly tough one for aviation. As any other sector that relies on the overall level of economic activity, the air transport industry is currently suffering from the global economic downturn. However, the effects of the crisis have just worsened some of the still unmitigated consequences of past shocks: the 9/11 terrorist attacks, the SARS outbreak, the ash clouds of the Eyjafjallajökull volcano, and other unfortunate events in recent years. However, it can be argued that it is precisely under adverse circumstances when the strengths and weaknesses of an institutional set-up should be tested. For that reason, it is quite opportune to provide a critical review of the main mechanisms that define air transport policy, particularly from the point of view of most European countries. In this chapter, we will first provide the background for the reforms and then analyse the implementation of the main policy measures and their effects.

The origins of this policy can be traced back to the Chicago Convention in 1944, when more than 50 signatory states acknowledged that the international nature of this sector would certainly require coordinated regulation. The International Civil Aviation Organization (ICAO) was thus established to oversee the main rules of air transport, in the form of compulsory standards (with essential specifications regarding the reliability and safety of services, air traffic control and airport operating rules), and recommended practices (covering many other technical and operational issues related to infrastructure, aircraft and services) (ICAO, 2010).

All of the European countries signed or later ratified this Convention on International Civil Aviation, and hence it defined the pillars of their national air transport policies. In the immediate post-war era, aircraft remained a novelty on the Continent, but as technology improved and in-flight comfort increased, their advantages over land or sea journeys became more and more evident. As the sector grew during the following decades and air travel progressively became the dominant means of transport for long-distance passenger movements,[1] it was clear that new rules and more pieces had to be implemented in order to keep the machinery tuned. Simultaneously, the economic and political union born after the Treaty of Rome (1957) and reinforced through the concept of a 'single market' introduced by the Single European Act (1986) rendered the previous design incomplete.

Until that moment, air transport markets in Europe were drawn within national boundaries with a large presence of domestic flag carriers. Most of them were government supported and operated oligopolistic or monopolistic routes. Beyond ICAO recommendations on technical issues, economic regulation was the sole competence of national authorities. Airlines' fares, flying frequencies, airport access conditions and capacity rules were all subject to approval or control. There was little infrastructure policy, and international flows were mostly the result of bilateral or multilateral agreements. Without the existence of an effective European internal market, competition was weak, and despite the increasing traffic figures, the overall performance of the sector exhibited a progressive lack of competitiveness as compared to the consolidated United States (US) market or the emergence of the Asian hubs.[2]

In the mid-1980s, the situation already required urgent action. In 1985 the European Court of Justice (in the *Nouvelles Frontieres* case) explicitly stated that the transport sector could not be left aside from the common market principles and that both passenger and freight traffic should be open to any European operator in any member state, regardless of its nationality status. This ruling paved the way for the definitive launching of 'a single market of transport services' as stated in a seminal White Paper (European Commission, 1985). This became the central objective of the European Union (EU) transport policy.

To achieve this goal, the required changes were based on two key ideas: the liberalization of services by dismantling internal barriers and removing the obstacles that hindered competition; and the harmonization of the rules that blocked the integration of national markets and limited fair trade. These elements were not new in the air industry: domestic passenger deregulation had already started in 1978 in the United States, spreading to other countries during the next decade (McGowan and Seabright, 1989). The resulting evidence was mixed, featuring both positive and negative results. This showed European countries that prior to embarking on a complete deregulation of the whole industry, it was reasonable to test it on a small scale. The pace for this experiment was thus to proceed firstly at a strictly national level by extending the agreements already negotiated between pairs of countries (namely, Britain, Ireland and the Netherlands).[3] Then, the reform was followed by measures at the EU level, as explicitly intended by several deregulation packages released in 1987, 1990 and 1992 with their corresponding Directives and regulations. Of course, this two-step approach was not particular to the aviation industry, but it also reflected the slow political process of mutual acquaintance that has slowly helped to build all of the European institutions (Betancor and Campos, 2000).

Once this initial context has been provided, the next section (2.2) examines in more detail the main components of the reforms that helped to shape the current European air transport policy from a national model to a coordinated system. I will combine a chronological and analytic perspective, considering not only when the changes were introduced but also their circumstances and how they were combined with the other pieces that define the entire artefact. Section 2.3 is then devoted to a critical review of the performance of the measures, particularly evaluating to what extent the main policy objectives have been achieved, what areas are to be reinforced, and what is the current situation of the regulatory framework in the sector. Using these ideas, section 2.4 provides some final conclusions to this chapter.

2.2   THE REFORM OF EUROPEAN AIR TRANSPORT REGULATION

Moving the entire air transport industry from a mostly national system (under technical supervision by ICAO on international issues and technical standards) to a supra-national scheme in order to create a single market was not an easy task. It required numerous political agreements and concessions. The initial examples provided by unilateral and bilateral liberalization processes in some countries contributed to mitigate the resistance of some of them, and the strong pro-European impetus that animated the reforms in other sectors by that time finally convinced a majority of EU members that it was the right time to implement new measures in the transport markets. Two periods can be identified and separately analysed within this process: the first decade (1987–2000) and the more recent years (2001–2011).[4]

2.2.1 The Core Engine: Implementing the Deregulation Packages, 1987–2000

Although it had been anticipated in some previous documents, the deregulation process in the air industry was formally started in 1987, and its completion took almost a whole decade. The liberalization of passenger and cargo services gradually evolved from that year onwards by means of a series of legislative measures that required a short implementation process at national level. The first 'package' was put into practice in January 1988 and only affected regular services among member states. It was aimed at reducing the national jurisdiction to regulate competition at the intra-European level by allowing airlines to offer discount fares within set zones. It also allowed multiple accesses on selected routes defined by traffic thresholds. In addition, it permitted the combination of flying rights within two destinations for the same flight and between regional and main airports. Since several countries were still not fully convinced, and in order to soften the final impact, block exemptions were granted for some existing practices regarding, for example, revenue pooling (now limited to 1 per cent of revenue earned on the route); fares and capacity coordination; airport slot allocation; and joint ownership of computer reservation systems.

Following the meeting of the Council of Transport Ministers in June 1990, a second deregulation package was adopted with the aim of eliminating some of the previous exceptions, particularly those related to revenue and capacity pooling agreements. From 1992 onwards, airlines were granted even greater freedom in their fare-setting procedures, with a provision for a lower fare being rejected only if both concerned governments disapproved. Notably enough, these rules were now to be applied not only to internal air services between member countries but also to existing and future agreements with non-members, which brought obvious implications for non-EU carriers. The second package also extended the liberalization process by allowing total freedom to operate third and fourth freedom routes in terms of the Chicago Convention,[5] only restricted by infrastructure limitations (e.g., runway capacity, slot allocation limits, or air traffic control safety considerations). Freedom rights were also increased to allow 50 per cent of any aircraft's capacity to be allocated to fifth freedom passengers. For the first time, the regulation provided support for cabotage at the European level (i.e., the transport of passengers between two points in the same country by an aircraft registered in another country), although subject to certain restrictions. Finally, it was also required that all member countries should license any airline registered in another member state, providing the airline satisfied the national requirements for the issuance of a valid operator's certificate.

Only a couple of years later, the final liberalization step was taken through a third package approved by the Council of Ministers in June 1992. This was also the year when the first White Paper entirely dedicated to the common transport policy (European Commission, 1992) was published. Its focus on opening the market was reflected in the package by eliminating some of the previous concessions that had not been agreed upon before, and by stating new access rules. Start-up airlines from member countries were now subject to common licensing requirements, simultaneously limiting the validity of the licences for existing carriers to a three-year period. After the expiration of this term, the rules for new carriers would apply to any renewal procedure. Furthermore, market access was also eased by removing the remaining differences between charter and scheduled services regulations, and unrestricted access for all European registered carriers to all airports was granted, except where it was considered that such a policy could be damaging for a country's justified national interests. The possibility of introducing public service obligations on low-density routes, and the protection of consumers and operators against abusive or predatory pricing practices, were also considered as a necessary complement to increased competition. Finally, in response to similar policies outside Europe, the package also defined the concept of 'a European operator': the airline ownership should effectively remain under the majority control of EU nationals, and its primary place of business had to be in the licensing member country.

It is generally considered that in April 1997, when most of the provisions of the third package came into force, the main foundations of the liberalization of air transport in Europe had been completed. All of the major measures and policy mechanisms were implemented, and the sector was ready to enter a new century under a new institutional set-up. The basic elements of a single market had been laid down: any technically qualified EU airline could now operate in any region of the European Union, even on wholly domestic routes, without the restraints on fares or capacity that had prevailed before.

2.2.2 From Fine-Tuning to Setting New Course: the 2000–2012 Period

The initial assessments made during the 1990s were moderately positive. As in the United States, the liberalization of air transport in Europe started to bring a proliferation of travel options for consumers through new types of rates and greater benefits associated with loyalty programmes. However, with few exceptions, no significant changes in the market structure took place at the beginning. Two of the reasons identified to explain this result were related to infrastructure inefficiencies: on one hand, important technical and economic capacity restrictions remained at airports; and on the other, airspace congestion in the European Union was an increasing problem as traffic figures rose more and more every year.

Thus, almost immediately after the implementation of the third package, the European air transport policy embarked on a revision process to adjust several pieces that did not appear to work properly within this machinery. In 1998, another White Paper (European Commission, 1998) proposed new measures to promote better access to airport infrastructure, still dominated by operators' established rights. Although the 1992 regulations had already included several provisions for the allocation of time slots, their results had not been strong enough. In many airports, the status quo remained almost unchanged. The 'use-it-or-lose-it' rule and other technical issues were improved. In addition, the regulation attempted to build a code of conduct that ensured a more transparent and efficient system, limiting the 'grandfather rights' and providing non-discriminatory mechanisms at major airports. It recommended better governance rules and set out the objective conditions of access for new entrants, with several safeguard mechanisms in place to avoid excessive disequilibria among operators. The lack of significant entry into the industry during these years suggests that the dominant position that the incumbent airlines enjoyed did not suffer too much until the emergence of low-cost carriers, many of them based at secondary airports.

Congestion was a structural problem due to the saturation and fragmentation of the airspace, which was technically characterized by the existence of central controls operated from different land systems that coordinate their tasks very closely on safety grounds. Efforts to unify the European airspace included in the White Paper did not find enough support among the member states until 1999, when the Single European Sky initiative was launched, and it was to be progressively implemented during the following decades. It established targets in key areas of safety, network capacity, effectiveness and environmental impact, and drove a major transformation of the role of Eurocontrol to become the network manager of the European air traffic management (ATM) system.

The next major adjustment in the European air transport policy was presented in the 2001 White Paper (European Commission, 2001), where the new design for the next decade was clearly outlined. As summarized in Figure 2.1, a crucial change in focus was introduced: the policy objectives progressively shifted from its main target so far (the consolidation of the

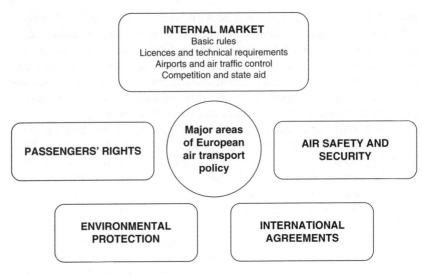

Figure 2.1   Major areas of European air transport policy since 2001

internal market, including the rules for service, infrastructure operation, and all of the issues connected to competition). The shift was made to new areas such as the protection of passengers' rights, the relevance of safety and security procedures, and the central role of environmental sustainability and international affairs. The White Paper's main innovation resided in proposing for the first time a strategy to gradually break the strong link between economic growth and the ever-growing transport demand. This was necessary in order to soften the pressure that this relationship implied for the environment. The White Paper advocated a qualitative change in the direction of transport policy, which should be refocused on the citizens rather than on institutions or markets. The European Commission considered that the internal air transport market had become a reality and an engine for growth. Simultaneously, it identified as main challenges the imbalance in the development of the different modes; congestion on routes, in cities and in airspace; and the impact on the environment. Accordingly, to adjust the balance, new policies were proposed to do away with bottlenecks in the major trans-European networks and to reduce external effects. It called for an effective policy on infrastructure charging and argued that the community should strengthen its position in international organizations.

At the mid-term review in 2006 (European Commission, 2006) most of the regulatory developments on air transport policy had been re-oriented towards the integrated and cooperative development of the different modes. The experience since 2001, as well as the optimistic projections available at that time, suggested that the measures envisaged in the White Paper would require additional tuning to contain the negative environmental impacts and other effects of transport growth while facilitating sustainable mobility as the new essential purpose of the transport policy.

All of these conclusions had been finally revised in the 2011 White Paper, the most recent piece added to the mechanism, which again defines 'a roadmap to a Single European Transport Area' (European Commission, 2011). It essentially encourages the development of a competitive and resource-efficient transport system. Although the paper reckons that 'a lot needs to be done to complete the internal market for transport, where considerable bottlenecks and other barriers remain', it does not propose many specific actions for air transport, implicitly assuming that the sector is now governed by autopilot interfaces and that only minor course corrections are needed. The next section attempts to evaluate to what extent this judgement is right.

2.3   THE RESULTS OF THE REFORMS AND THE CURRENT EUROPEAN AIR TRANSPORT POLICY

Deregulation policies have been widely reckoned as a major factor contributing to the worldwide increase in air travel during the past two decades (Button and Taylor, 2000). Most European airlines enjoyed a consistent positive trend in their figures during the 1990s. This only started to drop at the beginning of the new millennium. On average, however, traffic levels grew by an average annual rate of above 5 per cent between 1990 and 2007 in Europe; the number of routes doubled, and by 2008, about 800 million passengers were carried through about 400 airports, 65 per cent of them on domestic or intra-European flights. The estimated level of business activity for the sector amounted to €135 billion, including both airlines and airports, sustaining more than 3.2 million direct and indirect jobs, which represented 3 per cent of the EU workforce (European Commission, 2009). These figures confirm the relevance of an economic activity that, by its own nature, has become essential for the European Union as an element that guarantees the mobility of its citizens and the integration of its markets. Although the industry slowed its pace in 2008 as a result of the economic downturn, signs of recovery have emerged in 2011, showing again an increase of 5.9 per cent as compared with 2010, according to Eurostat data in Figure 2.2.

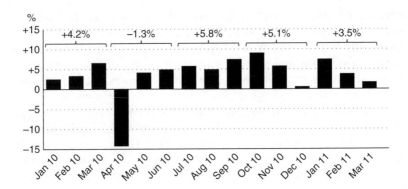

Figure 2.2   Evolution of EU air passenger transport in recent years

Table 2.1   Ranking of European airports as compared to the world's

Airport (city)	Passengers (2011) (mill.)	Passengers (2010) (mill.)	% change	World ranking
Heathrow (London)	69.4	65.8	+5.4	#3
Charles de Gaulle (Paris)	60.9	58.1	+4.8	#7
Frankfurt (Frankfurt)	56.4	53.0	+6.5	#9
Schiphol (Amsterdam)	49.7	45.2	+10.0	#14
Barajas (Madrid)	49.6	49.8	−0.4	#15
Munich (Munich)	37.7	34.7	+8.8	#27
Fiumicino (Rome)	37.6	36.3	+3.6	#29

Source: National Authorities' statistics.

However, some clouds remain on the horizon. Most of the domestic traffic is still highly correlated with touristic flows. Companies' balance sheets have been hit by shrinking demand and higher fuel costs. Only five airports operate with annual demand levels close to or above 50 million (see Table 2.1), while another 100 airports have traffic levels that range from 1.5 million to 10 million passengers per year. Public financial support and infrastructure investment is being reduced, and competition from high-speed rail services is gaining momentum on selected dense corridors (Gillen and Niemeier, 2008). The threat of higher costs due to the implementation of mechanisms aimed at internalizing external costs, enhancing travel security or protecting passengers' rights also reduces the future profitability of the sector. However, this is just a global view; the analysis of the results of the liberalization process requires some additional details that will be provided below, disaggregated by each major policy area.

2.3.1 The Relative Success of the Internal Market

As any other transport activity, the functioning of air transport markets is decided as a result of adequate provision of services by airlines, a smooth connection between them and the infrastructure, and the existence of a clear set of rules governing the relationship between these two parties and the consumers.

Service provision and the segmentation of the market

Although, in theory, most controls had been already removed and free market competition existed since April 1997, it was soon evident that the transposition to national laws of the third package regulations had not been homogenous throughout member states, whose national authorities still retain many powers. In 2008, a new basic regulation was produced that redefined common rules for the operation of air services. In particular, it redefined the licensing procedures of community air carriers, the law applicable to them, and the pricing of air services. These common rules define who the service providers are (what conditions and requirements they should meet) and how they should behave (pricing behaviour and access to routes). They constitute the most relevant part of current operating conditions.[6]

Since the deregulation also fully transformed the nature of the markets, the companies' strategies had to face a more challenging business environment. A natural consequence was their segmentation into three well-differentiated models: traditional or full-service carriers, low-cost or value-based airlines, and charter airlines (which were less affected by the changes and still focused on touristic flows). As shown in Table 2.2, the first group mainly included former flag carriers, many of them now privatized and merged, operating scheduled services on hub-and-spoke networks in order to exploit economies of density. Despite the growing demand, the economic performance of traditional carriers has weakened in recent years, reducing their market share. Without the recourse to public funds, some of them have recently gone bankrupt. Others have been forced to enter into concentration processes, as explained below, to become players in global alliances – such as Oneworld, SkyTeam or Star Alliance – or to copy their rivals' business models. In fact, the emergence of the low-cost business model has been considered an unexpected consequence of the changes in European aviation, very positive in terms of fares and new services but less positive, in several cases, in terms of service quality. Low-cost carriers have quickly taken over several routes formerly dominated by flag carriers and charter companies (Williams, 2001), and their growth expectations remain high.

Table 2.2 The international nature of major European Union airlines: fleet and passengers by group

Group	Airlines	Countries	Alliance	Major airports	Fleet in 2011	Passengers (mill.) in 2011	Passengers (mill.) in 2010
LUFTHANSA GROUP	Lufthansa, Lufthansa CityLine, Air Dolomiti, Swiss International Airlines, Bmi and Austrian Airlines	Germany	*Star Alliance*	Frankfurt Munich	710	106.33	90.20
RYANAIR	Ryanair	Ireland	*ELFAA*	Dublin London (Stansted)	295	76.40	72.72
AIR FRANCE-KLM	Air France, KLM, CityJet, VLM Airlines and Transavia	France Netherlands	*SkyTeam*	Paris (Charles de Gaulle) Amsterdam	616	75.78	70.75
EASYJET	EasyJet, EasyJet Switzerland	United Kingdom	*ELFAA*	London (Gatwick, Luton)	193	55.47	49.72
INTERNATIONAL AIRLINES GROUP (IAG)	British Airways, Iberia, Air Nostrum and BA CityFlyer	United Kingdom Spain	*Oneworld*	London (Heathrow) Madrid	420	51.68	57.30
AIR BERLIN GROUP	Air Berlin, Niki, Dba, LTU and Belair	Germany	*Oneworld*	Berlin Düsseldorf	153	31.78	31.77
SAS GROUP	Scandinavian Airlines, Blue1 and Wideroe	Sweden Norway Denmark	*Star Alliance*	Stockholm	173	27.20	25.23

Source: Own elaboration from the companies' annual reports.

The relationship between infrastructure and services

Beyond their obvious technical connections, a smooth economic relationship between the provision of air transport services and the airports is crucial to gain full advantage of the liberalization process. Otherwise, the infrastructure becomes a bottleneck and transfers its inefficiencies to the entire transport chain. This problem was explicitly recognized by the European Union in 2006, which admitted the possibility of a capacity shortfall both at airports and ATM systems. An 'infrastructure package' was thus launched concerning some aspects of the airport activities including slot allocation, groundhandling services, air navigation charges and airport charges.

In a context of reduced funding for investments other than those included within the Trans-European Networks (TENs), the general idea governing these provisions is the need for reorganization to make better use of existing capacity. In the case of slot allocation, attempts have been made to limit the incumbents' rights, although these restrictions have been eased under the current circumstances of the economic crisis.[7] Other amendments to this regulation have been made to clarify slot mobility and to monitor the compliance in exchanges. In fact, using the United Kingdom (UK) experience, secondary trading was recognized for the first time in 2008 as an acceptable system of swapping slots among airlines. As a result, this legislation is being revised, and the European Commission has decided to carry out an impact assessment of different scenarios (Betancor and de Rus, 2013).

With respect to groundhandling and infrastructure charges, most services at medium-sized and large airports had been liberalized since 1998, although some amendments were made in 2003 to extend their provisions.[8] Harmonization of charges has taken more time and is still incomplete. The regulation, effective since 2011, establishes the need for member states to create an independent charging authority to which most issues related to price-setting are delegated.[9]

In addition to an efficient airport network, the construction of the common internal market relies on the existence of a Single European Sky with an ATM system capable of providing safe and efficient operations. The initiative was started in 2004, and its objectives were the following: to improve safety; to restructure European airspace as a function of traffic flows rather than national borders; to create additional capacity; and to enhance the system's overall efficiency. All of these elements are under revision. A second package of legislation is expected in the near future, as described in the 2011 transport White Paper (European Commission, 2011). The White Paper also presents the Single European Sky ATM Research (SESAR) project as the key technological element, which targets the modernization of air traffic control infrastructure in Europe, in coordination with Eurocontrol.

Competition, prices and state aid
The third component of the internal market comes from the rules governing the relationship between operators (of infrastructure and services) and consumers. The liberalization of air transport has facilitated the entry of new carriers and increased the competitive pressure on a number of routes. Between 1992 and 2009, intra-European routes doubled, and the number of routes with more than two competitors tripled. The degree of rivalry among air carriers has increased dramatically: British Airways, for example, established a presence in the French market; Lufthansa introduced short-term discounts and started domestic services in Italy; Air France introduced discounted air passes and commenced cabotage services in Greece; and Alitalia started cabotage schedules in Portugal and Spain. The emergence of low-cost carriers such as Ryanair or EasyJet provided incentives for these responses, although in most cases, they were not enough. Most traditional companies had finally accepted merger processes, such as Air France–KLM or the International Airlines Group (British Airways plus Iberia). Even so, too many carriers probably still exist in the European Union compared with, for instance, the United States.

Although cases of collusive practices have increased, they are not widespread, and passengers are now offered a great variety of services with a wide range of fares from which to choose. This effect on fares has been claimed as one of the largest successes of the liberalization packages. A fairly strong relationship appears to exist between average fares and level of competition on a route, especially for unrestricted economy fares. However, even though an increasingly large number of promotional fares have become available, flexible fares kept on increasing, and large differences still remain in fares per kilometre across Europe. Note also that some of the airlines' responses to this environment could undermine these benefits. The excessive proliferation of tariffs, overbooking practices and even code-sharing and airline alliances can all make it harder for consumers to compare alternative offers. As competition increases, market transparency needs to be assured if consumer confidence is to be maintained.

On the contrary, European airports have been moving at a slower pace. Competition among them is limited, which is probably associated with their low degree of private participation, as noted by Winston and De Rus (2008), who also argue that this is a global trend. Oum et al. (2008) discuss how the ownership structure affects airport efficiency and show that the most cost-efficient airports are those that are either totally private or fully state-owned, while the models with mixed structures, especially those where the majority shareholder is a public body, are the least efficient. The authors' explanation for this is that airports with mixed governance criteria often have conflicting objectives, but this remains an issue that has not been treated in depth by the European air transport policy.

Another final issue related to the effects of public sector intervention on aviation markets is the case of state aid in the form of public sector obligations (PSOs). They play a relevant role in many national markets to ensure the provision of services in certain regions, although they also represent an exception within the general deregulatory framework (as PSO routes are fully regulated with respect to fares, frequencies and capacity, among other variables). Although the new legislation made a simplification and clarification effort, some rules are still unclear. In fact, PSO declarations are subject to very different interpretations and applications of provisions throughout Europe, which poses some regulatory risks (Williams and Pagliari, 2004).[10] In any case, and despite several elements to be completed in the near future, the achievement of the common internal market is a reality as compared with the situation prior to 1987.

2.3.2 The Improvement of Passengers' Rights

Although an efficient market performance should suffice to ensure customer satisfaction in terms of fares or frequencies, several quality dimensions in air travel have not been considered above, and that also plays a relevant role in consumers' welfare. In fact, the deregulation packages included a few provisions regarding the protection of passengers' rights (with respect to their purchases through computer reservation systems, in 1989; regarding the carrier's liability and the level of compensation in case of accidents, in 1997). However, it was not until 2000 that a 'charter of passenger rights' (which included clauses on denied boarding or overbooking) was effectively promoted. In 2006, the rights of people with reduced mobility were also reckoned.

The charter has been functioning fairly well, and it is now very common to see, at every corner of European airports, information about passengers' rights. With the exceptions of major incidents (strikes, security concerns or volcano ash), the companies usually meet expectations, although some low-cost carriers are often the target of many complaints due to the lack of sufficient ground staff and other practices. A second relevant exception occurs when air passengers become stranded away from home due to an airline bankruptcy or similar event. The possibility of airline bankruptcy is one of the implications of air transport liberalization. During the past few decades, this has affected national flag carriers such as Swissair and Sabena, larger companies such as Spanair, or smaller airlines such as AirLib, Air Exel or Duo. Since financial health criteria were introduced for the granting of airlines' licences, specific regulation does not exist on this issue at the EU level. The situation is changing, and several regulatory options are being considered: an insurance policy (individually purchased by each airline or passenger), agreements between companies, or collective guarantees. In all three cases, distortive impacts would be made on the markets: internalizing the risk conveys a higher cost of flying (Transport Studies Unit, 2005).

2.3.3   The Costs of Higher Safety and Security

After 1997, when the three deregulation packages were already implemented and the newly born common internal market for aviation services was ready to take off, two pieces of the system surprisingly became more evident than ever. On the one hand, it was clear that enhanced competition could not be accomplished by means of a reduction in safety standards; on the other, the shocking effects of the 9/11 attacks in 2001 exposed the risky nature of air travel and brought security to the front line of transport policy.

Historically, the accident rates in European civil aviation had remained fairly constant during the past few decades, but it was felt that an increasing risk was emerging, as traffic was expected to grow fast within the internal market. Although ICAO and other international bodies had so far dealt with safety procedures, the European Union reacted in 2003 by improving the procedures in an effort to collect and analyse the information of occurrences, accidents and incidents. It later forced each member country to establish a permanent national civil aviation safety investigation authority, to be coordinated with the European Aviation Safety Agency (EASA), created in 2002. The agency's main tasks were to develop common safety rules for the internal market in coordination with ICAO; to conduct inspections to verify that the rules were correctly applied; and to issue safety certificates to aircraft, air carriers, maintenance organizations and training programmes.

Most of EASA's actions so far have contributed to maintaining a high safety standard in European aviation, with some minor exceptions. As a consequence of several incidents, it has particularly devoted its efforts to third-country carriers using community airports by developing a 'black list' of those who do not comply with minimum safety standards. However, as the financial position of many carriers has deteriorated as a consequence of either increased competition or the economic crisis, the existence of a potential link between an operator's financial health and its safety procedures should not be disregarded, as well as the fact that national authorities have lost several parts of their supervision capacity due to the multinational nature of most operators.

With respect to security issues, the closure of the global airspace in September 2001 and the health hazards that brought similar consequences in later years (SARS in 2003–04, and swine flu in 2008–09) have shown the fragility of the civil aviation system and the need to introduce adequate regulatory mechanisms (Alderighi and Cento, 2004). In 2002, the European Union defined common security rules in airports and flights. It included an increase in the surveillance procedures whose costs were transferred to airlines and passengers in the form of both higher prices and longer waiting times. In a 2008 revision, some of the procedures were simplified but still constitute a major nuisance for most travellers, whose privacy has also been invaded due to data requirements. If flying continues to become such an unpleasant experience, it is no wonder that on certain routes, high-speed rail services have regained market share. Certainly, some technological improvements at airports are socially demanded to correct this trend.

2.3.4 Air Transport and Environmental Policy

If achieving an efficient allocation of resources is considered a central objective of the European air transport policy, it is clear that setting the rules for the economic functioning of the market is not enough: the policy must ensure that prices reflect the marginal social costs of air transport, including their three major external effects: noise, pollution and global warming.

The European Union's management of the noise problem closely follows the so-called 'balanced approach' defined by ICAO in 2001, which consists of identifying and quantifying the noise at airport areas and subsequently analysing alternative abatement measures: reduction at source; land use and planning; operational procedures; and operating restrictions on aircraft operations. In 2002–03, several Directives and regulations were developed to define rules regarding the introduction of restrictions on airlines' operations in sensitive areas and to establish several common procedures to elaborate noise maps that would allow determining the level of exposure in each case. Neither ICAO's approach nor the European Commission's approach specifically favoured setting Pigouvian charges as the main policy option to tackle this problem. It was simply recommended that, if used, charges should be non-discriminatory and designed to recover no more than the costs applied to noise alleviation or prevention.

However, in spite of increasing amount of technical literature on this issue,[11] the lack of a standardized methodology and the fact of noise being a very local externality have prevented general pricing schemes spreading over most EU airports.

As analysed in detail by Betancor and de Rus (2013), the approach to the treatment of air pollution has been very similar to the case of noise. Most of the regulatory mechanisms implemented by the European Union seek to introduce restrictions on the airlines' level of activity ('command and control' measures), whereas 'market measures' (through prices) are less frequent. In particular, emission charges at the airports are found in Europe only in a few instances (e.g. in Sweden, the United Kingdom and Switzerland).

Finally, although European aviation's share of overall greenhouse gas emissions is just below 3 per cent, its rapid growth jeopardizes the advances in other sectors and the targets set in the Kyoto Protocol. Since 2001, the climate change impact of aviation has been at the forefront of EU air transport policy, whose main efforts in the last decade have been devoted to: promoting research and development (R&D) on 'greener' technologies; improving the efficiency of the ATM systems through the effective implementation of the Single European Sky and SESAR initiatives; reconsidering the taxation of aviation fuel in line with its external costs; and favouring the reduction of aircraft emissions through their environmental certification.

As a relevant piece of the Greening Transport Package of 2008, aviation was finally included within the European Emission Trading Scheme (ETS). This change, effective since January 2012, constituted a major step towards a real reduction in emission figures, in line with the specific targets recently revised in the 2011 White Paper (usage of 40 per cent less low-carbon sustainable fuels). The scheme sets decreasing caps on the number of allowances to be allocated to each air carrier: in the first year of operation, the cap would be equivalent to 97 per cent of the historical aviation emissions, whereas it would be lowered to 95 per cent for each subsequent period. In the beginning, only 15 per cent of the allowances would be auctioned, and operators could trade allowances in order to allocate emissions reduction where they are most cost-effective.

The long-term impacts of these measures are controversial. Forsyth (2008) estimates that the potential impact of ETS in terms of percentage increase in fares ranges from 1.6 to 6 per cent depending on factors such as the market structure, the short-run versus long-run impacts, or the existence of other constraints. Similarly, CE Delft (2005) calculates that price increases would be in the range of €0.2 to €9 for a round trip, depending on the prices of allowances, routes and distances. In all cases, the internalization of external cost is not neutral. 'Greener flights' are more expensive; what remains to be decided is how the surcharges should be distributed among all the players. Otherwise the game is too boring: the consumers always lose.

2.3.5 The Internationalization of Air Travel Regulation

Extending the apparent success of the liberalization from the internal markets to the so-called Common Aviation Area (which comprises the European Union plus all its partners located along its southern and eastern borders) was the final development area of the EU air transport policy as envisaged in the 2001 White Paper. Prior to this date, member states frequently negotiated their own bilateral agreements with third countries, something that often derived into a source of conflict between the parties and the European Commission. Following the 'open skies' ruling by the European Court of Justice in 1992, this situation was reverted: member states' national authorities could no longer act in isolation when negotiating international air service agreements, since they were to be treated as a subject of Community interest (European Commission, 1992). A new set of principles and procedures was designed to ensure an adequate exchange of information, so that member states, in their bilateral relations with third countries in the area of air transport, did not risk infringing EU law.

The international agenda for the European Union's external policy was then extended to achieve global agreements in the major regions of the world, with the aim of strengthening the prospects for promoting European industry and ensuring fair competition in the most dynamic markets, while at the same time helping to reform international civil aviation by supporting ICAO's own initiatives.

The most relevant success in this area was the Open Skies Agreement between Europe and the United States, which went into effect in March 2008. Among other provisions, the agreement allows EU airlines to operate flights to the United States from any European airport, regardless of their nationality, thus giving full open access over transatlantic routes. It also includes an arrangement to develop the consensus further on matters such as safety, security, competition policy, state aid, consumer protection and the environment. With respect to the critical issue of airline ownership (in general, under US law, foreigners may not hold over 25 per cent voting shares in an American company and may not control it), an exception to the general rule was made. Europeans were allowed to hold more than a 50 per cent share in American carriers but not to gain overall control. The EU side reserved a right to restrict US investment in European companies to the same level.

The ultimate objective of the Open Skies Agreement seems to be the creation of a single aviation market between both signatories, with minimal restrictions on service provision, including access to domestic routes in the near future. Guided by this purpose, negotiations still go on since the benefits arising from the removal of restrictions in these markets have been estimated at an additional demand of 26 million passengers over a five-year period, with an increase in consumers' surplus that ranges from €6 billion to €12 billion (Booz Allen Hamilton, 2007). This agreement has also served as a model for negotiations with other countries (Eastern Europe and the Mediterranean Balkans neighbours), although their success is much more limited.

In general, by developing an external aviation policy, the European Union can lead the initiative towards reforming international civil aviation and opening up global markets to the efficiency benefits brought from fair competition. Quite likely, this is the most underdeveloped area within current EU air transport policy, and the recent 2011 White Paper explicitly proposes the 'completion of a European Common Aviation Area of 58 countries and one billion inhabitants by 2020'. Again, under a global economic downturn, this optimistic target may seem too far away. The flight will be long and with plenty of turbulence.

2.4   CONCLUSIONS

Although not initially included in the original articles of the Treaty of Rome, air travel is now widely viewed as a model sector where the impact of European policies is clear and effective, having reached full liberalization from a purely domestic market structure. The long deregulation process of air transport services that took place in Europe during the last decades of the twentieth century is now saluted by most analysts as a definitive and final step towards the integration of EU domestic markets beyond national borders. It is a necessary measure to increase the relevance of European companies in the global context and the possibility for European travellers to gain access to better and more efficient services for both their work and leisure flights.

Ten years later, the results of this regulatory reform seem mixed. On the positive side, airlines can now operate in most domestic and international markets liberated from national restrictions or the need for bilateral agreements. Traffic levels have increased, the degree of competition has enjoyed dramatic growth, particularly in routes served by low-cost carriers, and passengers face a wider range of services and fares.

Several clouds still overshadow these encouraging results. Firstly, the global relevance of European airlines and airports is still declining as compared to their US or Asian counterparts. Too many carriers probably still exist in the European Union compared with other places. In addition, the participation of European carriers in international alliances and their concentration through transnational mergers has not brought a much brighter business performance or a better positioning of European airports as compared with the pre-liberalization period. Secondly, intra-European traffic figures are mostly explained via tourist flows, affected by seasonal variations and the emergence of high-speed rail as an intermodal competitor. Meanwhile, transatlantic flights are still highly exposed to external shocks. Most travellers are concentrated on a reduced number of airports, while less dense routes suffer from chronic financial problems and the need for explicit support in the form of (tolerated, but regulated) public service obligations or (less tolerated) state or local government aid. Finally, substantial obstacles to competition still arise from differences in member states' implementation of the liberalization packages. Management and access to airport and other infrastructure services (including air traffic control and land support services), along with the increasingly restrictive effects of the regulation of externalities (noise, pollution and safety) in a context of global financial crisis definitely constitute some of the most relevant regulatory challenges that will face the air transport industry in the coming years.

The main aim of this chapter has been to discuss each of these results by considering how regulation affects market performance and vice versa, putting together the pieces of a process that not only explains the evolution of the European air transport in recent years but also provides some insights on future initiatives in this sector in order to ensure an efficient regulatory framework. The plane is already in flight, but having a safe and pleasant journey will depend on the pilot's ability to face current stormy weather, so to speak.

NOTES

1. In the 1950s and 1960s, annual growth rates of 15 per cent or more were common in the United States (US) market, whereas other countries such as Britain or France enjoyed slightly lower rates. In the 1970s, in spite of the first oil crisis, the touristic boom kept the figures positive, although the expansion rates were reduced by 50 per cent. In 1975, air transport accounted for 9 per cent of all international passenger movements, whereas sea transport maintained its traditional dominance for freight (Heppenheimer, 1995).
2. An extensive literature covers the situation of the European air transport markets prior to their reform and compares them with different cases. The subsequent liberalization process and some of its results has been studied by, among others, Abbot and

Thompson (1991), Button et al. (1998), and more recently by Gillen and Niemeier (2008).

3. In fact, as noted by Hakfoort (1999), the initial proposals for change had been put forward to member countries in 1984 within an internal memorandum that suggested dismantling of pooling agreements, reduction of capacity controls and greater flexibility in the approval of fares and tariffs. Concurrent with these ideas, a new bilateral agreement between the United Kingdom and the Netherlands was completed. This showed that a liberalizing shift away from the traditional regulation was possible by allowing new carriers to operate on the routes, providing access to any airport by designated carriers, removing capacity controls and addressing the double-disapproval of fares.

4. Of course, a detailed analysis of the entire European legislation for the air transport sector is beyond the scope of this chapter. This section simply provides an overview of the main policy actions within their context. The Appendix includes a summary of the main regulatory Acts organized around their corresponding policy areas. Further details are online at http://ec.europa.eu/transport/air/handbook/handbook_en.htm.

5. First and second freedoms include the right to overfly a foreign country and make technical stopovers, as defined in the Chicago Convention. Third and fourth freedoms are commercial rights that appear in bilateral agreements between countries. The third one is the right to carry passengers or cargo from one's own country to another, whereas the fourth implies the right to carry passengers or cargo from another country to one's own. Finally, the fifth freedom allows an airline to carry revenue traffic between foreign countries as a part of services connecting the airline's own country (ICAO, 2010).

6. The requisites are not too restrictive: they include the exigency that the company hold an Air Operator Certificate (defined in line with ICAO recommendations), comply with insurance and ownership requirements, and provide financial guarantees. In addition, the management will be requested to provide proof that the undertaking is of good repute. With respect to pricing rules, they are minimal. Regulation 1008/2008 states that fares are freely set, but they should be informative and non-discriminatory.

7. This is also known as the '80:20 rule', according to which an airline might continue to use its 'grandfather rights' as long as they are used 80 per cent of the time. Non-used slots and newly created ones must go to a pool, with 50 per cent of them being reserved for new entrants. Initially, mobility of slots was reduced to transfers between sister companies or to one-by-one exchanges.

8. Directive 1996/67 stipulated that for certain categories of services (baggage handling, ramp handling, fuel and oil handling, and freight and mail handling) member states could limit the number of suppliers to no fewer than two for each category of service, although at least one of these suppliers had to be independent of the airport or the dominant airline. To reduce the differences that this regulation created across countries, the European Commission in December 2011 introduced new proposals to ensure that airlines had an increased choice of groundhandling solutions (from two to three operators, self-handling liberalization, new coordination rules, etc.).

9. After reviewing airport charges at European airports, Gillen and Niemeier (2008) note that when regulation is in place, it is most frequently of a cost-based type. Only in cases of privatization do price caps exist. They also conclude that independent regulators and incentive-based regulation lead to greater efficiency levels, peak pricing and the development of non-aviation commercial activities.

10. PSOs often end up becoming a double-edged sword. On one side, they guarantee the accessibility to remote regions; on the other, they restrict competition and often lead to inefficient outcomes. Within the European Union, it is up to the member states to decide upon which routes are 'essential air services' and to decide upon whether the central government or the regional governments should have responsibility for the PSO tenders. This has led to a certain degree of diversity. Norway has the largest number of PSO routes (61), followed by France (41). Spain, Portugal and Scotland have 10–12 routes each. The share of domestic seats that are offered under the PSO regime is highest in

Portugal (40 per cent) and Ireland (23 per cent). Several other countries, such as France and Norway, have around 10 per cent (Braathen, 2011). The average flight leg, capacity and subsidy per passenger also vary across countries (Reynolds-Feighan, 1995).

11. See, for example, Nelson (2004) or the IMPACT study by Maibach et al. (2007).

REFERENCES

Abbot, K. and D. Thompson (1991), 'De-regulating European aviation: the impact of bilateral liberalization', *International Journal of Industrial Organization*, **9**, 125–140.

Alderighi, M. and A. Cento (2004), 'European airlines conduct after September 11', *Journal of Air Transport Management*, **10** (2), 97–160.

Betancor, O. and J. Campos (2000), 'The first decade of European air transport deregulation: an empirical note', *Journal of Public Works and Management*, October, 135–146.

Betancor, O. and G. de Rus (2013), 'Aviation regulation in Europe', in D. Jenkins (ed.), *The Handbook of Airline Economics: A Global Approach*, Cheltenham, UK and Northampton, MA, USA: Edward Elgar Publishing.

Booz Allen Hamilton (2007), *The Economic Impact of an Open Aviation Area between the EU and the US*, report prepared for the Directorate General Energy and Transport, DG-TREN, Brussels.

Braathen, S. (2011), *Air Transport Services in Remote Regions*, ITF Discussion Paper 2011-13, Paris: OECD.

Button, K., K. Haynes and R. Stough (1998), *Flying into the Future: Air Transport Policy in the European Union*, Cheltenham, UK and Lyme, NH, USA: Edward Elgar Publishing.

Button, K.J. and S.Y. Taylor (2000), 'International air transportation and economic development', *Journal of Air Transport Management*, **6**, 209–222.

CE Delft (2005), 'Giving wings to emission trading: inclusion of aviation under the Emission Trading System', report prepared for the European Commission, DG Environment, Brussels.

European Commission (1985), 'Completing the Internal Market', White Paper from the Commission to the European Council, COM(85)310, June, Brussels.

European Commission (1992), 'The future development of the Common Transport Policy', White Paper from the Commission to the European Council, COM(92)494, December, Brussels.

European Commission (1998), 'Fair payment for infrastructure use: a phased approach to a common transport infrastructure charging framework in the EU', White Paper from the Commission to the European Council, COM(98)466, June, Brussels.

European Commission (2001), 'European transport policy for 2010: time to decide', White Paper from the Commission to the European Council, COM(2001)370, September, Brussels.

European Commission (2006), 'Keep Europe moving – sustainable mobility for our continent, mid-term review of the European Commission's 2001 Transport White Paper', Communication from the Commission to the Council and the European Parliament, COM(2006)314, Brussels.

European Commission (2009), 'Facts and key developments on air transport', available at http://ec.europa.eu/transport/air/doc/03_2009_facts_figures.pdf.

European Commission (2011), 'Roadmap to a Single European Transport Area – towards a competitive and resource efficient transport system', White Paper from the Commission to the European Council, COM(2011)144, March, Brussels.

Forsyth, P. (2008), 'The impact of climate change policy on competition in the air transport industry', ITF Discussion Paper No. 2008-18, prepared for the Round Table on Airline Competition, Systems of Airports and Intermodal Connections, Paris: OECD.

Gillen, D. and H.M. Niemeier (2008), 'The European Union: evolution of privatization, regulation and slot reform', in C. Winston and G. de Rus (eds), *Aviation Infrastructure Performance: a Study in Comparative Political Economy*, Washington, DC: Brookings Institution.

Hakfoort, J.R. (1999), 'The deregulation of European air transport: a dream come true?', *Tijdschrift voor Economische en Sociale Geografie*, **90** (2), 226–233.

Heppenheimer, T.A. (1995), *Turbulent Skies: The History of Commercial Aviation*, New York: John Wiley & Sons.

ICAO (2010), *Convention on International Civil Aviation* (with amendments), Montreal: ICAO Publications.

Maibach, M., C. Schreyer, D. Sutter, H.P. Van Hessen, B.H. Boon, R. Smokers, A. Schroten, C. Doll, B. Pawlowska and M. Bak (2007), *Handbook on Estimation of External Costs in the Transport Sector*, Delft: IMPACT (Internalisation Measures and Policies for All External Cost of Transport), European Commission.

McGowan, F. and P. Seabright (1989), 'Deregulating European airlines', *Economic Policy*, October, 284–335.

Nelson, J.P. (2004), 'Meta-analysis of airport noise and hedonic property values', *Journal of Transport Economics and Policy*, **38** (1), 1–27.

Oum, T.H., J. Yan and C. Yu (2008), 'Ownership forms matter for airport efficiency: a stochastic frontier investigation of worldwide airports', *Journal of Urban Economics*, 64, 422–435.

Reynolds-Feighan, A. (1995), 'European and American approaches to air transport liberalization: some implications for small communities', *Transportation Research A*, **29**, 467–483.

Transport Studies Unit (2005), 'Functioning of the internal market for air transport', AIRREG final report prepared for DG TREN.

Williams, G. (2001), 'Will Europe's charter carriers be replaced by "no-frills" scheduled airlines?', *Journal of Air Transport Management*, **7**, 277–286.

Williams, G. and R. Pagliari (2004), 'A comparative analysis of the application and use of public service obligations in air transport within the EU', *Transport Policy*, **11** (1), 55–66.

Winston, C. and G. De Rus (2008), 'Introduction', in C. Winston and G. de Rus (eds), *Aviation Infrastructure Performance: A Study in Comparative Political Economy*, Washington, DC: Brookings Institution.

APPENDIX

Table 2A.1 A summary of main European legislation in the air transport sector classified by major policy areas

Internal market:	
Basic rules	Regulation 1008/2008 on common rules for the operation of air services
Competition and state aid	Community guidelines on financing of airports and start-up aid to airlines departing from regional airports
	Regulation 868/2004 concerning protection against subsidization and unfair pricing practices causing injury to community air carriers in the supply of air services from countries not members of the European community
	Regulation 487/2009 on the application of Article 81(3) of the treaty to certain categories of agreements and concerted practices in the air transport sector
Licences and technical requirements	Directive 1991/670 on the mutual acceptance of licences for persons working in civil aviation
	Regulation 3922/91 on the harmonization of technical requirements and administrative procedures in the field of civil aviation
	Directive 2006/23 on a community air traffic controller licence
Airports and air traffic control	Regulation 95/93 on common rules for the allocation of slots
	Regulation 1794/2006 laying down a common charging scheme for air navigation services
	Directive 2009/12 on airport charges
Passengers' rights:	Regulation 785/2004 on insurance requirements for air carriers and aircraft operators
	Regulation 261/2004 establishing common rules on compensation and assistance to passengers in the event of denied boarding and of cancellation or long delay of flights, and repealing Regulation (EEC) No 295/91
	Regulation 2111/2005 on the establishment of a community list of air carriers subject to an operating ban within the Community and on informing air transport passengers of the identity of the operating air carrier, and repealing Article 9 of Directive 2004/36/EC
	Regulation 1107/2006 concerning the rights of disabled persons and persons with reduced mobility when travelling by air
	Regulation 80/2009 on a code of conduct for computerized reservation systems and repealing Regulation 2299/89

Table 2A.1 (continued)

Air safety and security:	Directive 94/56 establishing the fundamental principles governing the investigation of civil aviation accidents and incidents
	Regulation 889/2002 amending Regulation 2027/97 on air carrier liability in the event of accidents
	Directive 2003/42 on occurrence reporting in civil aviation
	Directive 2004/36 on the safety of third-country aircraft using community airports
	Directive 2004/82 on the obligation of carriers to communicate passenger data
	Regulation 216/2008 on common rules in the field of civil aviation and establishing a European Aviation Safety Agency, and repealing Council Directive 91/670/EEC, Regulation 592/2002 and Directive 2004/36/EC
	Regulation 300/2008 on common rules in the field of civil aviation security and repealing Regulation 2320/2002
Environmental protection:	Directive 2002/30 on the establishment of rules and procedures with regard to the introduction of noise-related operating restrictions at community airports
	Directive 2002/49 relating to the assessment and management of environmental noise
	Regulation 1702/2003 implementing rules for the airworthiness and environmental certification of aircraft and related products, parts and appliances, as well as for the certification of design and production organizations
	Directive 2006/93 on the regulation of the operation of airplanes covered by Part II, Chapter 3, Volume 1 of Annex 16 to the Convention on International Civil Aviation
	Communication from the Commission COM (2005) 459: 'Reducing the Climate Change Impact of Aviation'
	Regulation 71/2008 setting up the Clean Sky Joint Undertaking
	Directive 2008/101 amending Directive 2003/87/EC so as to include aviation activities in the scheme for greenhouse gas emission allowance trading within the Community
International agreements:	Regulation 847/2004 on the negotiation and implementation of air service agreements between member states and third countries
	Decision 2007/339 on the signature and provisional application of the Air Transport Agreement between the European Community and its member states as well as the United States of America

3. Rail transport

Chris Nash

3.1 INTRODUCTION

Rail transport has long been seen as important by the European Union because of its ability to ease road congestion and its low environmental impact compared with road or air, and a major expansion in its market share is seen as an important element of the policies in the new European transport policy White Paper (European Commission, 2011), particularly regarding achievement of its greenhouse gas targets. Up to 1989, the normal approach to delivering rail services within Europe was for a single state-owned company to provide both infrastructure and all services, under the supervision of the relevant ministry, and there was no question of independent external regulation. However, there was great concern that rail was losing market share, particularly in international freight transport, where services were offered by cooperation between national railway companies, each handing over to the next at the border. It was believed that this seriously detracted from quality of service, and that having a single through international operator responsible for the complete transit would make rail more competitive. In that year, the European Commission issued a communication (European Commission, 1989) setting forward a new policy, in which infrastructure would be separated from operations, and operations thrown open to competitive entry. The first measure in pursuit of this (Directive 91/440) did indeed require open access for certain categories of freight train operations, and at least accounting separation of infrastructure from operations. Further measures followed, culminating in the three railway packages of 2001–07, which resulted in complete open access in the freight market (domestic and international) and open access for international passenger services, and required establishment of a regulator, independent from the infrastructure manager.

The next section will describe the measures contained in these packages. We then describe in turn the ways in which these measures were implemented, the resulting structure of the rail industry and the results of research on their impacts. Finally we comment on current proposals as to future measures to deal with the continuing problems, before reaching our conclusions.

3.2   OVERVIEW OF LEGISLATION

The first railway package of 2001 comprised three Directives, which between them required the following (Drew and Ludewig, 2011):

1. A degree of vertical separation. Infrastructure, passenger operations and freight operations had at least to be in separate divisions with their own balance sheets and profit and loss accounts, so that what the incumbent was paying for track access relative to new entrants was transparent. Non-discriminatory rules had to be established for establishing track access charges and allocation of capacity. Moreover, if the infrastructure manager was not completely independent in decision-making from any railway undertaking then it could no longer be responsible for these functions – a separate independent body was needed.
2. Track access charges based on direct cost. Track access charges had to be based on the direct cost of providing for the service in question, although non-discriminatory mark-ups, based on what the traffic could bear, were permitted when needed for financial reasons. These charges could include reservation charges, charges for scarce capacity (although in that case the infrastructure manager was required to undertake a capacity review to examine solutions to the problem) and environmental costs (although these could only raise the average level of charges if environmental costs were charged on other modes as well).
3. Open access for freight. Open access was provided for freight operators to an extensive network for international freight. Subsequently, and with effect from 2007, this was extended to cover the entire network, and to cover domestic as well as international freight; open access for international passenger services was established with effect from January 2010 (through the Third Railway Package).
4. Regulation. A regulator was required to which appeals could be made by operators which believed they were the subject of discrimination. This regulator must be independent of the infrastructure manager and any railway undertaking, but not necessarily of the Ministry.
5. Financial equilibrium. Governments were responsible for ensuring that a plan existed which put pressure on the infrastructure manager to be cost-effective but subject to this ensured financial equilibrium.

This plan could take the form of a multi-annual contract between the state and the infrastructure manager, or be achieved by a periodic review of the infrastructure manager's finances by the regulator with a duty on the regulator to ensure that the infrastructure manager had adequate finance.

As already noted, the two packages extended open access; they also set the rules for interoperability and safety, establishing the European Railway Agency to advise the Commission in these areas. Lack of interoperability and inconsistent safety legislation had proved major barriers to entry. Firstly, the fact that there are technical differences between the national rail systems of Europe (for instance in track and loading gauge, signalling systems and electrification) means that rolling stock that can run in one country may not necessarily be able to do so in another, or may need additional equipment in order to do so. This added to the costs of train operators and of manufacturers which could not deliver a standard product to a Europe-wide market. Secondly, and partly for this reason, the fact that rolling stock was accepted as safe to run in one country did not give it the right to run in any other; there were lengthy, expensive and inconsistent procedures to go through to get authorization in each country through which it was proposed to run. The legislation established procedures to determine common standards to be adopted in all new and upgraded infrastructure, so that incompatibilities would gradually be overcome; and common rolling stock authorization procedures, although it obviously remained necessary to have a two-part procedure in which the second part took account of particular national requirements.

3.3 IMPLEMENTATION

There were major differences in the way in which the legislation was implemented in different countries (European Commission, 2012b). Regarding vertical separation, three structures have emerged: complete separation, a holding company and separation of key powers. Even before the legislation, in 1988, Sweden had already completely separated its rail system into an infrastructure company and a train operating company, both owned by the state. Its reason for doing this initially had nothing to do with introducing competition (Alexandersson, 2011). Rather, it was to ensure transparency of financial flows, so that the government could finance the infrastructure in the same way and on the same cost–benefit criteria as it did roads, with no suspicion that these funds would be used to support operations. In 1994–97, Britain[1] went further, privatizing its infrastructure (since transferred to a not-for-dividend company) and splitting up and completely privatizing its train operators. This pattern of complete separation was adopted by many other countries, although elsewhere there remain a state-owned infrastructure company and a dominant state-owned operator, at least for passenger traffic.

Germany adopted the holding company model, establishing its infrastructure, passenger and freight companies as separate subsidiaries of a common holding company. A handful of other countries, including Austria, Italy and Belgium, followed this approach.

The third approach, the so-called separation of key powers, is more diverse, but designed to ensure that whilst the incumbent operator remained responsible for many functions regarding the infrastructure, it satisfied the requirement that it was not responsible for setting track access charges or for allocation of capacity. In addition, the structure often provided also for the wish for government to have a body other than the operator responsible for planning and investing in the infrastructure and providing advice on these matters. A good example is France, where RFF was established to take over planning and investment, allocation of capacity and charging, but contracts back all operations, such as time-tabling, signalling and maintenance work on the infrastructure, to the lead operator, SNCF.

By 2012, a majority of European Union (EU) countries had implemented complete vertical separation, although five had holding companies and six some form of hybrid involving separation of key powers (Table 3.1). The advantage of complete vertical separation is obviously that it removes the incentive for the infrastructure manager to favour train operations by its own sister companies. On the other hand, it is argued that the holding company model permits better integration, for instance in timetabling and in the planning of investment, whilst still having adequate safeguards to protect new entrants. The hybrid model is in between the two. For instance, in France, the fact that infrastructure operations and maintenance are with the leading operator may lead to better coordination, but also certainly to allegations that SNCF favours its own services over those of other operators. To the extent that the regulator now requires complete independence of decision-making by the infrastructure division of SNCF, this model becomes more like complete vertical separation and both the benefits and the costs of the hybrid model are removed.

Despite the provisions of this legislation, track access charges remain diverse in both level and structure (Nash et al., 2005). Figures 3.1 and 3.2 illustrate these differences. For freight (Figure 3.1), whilst some Western European countries simply charge short-run marginal costs (or arguably less), most Eastern European countries have very much higher charges

*Table 3.1   Rail freight market share of all but the principal railway
undertakings by railway structure (%), 2010*

Vertically separated		Hybrid		Holding Company	
Britain	51	Estonia	45	Austria	15
Bulgaria	22	France	20	Belgium	12
Czech Rep	13	Hungary	19	Germany	25
Denmark	25	Latvia	23	Italy	24
Finland	0	Luxembourg	0	Poland	36
Greece	n.a.	Slovenia	0		
Lithuania	0				
Netherlands	40				
Portugal	n.a.				
Romania	55				
Slovakia	2				
Spain	8				
Sweden	40				
Mean	20		18		22

Source: European Commission (2012b).

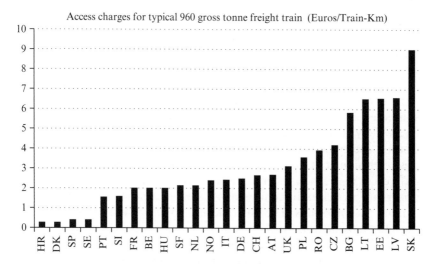

Source: International Transport Forum (2008).

Figure 3.1   Typical freight access charges, € per train-km in 2008

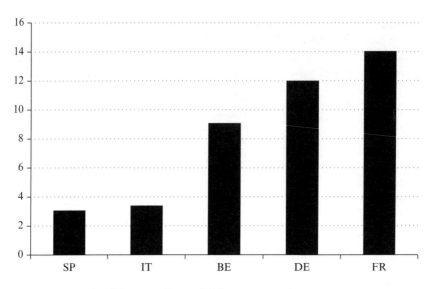

Source: International Transport Forum (2008).

*Figure 3.2   Typical access charges for high-speed passenger trains, € per
train-km in 2008*

designed to recover full costs. There are similarly large differences for passenger trains, and especially for high-speed trains (Figure 3.2). Obviously,
high charges affect the competitive position of rail, including for international traffic to and from countries where charges are lower.

The legislation recognizes the need for differing levels of track access
charges according to the financial needs of the infrastructure manager
concerned, but less expected is the variety of structures, with charges based
on a variety of measures including train kilometres (usually varying by type
of train and sometimes characteristics of the track), gross tonne kilometres (with similar variations), and path kilometres reserved. These reflect
differences in the view taken of what constitutes direct cost and what its
drivers are, as well as differences in the extent to which there are charges for
scarcity and mark-ups. The differences in structure add to the complica-
tions faced by international operators and manufacturers of rolling stock
in planning their services and in responding to the incentives provided by
track access charges. For instance if one country (e.g. Britain) has a sophis-
ticated system of track access charges reflecting variables such as unsprung
mass, which cause wear and tear on the track, and another only charges
a flat charge per train kilometre, then it will be worth spending money to
reduce unsprung mass of vehicles in some countries but not in others.

Regarding regulation, there are at least three different approaches (IBM, 2006). Some countries, such as Britain, have a specific rail regulator (Office of Rail Regulation, ORR), with wide-ranging powers and responsibilities. In Britain these include overseeing not just charges and capacity allocation but also whether the infrastructure manager meets the reasonable needs of its customers in terms of capacity and quality of service, and conducting a periodic review of the financial needs of the infrastructure manager, alongside benchmarking to determine the degree to which it can reduce those needs by increased efficiency. The British regulator is not subject to government direction. It is rare for the regulator of the rail sector to have these powers and responsibilities. In Britain the regulator is also responsible for regulating safety, whereas in many countries this is a separate body.

In other countries, such as Germany and the Netherlands, regulation of the rail sector has passed to a sector regulator, responsible also for (for instance) air transport and telecommunications. A third solution is for the regulator to be within the Ministry. Many countries, including France and Italy, initially adopted this model, in which the regulator was largely advising the government and had no powers or independent staff of its own. The obvious problem with this is that in general the same ministry was responsible for the infrastructure manager and the incumbent train operator, leading to a clear conflict of interest and suspicion as to how independent the regulator really was. Most countries are gradually moving away from this model to a more independent body.

Regarding finances, again Britain is unusual in placing the key responsibility for ensuring adequate finance on the regulator. As part of the periodic review, the British government sets out what it expects of the infrastructure in terms of capacity and capability (the high-level output specification) and what it is prepared to pay (the statement of funds available). If these are inconsistent, then the regulator has to find a solution, if necessary reducing the outputs required of the infrastructure manager. In most countries, as in Germany, financial equilibrium is achieved by direct negotiation between the government and the infrastructure manager of a multi-annual contract, although there are complaints in a number of countries (particularly in Eastern Europe) that the government imposes solutions that do not ensure financial equilibrium, or even fails to make the promised payments.

It should be said that there has been much dispute over the way in which the legislation has been implemented. In 2008, the Commission wrote to all but one member states with a rail system warning them that it considered their implementation of the legislation insufficient. Whilst many of the issues were minor and easily resolved, the Commission took legal action against 13 member states in 2010. Major issues are the degree of separation of infrastructure from operations, lack of a performance regime and lack of measures to ensure the efficiency of the infrastructure manager (European Commission, 2012b).

3.4   STRUCTURES

We have already explained that, everywhere but Britain, there remains a state-owned dominant passenger operator, sometimes part of a holding company with the infrastructure manager and sometimes completely separate. (Only Ireland, which up to now has had a derogation, and Switzerland as a non-EU member, retain completely vertically integrated structures.) In a number of countries, the state-owned freight train operator has been sold, but usually to the state-owned rail company of another member (Deutsche Bahn – German Railways – owns the main freight operator in Britain, Denmark and the Netherlands; and Austrian Railways owns that in Hungary).

New entry varies greatly, with none in some countries, but typically some 20 per cent of the freight market is now in the hands of entrants (see Table 3.1). According to the Rail Market Monitoring Study (European Commission, 2012a), the share of new entrants in the rail freight market remains very variable, with some countries still having none and others up to a maximum of 51 per cent. But there is no clear difference in the extent of new entry in countries with complete vertical separation as opposed to the holding company model or separation of essential functions. The major new entrants into the freight market remain the state-owned operators Deutsche Bahn (DB) and Société Nationale des Chemins de fer français – French National Railways (SNCF) (the latter having acquired the foreign freight operations of the largest private operator, Veolia) but a number of private operators do remain, particularly in the bulk and container markets. No new operator has emerged in the wagonload freight business, offering services for individual wagonloads of traffic over an entire network. Whilst there may still be barriers to entry in gaining access to marshalling yards and terminals, it is hardly surprising that no one has entered this field: wagonload services generally offer poor profitability and involve high overheads to set them up.

Although not required by European law, some countries have implemented competition in passenger operations in one of two ways: either by allowing commercial operators to introduce services at their own risk, or by inviting bids for franchises to run certain, usually subsidized, services. Several countries, including Germany, Austria, Italy and now Sweden, and to a limited extent Britain, allow the former form of entry, but little entry has occurred so far. In particular, a couple of open access operators run on the East Coast Main Line in Britain (one owned by First Group and the other by German Railways) and German Railways in particular is seeking to expand on to other routes. In Germany, Veolia operates through services on a few routes abandoned by German Railways. A private operator is running between Vienna and Salzburg in Austria and another one in the Czech Republic. But the most interesting development is the recent entry in Italy of NTV, a private company but with a 20 per cent shareholding by French Railways, providing frequent high-speed train services over the Italian high-speed network in direct competition with Italian Railways (Johnson and Nash, 2012).

Where entry has occurred, typically fares are lower and passengers are offered more choice of services, including through trains on routes where otherwise a change of train would be necessary. In countries where there is a mark-up on track access charges, such entry may also produce additional revenue for the infrastructure manager, and the additional competition may also provide more competition on costs. On the other hand, splitting the service between different operators loses economies of density, and may reduce the profitability of the incumbent, leading to less revenue from franchising or reduced ability to cross-subsidize other services.

There is more entry into the passenger sector through competitive tendering, mainly in the regional sector, although Britain uses competitive tendering for virtually all services and Sweden for all subsidized services whether short-distance or long (Alexandersson, 2009). There is a growing trend towards competitive tendering of regional services in Germany, and some tendering in a number of other countries including Denmark and the Netherlands. Whilst there are other companies active in this market, so too are foreign railways, especially since the acquisition of the biggest Europe-wide private passenger operator (Arriva) by German Railways; when it was required to dispose of Arriva's German operations, these were bought by Italian Railways.

Of particular interest is the growth of German Railways into a major Europe-wide freight and passenger operator, largely by acquisitions, and the attempts by other railways, notably SNCF and Trenitalia, to follow suit. For instance, as noted above, SNCF has acquired the overseas freight operations of Veolia. It seems clear that the future pattern of passenger and freight competition will be competition between a small number of Europe-wide giants, mostly state-owned, with some smaller state-owned or private companies remaining in particular markets.

The question is often asked why there has not been more market entry and why incumbents remain so dominant. In part, the answer may be that rail transport is not a very attractive field, with relatively few profitable opportunities (a large proportion of passenger services are subsidized, and many freight operations lose money: the freight operations of French and Belgian railways are particularly heavy loss-makers). But other barriers to entry remain. Rail systems tend to experience economies of density; splitting the traffic on a particular route between a variety of operators, other things being equal, will raise costs (see below). But also there has been concern that other barriers remain. A new entrant will need to train its drivers, clean and maintain its rolling stock, sell tickets and provide information to its passengers, and buy fuel and power. In a country with a dominant incumbent, often the incumbent will be the only source from which these can be purchased, and there remain allegations of discrimination in all these functions (SDG, 2006).

3.5 EFFECTS

In this section, we consider first the likely costs and benefits of vertical separation and liberalization, then attempts to measure the impact on costs, and finally studies of the impact on demand and modal split.

A number of studies (e.g. Mizutani and Uranishi, 2012) discuss the likely costs and benefits of vertical separation. They generally conclude that the principal benefit of vertical separation is in the promotion of competition. Complete separation of infrastructure from operations means that there is no reason for the infrastructure manager to wish to favour one operator over another, and it gives new entrants confidence of equality of treatment. It also simplifies regulation of the infrastructure manager by promoting clarity of relationships and financial flows within the industry, and encourages specialization, which may improve cost-efficiency and marketing. As opposed to that, vertical separation may lead to additional costs resulting from complexity of interfaces and duplication of facilities and services, and to misalignment of incentives regarding pricing, investment, capacity allocation and provision of information.

Overall it seems likely that vertical separation would raise costs and reduce service quality for a given level of competition, and do so more the more complex and heavily used the system. The benefits of specialization may counter this, however, for instance resulting from separation of responsibility for freight and passenger services. The benefits of vertical separation largely flow from the postulated increase in competition, leading to lower costs and higher quality of services.

It should however be noted that both British (Wheat and Smith, 2010) and United States (US) (Caves et al., 1987) evidence suggests that rail operations are subject to roughly constant returns to scale but increasing returns to density. Thus simply having more operators in a country should not raise costs, but splitting services on a particular route between operators will, other things being equal. This result tends to favour franchising rather than on-track competition provided that both forms of competition exert a similar pressure on costs.

A couple of papers have tried to quantify directly the additional transaction costs arising from vertical separation. Merkert (2010) takes a top-down approach, looking at the proportion of total rail systems staff classified as managerial and administrative in three countries with different structures: Germany, where infrastructure and operations are separate subsidiaries of the same holding company; Sweden, where there is total vertical separation; and Britain, where there is total vertical separation and an attempt to deal with misalignment of incentives by means of complicated track access charging and performance regimes. He finds this category of staff costs to be around 10 per cent of total system costs in Sweden and Britain but only 4 per cent in Germany. However, this figure will reflect the transaction costs of all the differences between Britain and Sweden, and Germany, not just vertical separation, and also be very susceptible to differences in the classification of staff. In a further paper, Merkert et al. (2012) provide the only direct estimate that we have found of the level of transaction costs involved in interactions between the infrastructure manager and train operators. By means of interviews, they collected data bottom-up on the staff time involved in interactions between infrastructure managers and train operating companies in the same three countries. They found that the most time-consuming areas of interaction were train planning and day-to-day operations, but that transaction costs were at most 2–3 per cent of total cost, and vertical separation added less than 1 per cent to total costs compared with the holding company model.

In Britain, the McNulty study (McNulty, 2011) was set up jointly by the Department for Transport and the Rail Regulator to examine why rail costs in Britain are so high. Overall, McNulty concluded that the costs of the British rail system should be reduced by 30 per cent by 2018–19 by comparison with European best practice. Of this, some 2 per cent might be achieved by reduced transaction costs, and 2–20 per cent (according to different case studies) by better-aligned incentives. The key point here is that, whilst charges to train operators in Britain are designed to reflect the wear and tear caused by different types of vehicle and (very roughly) the contribution trains make to congestion on the system, train operators do not pay directly for the quality and capacity of the infrastructure they use. Moreover, the franchising system protects franchised operators from any increase in Network Rail costs, in that any change in track access charges leads to an equal change in franchise payments from or to the government. Thus they have no incentive to help or pressure Network Rail to deliver capacity in the most cost effective way. The solution to this problem was seen as closer arrangements between Network Rail zones and franchised train operating companies, taking the form of alliances, joint ventures or even the leasing of infrastructure to the franchisee. Different solutions were seen as appropriate for different circumstances; for instance, the latter was only seen as appropriate were there was a single dominant train operator, as there are in some parts of Britain given the comprehensive franchising system and the dominance of passenger services.

In a study specifically of the Swedish experience, Jensen and Stelling (2007) estimate cost functions with time series data for Sweden for 1970–99, and find that vertical separation there raised costs, but that this is more than outweighed by the favourable impact of competition.

A number of studies of individual countries have shown reductions in subsidy of 20–30 per cent as a result of passenger franchising (Alexandersson, 2009), with the big exception being Britain where costs have risen sharply (Smith et al., 2009). But the cost reduction seems to hold for Germany (with a holding company structure) as well as countries with complete vertical separation. Moreover, as noted above, franchising is compatible with a degree of vertical integration in the form of a joint venture between the infrastructure manager and the train operating company or complete leasing of the infrastructure to the train operator for the duration of the franchise.

But most of the relevant literature on costs comes from estimation of an overall production or cost function on a panel of European railways over time. Many of these studies are now quite old, so they do not take account of the major changes in the rail market in recent years. Most of them use data from the International Union of Railways (UIC) International Rail Statistics, supplemented to some extent from other sources such as individual company accounts. This source of data has some known deficiencies. Firstly, it generally only covers the main state-owned operator in each country, and Britain – where reform has been carried furthest – is excluded. Secondly, some of the physical data are incomplete or misleading. For instance, Abate et al. (2009) shows the inconsistency of the data on rolling stock; this appears to be the only study to systematically correct for this. Thirdly, in some cases (certainly for Germany) the data include subsidiaries in other countries, so the geography of the infrastructure and operations added together is inconsistent. Fourthly, there is a general problem with physical data such as staff numbers, in that subcontracted activities such as track and rolling stock maintenance and cleaning are not included. Subcontracting should be included in the cost data, and for that reason we consider it is generally more reliable, although it may have problems of its own particularly in the calculation of depreciation and financial charges given different assumptions about amortization and capital write-offs.

A further issue is the actual measurement of the reforms. Ideally we would like to account separately for the impact of different degrees of competition in passenger and freight markets and different degrees of vertical separation (at least using the three different categories identified in the Rail Market Monitoring Study: complete institutional separation, the holding company model and hybrid systems). Most studies take account of the date of legal reforms, such as rights of access, introduction of competitive tendering on one route or establishment of a regulator, but these often happened many years before any significant entry took place and in a situation when it was known that there were still effective barriers to entry.

Finally, there is a risk that the reforms carried out may be correlated with other variables relating to the operating conditions of the railway concerned, such as traffic density. This is particularly a problem given that vertically separated railways tend to be clustered around the periphery of Europe, and vertically integrated ones in the core. Thus it is necessary to introduce variables to control for these factors.

Given all these problems, plus the variety of techniques used, it is not surprising that no consistent pattern emerges from past studies. For instance, Wetzel (2008) found that separation has no significant impact on technical efficiency, whereas Growitsch and Wetzel (2009) found significant diseconomies from separation of infrastructure and operations in most countries. Friebel et al. (2010) find that in general introduction of open access, vertical separation (whether as a holding company or total separation) and creation of a regulator improve efficiency, but the results depend on the sequencing of the various reforms; undertaking them all together is damaging. All these studies rely on physical data, fail to take account of different operating conditions in different countries, and rely on dates of legal changes rather than actual reforms. Thus for instance Friebel et al. date open access in France as 1997, whereas in practice it remained impossible until 2005.

Asmild et al. (2009) had available an independent source of cost information from another study, and went to considerable lengths to clean up the UIC data used for other variables; exceptionally they also included Britain. However, their data only covered the period 1995–2001. They found both competitive tendering for passenger services and freight open access to improve efficiency, as did accounting separation of infrastructure and operations. There was no significant further effect of complete vertical separation.

The most recent studies are those of Cantos et al. (2010, 2011), Mizutani and Uranishi (2012) and van de Velde et al. (2012), which will be discussed in a little more detail. Cantos et al. (2010) uses data envelopment analysis on physical data for 16 railways for the period 1985–2005. In a first stage they use two outputs (passenger km and freight tonne km) and four inputs – employment, number of passenger carrying vehicles, number of freight wagons and route km – to compile measures of efficiency. They then regress these measures on variables reflecting the operating conditions of the railway concerned (percentage of train km that are passenger; traffic density in terms of train km per route km; mean passenger train load and mean freight train load) and on variables reflecting vertical separation and introduction of competition.

They find separate beneficial effects of vertical separation and introduction of competition in the freight market, whereas passenger franchising has no such effect. However, of the four countries in their sample in which passenger franchising has been introduced, only in Sweden and Germany has it covered a significant proportion of regional services and in none has it covered commercial services. That vertical separation has improved efficiency over and above the impact of competition is surprising; we worry that this may be because vertically separated systems undertake more subcontracting and that this has not been picked up in the physical data, but we have no evidence on this issue.

Cantos et al. (2011) uses a greater sample of 23 countries and a more up-to-date period of 2001–08. It repeats the data envelopment analysis approach of the earlier paper, but also applies a stochastic frontier approach, showing that this leads to much lower efficiency scores although the ranking of countries in terms of efficiency is similar. The results of the second-stage analysis are rather different however. Vertical separation has no significant effect on efficiency, whilst the strongest positive effect on efficiency comes from passenger tendering. Freight open access has a positive effect on efficiency that is significant in one of the models. Unfortunately, there seems to be a less adequate set of variables as controls in the second-stage analysis in this paper. Only population density and rail route length are included. The results could be considerably biased by the lack of data on passenger and freight train loads, which tend to be heavily influenced by the geography of the country and government policy, but which are major determinants of efficiency.

Mizutani and Uranishi (2012) estimate a translog cost function on data for 30 companies in 23 countries, adding together train operating companies with the manager of the infrastructure over which they run.

Their sample includes companies in Japan and South Korea, as well as Europe. They conclude that vertical separation leads to cost reductions for railways with low train density, while railways with higher train density experience cost increases (of European railways, only Switzerland and the Netherlands currently have high enough density for this to be the case). They explain this in terms of the transaction costs of operating a complex system with conflicts over the use of capacity. They also conclude that horizontal separation of freight from passenger operations has been beneficial. They do not measure the benefits of competition separately, so to the extent that vertical separation increases competition, the measured impact is the net effect of these two factors.

Van de Velde et al. (2012) take this work further by updating and improving the data set and introducing separate dummy variables for holding companies and complete vertical separation. They also introduce dummy variables representing passenger and freight market competition. They confirm the previous finding that, compared with complete vertical integration, vertical separation reduces costs at low levels of density but increases them at high levels; at mean European density levels costs are not affected by the change. They find weak evidence (significant at 10 per cent only) that the holding company model reduces costs compared with vertical integration, but this does not vary with density, so the holding company would be preferred to vertical separation at medium and high levels of density but not at low levels. Within the range of the data, the introduction of competition seems to have had no effect on costs. Horizontal separation of freight and passenger undertakings seems to have sharply reduced costs (perhaps because this has typically been associated with preparation of the freight undertaking for privatization), whilst a high proportion of revenue coming from freight rather than passengers tends to increase the costs of vertical separation (perhaps because planning freight services efficiently requires closer day-to-day working than passenger services, since freight services vary from day to day whereas passenger services are generally fixed for the duration of the timetable). They also provide qualitative evidence on the issue of how misalignment of incentives may raise costs, and show how whilst efficiently set track access charges and performance regimes are important, they do not provide incentives for railway undertakings to assist infrastructure managers in seeking the minimum-cost solution to infrastructure provision. Only a complete sharing of changes in costs and revenues, as provided for in some of the alliances now being negotiated in Britain, will achieve that.

Turning to the evidence on impacts on demand, there is far less evidence to go on. Impacts on demand may come because competition leads to improved services, or they may come indirectly if cost reductions lead to lower fares or to tendering bodies being able to afford to improve services. There are a couple of specific studies of franchising in Britain. Wardman (2006) concludes that whilst most of the major growth in rail passenger demand in Britain since the introduction of franchising is due to external factors such as rising incomes and increased road congestion, there is a small unexplained element that may be attributed to improved marketing and other 'soft' service quality attributes following franchising. He has already taken out the effect of increased train kilometres and the holding down of regulated fares over this period. Preston and Robins (2011) find a much greater increase in demand due to franchising taking these factors into account, but to the extent that these were government decisions, presumably government could have chosen to impose them on the former rail operator.

There is much less evidence on open access passenger operations as they have been very limited. Griffiths (2009) reviews the British experience and Seguret (2009) the German. In both cases competition has been mainly in niche markets, running at low frequencies on routes not served by the incumbent operator, but open access entrants do invariably offer lower fares than the incumbent as well as through services to places not otherwise served by through trains. Although head-on competition at high frequencies on key routes now exists in a number of countries, including Italy and Austria, this has started too recently for any analysis to be available in the literature. So for the effects of this form of competition we are forced to rely on modelling. A number of studies using the Praise model (Preston et al., 1999; Preston et al., 2002) conclude that head-on competition is only feasible where demand is strong and/or track access charges low, and even then it tends to lead to excessive service levels and therefore costs.

Fowkes and Nash (2002) reach similar conclusions to those on franchising regarding the growth of rail freight in Britain, that it was mainly due to external factors (such as the increased use of imported coal), but the fact that rail mode share had risen in most commodities suggested some improvement due to privatization and the introduction of competition in freight.

Looking more widely across Europe, Drew and Nash (2011) make simple comparisons of vertically integrated (holding company) and vertically separated railways. They find that there is more competition in the freight market in vertically separated railways (15 per cent of the market on average held by new entrants as opposed to 12 per cent in vertically integrated countries in 2008). However, on average vertically integrated railways have seen substantial growth, and vertically separated countries none. They acknowledge that there are many different factors determining the level of traffic growth and also that this comparison is heavily influenced by the case of France, which is in any case a hybrid with many of the functions of an infrastructure manager (track maintenance, signalling) still performed by the state-owned train operator. But even taking France out, vertically integrated railways still perform significantly better in terms of traffic growth.

In the passenger sector, vertically separated railways do perform better on average than vertically integrated railways. But here the countries that have performed best are Britain, France and Spain. In Britain, part of the growth does appear to be due to the reforms, as commented above. But in France and Spain, there has been no competition in the passenger market. In these countries, it is clear that a high level of investment, particularly in high-speed rail, is at least part of the explanation for the growth.

Laabsch and Sanner (2012) test these relationships further by means of a regression model relating mode split to various explanatory variables, including rail industry structure and market opening (measured by the IBM/Kirchner liberalization index) as well as measures of public spending on rail, strength of regulation and gross domestic product (GDP) per capita. Their results are very surprising. In the passenger sector, both vertical integration and liberalization have a strong positive impact on rail mode split, whilst public spending on rail has none. In the freight market no significant effect of either industry structure or liberalization can be found. Their hypothesis is that this may be because of the importance of international traffic in the freight sector, which depends on conditions in more than one country.

Again the most recent evidence is provided by van de Velde et al. (2012). For 26 Organisation for Economic Co-operation and Development (OECD) countries from 1994 to 2010, they examined the relationship between passenger and freight mode split and railway structure and competition. For freight, there was no evidence that either vertical separation or the introduction of competition increased rail market share. For passengers, there was weak evidence (significant at the 10 per cent level) that the introduction of competition (within the sample almost entirely by competitive tendering) combined with moving away from complete vertical integration improved rail mode split, but no significant difference between the holding company model and complete vertical separation.

In summary, then, there are many inconsistencies in the results of studies of the impact of European rail policy, and these may partly be explained by differences in methodology and by the difficulty of getting appropriate and consistent data. Also, many of the reforms have only started to take full effect in recent years. The most recent research finds some evidence of benefits on costs from vertical separation for least densely trafficked lines, particularly when these are predominantly passenger lines, and from the holding company model for more densely trafficked lines; also evidence of strong cost savings from horizontal separation of freight and passenger services. That vertical separation causes more costs in densely used systems makes sense, as the need for efficient coordination in such systems may be greater than elsewhere, but the source of the benefits for more lightly used systems is less clear. We find no evidence that complete vertical separation leads to more competition in the freight market, and the scope for competition may be less in less densely trafficked systems. In the passenger market, the level of competition has depended mainly on whether passenger services are franchised out, and franchising systems seem to work equally well with complete vertical separation or the holding company model. It is been suggested that vertically integrated franchises might make sense although there is no experience as yet of these on mainline railways (the development of alliances with complete sharing of changes in revenues and costs in Britain will provide important evidence on this). In terms of impacts on demand, we find some evidence of benefits from franchising but the evidence regarding freight competition is mixed.

3.6 CONCLUSION

The Commission's reforms have already led to major changes in the railways of Europe. In many cases infrastructure has been completely separated from operations. There is complete open access for new freight operators, and in many countries this has been used by a number of operators. Many countries also have a degree of competition in the passenger market, through either open access or competitive tendering, and this is growing.

However, there is a lack of clear evidence on the effectiveness of these reforms. Moreover, as has already been noted, there remains concern that the freight market is still subject to many barriers to entry, whilst there is as yet no requirement to open up the domestic passenger market. At the time of writing in November 2012 the Commission is proposing two further measures to deal with these issues (Nash, 2010).

Firstly it is proposing a recast of the first railway package to clarify a number of points. These include the principles for track access charges and mark-ups, access to rail-related services and the need for international cooperation between regulators.

More radically it is also proposing a fourth railway package. This will propose complete opening up of the domestic passenger market for competition either in the market or for the market by means of competitive tendering. It will also make further proposals regarding the structure of the rail industry. The European Commission has made it clear that it would like to see complete separation of infrastructure and operations as the most effective way to ensure non-discrimination (European Commission, 2011). But whether member states will agree to that remains to be seen.

Whether any of these measures would lead to a change in the situation where the industry is dominated by a few large, mainly public sector groups is doubtful. This concerns some people, who worry that such organizations have the ability to cross-subsidize in order to compete unfairly. For this reason, as well as the inevitable monopoly of the infrastructure manager, it is clear that regulation will continue to play an important role in the European rail industry.

ACKNOWLEDGEMENT

I wish to acknowledge the very helpful comments given by Torben Holvad on an earlier draft of this chapter; responsibility for any errors remaining is solely my own.

NOTE

1. 'Britain' in this chapter refers to the three countries of Great Britain, that is, England, Wales and Scotland. It excludes Northern Ireland, the small railway network of which remains a vertically integrated monopoly.

REFERENCES

Abate, M., M. Lijesen and A. Roeleveld (2009), 'Estimating efficiency of reliable railroad companies', Department of Spatial Economics, Amsterdam: VU University.

Alexandersson, G. (2009), 'Rail privatisation and competitive tendering in Europe', *Built Environment*, **36** (1), 37–52.

Alexandersson, G. (2011), 'Sweden', in J. Drew and J. Ludewig (eds), *Reforming Railways – Learning from Experience*, Brussels: Eurail Books.

Asmild, M., T. Holvad, J.L. Hougaard and D. Kronborg (2009), 'Railway reforms: do they influence operating efficiency?', *Transportation*, **36** (5), 617–638.

Cantos, P., J.M. Pastor and L. Serrano (2010), 'Vertical and horizontal separation in the European railway sector and its effects on productivity', *Journal of Transport Economics and Policy*, **44** (2), 139–160.

Cantos, P., J.M. Pastor and L. Serrano (2011), 'Evaluating European railway deregulation using different approaches', paper given at the workshop on Competition and Regulation in Railways, FEDEA, Madrid, 12 March.

Caves, D.W., L.R. Christensen, M. Tretheway and R.J. Windle (1987), 'Network effects and the measurement of returns to scale and density for US railroads', in A.F. Daugherty (ed.), *Analytical Studies in Transport Economics*, Cambridge: Cambridge University Press.

Drew, J. and J. Ludewig (2011), 'Introduction', in J. Drew and J. Ludewig (eds), *Reforming Railways – Learning from Experience*, Brussels: Eurail Books.

Drew, J. and C.A. Nash (2011), 'Vertical separation of railway infrastructure – does it always make sense?', paper given at the Kuhmo-Nectar conference, Stockholm.

European Commission (1989), 'Communication on a Community rail policy', COM (89) 564, Brussels: European Commission.

European Commission (2011), 'Road map to a single European transport area', Transport White Paper, COM(2011) 144, Brussels: European Commission.

European Commission (2012a), *Rail Market Monitoring Study, 2011*, Brussels: European Commission.

European Commission (2012b), Commission Staff Working Document accompanying European Commission, *Rail Market Monitoring Study, 2011*, Brussels: European Commission.

Fowkes, A.S. and C.A. Nash (2002), 'Rail privatisation in Britain – lessons for the rail freight industry', ECMT Round Table on Rail Privatisation, Paris: OECD.

Friebel, G., M. Ivaldi and C. Vibes (2010), 'Railway (de)regulation: a European efficiency comparison', *Economica*, **77** (305), 77–91.

Griffiths, T. (2009), 'On rail competition: the impact of open access entry on the Great Britain rail market', paper presented to the International Conference on Competition and Ownership in Land Passenger Transport, Delft, September.

Growitsch, C. and H. Wetzel (2009), 'Testing for economies of scope in European railways: an efficiency analysis', *Journal of Transport Economics and Policy*, **43** (1), 1–24.

IBM (2006), 'Rail regulation in Europe: comparison of the status quo of the regulation of rail network access in the EU-25 countries, Switzerland, and Norway', Zurich: IBM.

International Transport Forum (2008), 'Charges for the use of rail infrastructure', Paris: OECD.

Jensen, A. and P. Stelling (2007), 'Economic impacts of Swedish railway deregulation: a longitudinal study', *Transportation Research E*, **43** (5), 516–534.

Johnson, D. and C.A. Nash (2012), 'Competition and the provision of rail passenger services: a simulation exercise', *Journal of Rail Transport Planning and Management*, **2** (1–2), 14–22.

Laabsch, C. and H. Sanner (2012), 'The impact of vertical separation on the success of the railways', *Intereconomics – Review of European Economic Policy*, **47** (2), 120–128.

McNulty, Sir R. (2011), 'Realising the potential of GB rail: final independent report of the Rail Value for Money Study', London: Department for Transport and Office of Rail Regulation.

Merkert, R. (2010), 'An empirical study on the transaction sector within rail firms', *Transportmetrica*, **8** (1), 1–16.

Merkert, R., A. Smith and C.A. Nash (2012), 'The measurement of transaction costs – evidence from European railways', *Journal of Transport Economics and Policy*, **46** (3), 349–365.

Mituzani, F. and S. Uranishi (2012), 'Does vertical separation reduce cost? An empirical analysis of the rail industry in OECD countries', *Journal of Regulatory Economics*. DOI: 10.1007/s11149-012-9193-4.

Nash, C.A. (2010), 'European rail reform and passenger services – the next steps', *Research in Transportation Economics*, **29** (1), 204–211.

Nash, C.A., B. Matthews and L.S. Thompson (2005), 'Railway reform and charges for the use of infrastructure', ECMT, Paris: OECD.

Preston, J.M., T. Holvad and F. Rajé (2002), 'Track access charges and rail competition: a comparative analysis of Britain and Sweden', paper presented at the European Transport Conference, Cambridge.

Preston, J. and D. Robins (2011), 'Evaluating the long term impacts of transport policy: the case of passenger rail privatisation', paper presented at the 12th International Conference on Competition and Ownership in Land Passenger Transport.

Preston, J., M. Wardman and G. Whelan (1999), 'An analysis of the potential for on-track competition in the British passenger rail industry', *Journal of Transport Economics and Policy*, **33** (1), 77–94.

SDG (2006), 'Servrail – assessment of present and likely future conditions of providing rail-related services', Brussels: European Commission.

Seguret, S. (2009), 'Is competition on track a real alternative to competitive tendering in the railway industry? Evidence from Germany', paper presented to the International Conference on Competition and Ownership in Land Passenger Transport, Delft, September.

Smith, A., C.A. Nash and P. Wheat (2009), 'Passenger rail franchising in Britain: has it been a success?', *International Journal of Transport Economics*, **36** (1), 33–62.

van de Velde, D., C.A. Nash, A. Smith, F. Mizutani, S. Uranishi, M. Lijesen and F. Zschoche (2012), EVES-rail. 'Economic effects of vertical separation in the railway sector', Brussels: Community of European Railways (CER).

Wardman, M. (2006), 'Demand for rail travel and the effects of external factors', *Transportation Research E*, **42** (3), 129–148.

Wetzel, H. (2008), 'European railway deregulation', Working Paper 86, Institute of Economics, Leuphana University of Lüneburg, available at http://ideas.repec.org/p/lue/wpaper/86.html.

Wheat, P. and A. Smith (2010), 'Econometric evidence on train operating company size', report for ORR, Institute for Transport Studies, University of Leeds.

4. Inter-urban road freight

Jan Burnewicz and Monika Bak

4.1 INTRODUCTION

Inter-urban road freight transport is one of the most important economic sectors of the European Union. The wide influence of transport on almost all aspects of life has long been generally known, but road transport plays a special role for the European Union (EU) economy since this transport mode fulfils the overwhelming majority of transport needs both for companies and individuals. From the macroeconomic and mezzo-economic perspective this impact is also crucial and can be perceived as a general effect for the economic growth, structural changes of the economy, regional development and cohesion, and so on. Interrelations between macroeconomic development and road transport condition influence the EU economic and industrial competitiveness.

In this chapter inter-urban road freight is perceived from the perspective of reforming regulatory frameworks and their effects. This regulatory reform should result in improving operational conditions or freeing it from unnecessary limitations needed in order to complete the creation of a Single European Transport Area including a competitive, efficient and fair road freight market.

The regulation of road freight transport in the EU has a long history and has already resulted in measurable positive effects. Its overall objective is to rationalize the numerous advantages of this transport mode. This objective requires various actions. On the one hand, it is necessary to strengthen the development of the sector; on the other hand, its negative environmental impacts should be limited. Progress is being made through a complementary package of instruments covering the EU common transport policy documents, regulations and technical standards, as well as financial and investment programmes, research development and innovation projects. The regulation of road freight transport must be consistent with general objectives of the common EU transport policy, including promoting transport as an accelerating factor of the European integration, strengthening the international competitiveness of the European economy, improving accessibility and ensuring sustainable development.

We have had a period of restrictive road rules (1960s to 1980s). At that time it was thought that the system would be efficient, effective and equitable if admission to the profession of road haulage operator and access to markets were regulated, prices of transport services were determined by public authorities rather than by the market, and international transport operations were controlled at the borders. This type of regulation faced great resistance from the market, and it failed. Economic progress in road freight transport of goods is ensured by full freedom of establishment rather than by the previous restrictions and standards. This freedom of establishment and freedom to provide services was achieved after 1985 through liberalization of the access to the occupation of road haulage operator and to all markets. The present period of regulation is quite different: driving forces for development of road freight transport are the competition between operators, free access to markets and promoting innovations in the road haulage market. In fact, road haulage is one of the most liberalized sectors, achieved through implementing uniform rules on access to the profession and principles of fair competition, as well as some harmonization of working time and taxation.

Technical, organizational, economic and fiscal changes, which were carried out in the EU for road freight transport in the years 1960–2010, had a positive impact on the economy in the form of a reduction of logistics costs, the emergence of new types of production, and the intensification of industrial cooperation and trade. If road transport operated in Europe as it was in the 1960s, the logistics costs would be considerably higher. These positive effects, however, are accompanied by negative impacts in terms of increased external costs of road transport. Specifically, negative effects consist of substantial losses resulting from a large number of road accidents, loss of time in traffic jams and congestion, the environmental degradation and the destruction of infrastructure. The scale of these effects requires the intervention of public authorities and the implementation of effective regulatory instruments influencing both operators and transport users.

There are some negative phenomena in freight road transport which have not yet been covered by the EU regulatory actions. The significant excess of supply of transport services can be treated as an acceptable negative effect of a free-market system (i.e. approximately 30 per cent more trucks on the market than required, taking into account transport demand). Additionally, a very high percentage of carriers with financial problems are operating. Drivers with poor qualifications and experience are still hired, and also working conditions are often inadequate. Rules limiting the movement of heavy vehicle traffic during the holidays and weekends differ between member countries.

Effectiveness and efficiency of road freight transport regulation in the EU requires research and analysis. As a basis it is necessary to have complete and reliable statistical information and market research results, including studies covering the long term. It has to be noticed that available Eurostat and other institutions (United Nations Economic and Social Council – UNECE; International Transport Forum – ITF; International Road Transport Union – IRU; European Union Road Federation – ERF) statistics are very fragmented and often unreliable. For the purpose of this elaboration a database of the most important EU transport data for the years 1990–2010 was developed consisting of a compilation of the statistics of many publications covering different periods and data ranges (especially for the years 1990–2000). Despite the implementation of EU Directives relating to road statistics, there is still a lack of complete information on the total network of all categories of roads, and data on the number of enterprises and employees in the road transport of goods (due to differentiated national classifications) is not reliable. Statistics are incomplete for all categories of transport (national, export and import, cross-trade and cabotage) and information about turnovers is fragmentary. We have developed a specific statistical basis which is partly based on estimations, but the method is limited to a margin of error of no more than 10 per cent and allows us to test several important hypotheses illustrating the operation of the road freight transport (in the years 1990–2010) in the light of regulatory framework. The results of these analyses are included in the following sections 4.3–4.5. Overall, the rest of the chapter is structured as follows. Section 4.2 provides an overview of the regulatory measures for road freight during the past two decades. In section 4.3 implementation issues are considered, while section 4.4 examines the new structures that are developing in this sector. The possible reform effects are outlined in section 4.5 while concluding remarks are contained in section 4.6.

4.2   OVERVIEW OF REGULATORY MEASURES

The European Union uses a range of instruments to implement the Common Transport Policy: (1) political documents (White and Green papers, various other EC – European Commission – communications); (2) legal measures (regulations, Directives, recommendations and decisions); (3) administrative instruments; (4) EU financial funds (e.g. the Trans-European Transport Network, TEN-T; regional and structural funds); and (5) results of scientific research (e.g. the EC research programme for research and technological development, RTD).

The EU policy objectives for road freight transport are therefore to promote efficient transport services, to create fair conditions for competition, to promote and harmonize safer and more environmentally friendly technical standards, to ensure a degree of fiscal and social harmonization, and to guarantee that road transport rules are applied effectively and without discrimination (these policy objectives are outlined in various EC documents and also available on the website of the European Commission Directorate-General on Mobility and Transport, DG MOVE).

The scope of this chapter does not allow for a detailed discussion on existing regulations relating to road freight transport. They are available in the Directory of European Union legislation in force (EUR-Lex) in 23 official EU languages (see: http://eur-lex.europa.eu/en/index.htm) and summaries of the most important regulations are posted on the website as 'Summaries of EU legislation' (see http://europa.eu/legislation_summaries/transport/index_en.htm). The political background of these regulations is explained on the DG MOVE website. In this chapter, attention is focused on those regulations most important for the functioning and development of this sector.

In order to create an efficient, environmentally sustainable and socially equitable internal market, the European Union has introduced many legislative and regulatory measures over the past decades. In 2012, EUR-Lex contained 731 Acts concerning transport policy (360 Acts on inland transport, of which more than 200 Acts concern road transport). Therefore, the largest number of legal regulations in the transport of the European Union applies to the road freight sector.

The transport sector is included as one of the most important sectors for achieving these objectives and the road freight sector is crucial as representing almost three-quarters of the total inland tonnage (tkm) transported in the EU (see Figure 4.1) and also mainly responsible for environmental damage and social problems related to transport. Environmental impacts are measured through calculations of external costs of transport, while the social dimension is perceived from the perspective of the high number of workers employed in the sector, working time, minimum level of training, mutual recognition of diplomas and qualifications, and other aspects linked to working conditions.

The major objectives of current EU policy for the road freight sector are the following:

- ensuring fair competition between transport operators;
- providing high-quality services to shippers;
- providing quality jobs for transport workers;
- minimizing the road haulage sector's environmental and climate change damage.

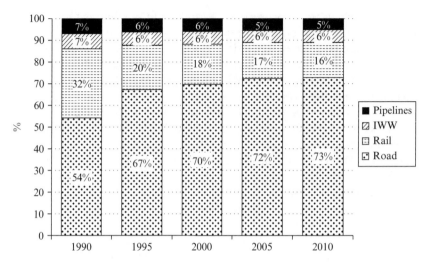

Sources: Eurostat (2012) and European Commission (2012b).

Figure 4.1 EU27 Freight Transport for Inland Modes (% of tkm) 1990–2010

These objectives are in line with the creation of the Single European Transport Area which should lead to substantial benefits for market efficiency.

The legal regulation of the EU road freight transport covers the following main aspects of the activity of the sector:

1. Administrative harmonization of activities (admission to the occupation of road haulage operator, monitoring of road transport undertakings, driving licences, hiring of vehicles for the carriage of goods).
2. Liberalization of access to the road haulage market (bilateral international transport, cross-trade, cabotage).
3. Social harmonization (working time, driver attestation).
4. Fiscal harmonization (fuel taxation, annual vehicle taxation, road infrastructure charging).
5. Technical harmonization (weights and dimensions, EC-type approval system for motor vehicles, roadworthiness testing of heavy goods vehicles, road infrastructure safety management, parking areas along the European road transport network).
6. Improvement of safety (driving time and rest periods, tachograph, transport of dangerous goods, safety in European road tunnels, community database on road traffic accidents).

Table 4.1 Objectives to be achieved through the implementation of different types of regulations in the road freight sector

Type of regulation:	Objectives:			
	To ensure fair competition between transport operators	To provide high-quality services	To provide quality jobs for transport workers	To minimize environmental and climate damage
1. Administrative harmonization	XXX	XXX	XX	-
2. Liberalization of access to the road haulage market	XXX	X	X	-
3. Social harmonization	XXX	X	XXX	-
4. Fiscal harmonization	XXX	X	-	XX
5. Technical harmonization	XXX	XXX	X	XX
6. Improvement of safety	X	XX	X	XX
7. Reduction of environmental degradation	X	X	-	XXX

Note: Level of relations between domain of regulation and policy objectives: XXX – very strong; XX – significant; X – weak; - – insignificant.

7.   Reduction of environmental degradation (reduction of pollutant emissions from vehicles, quality of petrol and diesel fuels, use of biofuels, clean and energy-efficient road transport vehicles, hydrogen-powered motor vehicles, reusing, recycling and recovering of motor vehicles).

An overview of how the above-mentioned domains of regulation are linked to the policy objectives is set out in Table 4.1.

Fair competition between transport operators can be achieved through legislative measures including common rules for access to the market and harmonization of the charging system for heavy goods vehicles as well as through the regulation of access to the profession. In addition, technical harmonization measures and to some extent also road safety and environmental regulation influence the competition conditions.

High-quality services can be developed in the conditions of harmonized rules governing technical standards of motor vehicles as well as administrative harmonization. Certain regulations of carriage of goods directed at ensuring a safer transport system as well as road safety measures aim at quality improvements. Also, working conditions seem to be important in this context.

In order to provide quality jobs for employees in the road freight sector different types of regulations of employment and working conditions as well as administrative harmonization have to be implemented. In particular, in the case of international and especially cabotage operations it is important to improve job conditions and attractiveness. From a social perspective long-distance haulage means spending nights away from home, often in uncomfortable circumstances, along with additional hazards and risks to road transport drivers.

All environmental and safety measures obviously are contributing to minimize environmental damage (including climate change). Also, technical and fiscal harmonization as well as implementation of measures promoting innovations in transport can contribute towards the reduction of environmental hazards.

The essential regulation in road freight transport in the EU concerns the rules of access to the business of carrier. This issue was regulated differently during the period 1974–2011. Originally, access was regulated separately for freight and passenger sectors. Consolidation of rules for both forms of transport took place in 1989. In the years 1990–2009 these issues were governed by Directive 96/26/EC amended by Directive 98/76/EC (Burnewicz, 2005). Available evidence shows that the Directive is being applied inconsistently by member states. Such disparities have several adverse consequences, in particular distortion of competition, lack of market transparency and of uniform monitoring, as well as the risk that undertakings employing staff with a low level of professional qualifications may be negligent in respect of, or less compliant with, the rules on road safety and social welfare, which may harm the image of the sector.[1] EC Regulation No 1071/2009 is therefore intended to reinforce the harmonization of the rules with the aim, in particular, of promoting fair competition between road transport companies and improving the level of professional qualifications of staff. This regulation applies to all undertakings operating in the road freight sector within the EU, and to undertakings which intend to start operating. It should be noted that the regulation does not apply to undertakings using vehicles with a weight not exceeding 3.5 tonnes, and certain special vehicles.

The undertaking and the manager in particular shall be deemed to be of good repute, in other words they shall not have been convicted for any infringement of national rules in certain fields such as commercial law, road traffic, or trafficking in human beings or drugs. The undertaking must be able to meet its financial obligations. To do so, it shall have at its disposal, every year, capital and reserves totalling at least €9000 when only one vehicle is used, increased by €5000 for each additional vehicle. The manager of the undertaking shall have passed a compulsory written examination which may be supplemented by an oral examination.

Another important Act regarding road freight transport in the EU concerns the rules of access to the road haulage markets in bilateral international transport, cross-trade and cabotage. The international bilateral carriage of goods and cross-trade by road within the European Union should be conditional on the possession of a Community licence, which can be obtained, provided they satisfy the conditions governing admission to road transport operations.[2] Cabotage is national transport carried out by a non-resident haulier. It is not yet fully liberalized in the EU. According to Article 8 of Regulation No 1072/2009, only up to three cabotage operations in a country are allowed during at most seven days following an international delivery to that country. Cabotage operations are covered by national legislation in the following areas: (1) prices and other conditions governing the transport contract; (2) standards relating to weights and measures; (3) requirements relating to the carriage of certain categories of goods; (4) driving and rest time for drivers; (5) value-added tax (VAT) on transport services.

The opening of transport markets in Europe significantly increased the competitive pressure on operators and their mobile workers. In this context social standards influencing the cost structure needed to be harmonized to create a level playing field between companies from different member states, to guarantee good working conditions, and to protect the health and safety of workers. The EU has thus established over the years a framework of social rules for goods and passenger road transport operators (driving time and rest periods, working time, enforcement, and the recording device tachograph) with three complementary goals: (1) to ensure the adequate social protection of road transport workers; (2) to guarantee fair competition between the undertakings; (3) and to improve road safety by averting road fatigue.

The fiscal harmonization regarding EU road freight transport sector is necessary in order to eliminate distortions of competition between undertakings, strengthen the environmental performance of vehicles and ensure optimum use of the existing road network. Legal regulations in this area include fuel taxation, annual vehicle taxation and road infrastructure charging. The EU has created a framework to encourage member states to use taxation and transport infrastructure charging in the most effective and fair manner in order to promote the 'user pays' principle.

The European Commission is working towards a form of mobility that is sustainable, energy-efficient and environmentally friendly. Environmental regulations for reduction of environmental degradation in road freight transport apply to: (1) reduction of pollutant emissions from vehicles (Regulations 715/2007 and 595/2009); (2) quality of petrol and diesel fuels (Directive 98/70/EC); (3) use of biofuels (Directive 2009/28/EC); (4) clean and energy-efficient road transport vehicles (Directive 2009/33/EC); (5) hydrogen-powered motor vehicles (Regulation 79/2009); (6) reusing, recycling and recovering of motor vehicles (Directive 2005/64/EC).

The harmonization of the existing technical standards in the member states is essential in order to eliminate a large number of obstacles to trade in goods within the EU. EC-led technical harmonization of motor road vehicles aims to: (1) eliminate the existing technical barriers to trade in vehicles and vehicle equipment; (2) ensure high levels of safety, environmental protection, energy efficiency and protection against theft. Regulatory measures in this field are numerous and so detailed that it is outside the scope of this chapter to cover these in detail (EC type-approval system for motor vehicles, roadworthiness testing of heavy goods vehicles, etc.). From an economic perspective the most important ones are regulations concerning the weight and dimensions of vehicles.

4.3   IMPLEMENTATION

The implementation of the EU *acquis*[3] in the road freight transport has lasted for over 50 years. During this period the European Community was enlarged several times, which naturally could cause differences regarding compliance with regulations in place for the sector. As such the new member states (EU-12) had limited time to implement the *acquis communataire*; while applying for membership these countries were under greater pressure and control of the European Commission compared to previous enlargements of the EU. The largest differences regarding implementation of the *acquis* in the European Union appear for the newest and/or most radical regulations (revised in 2009 rules regarding access to the occupation and to the market for carriage of goods, installation of digital tachographs, reduction of CO_2 emissions from road transport, etc.). Today there are no substantial differences in formal implementation of the *acquis* in the member states, but there remain noticeable variations regarding fiscal, social and technical aspects.

Key factors of effective implementation of the road regulations within the EU consist of: (1) full integration into the national legislation of the EU member states (especially transposition of the Directives); (2) effective enforcement to ensure compliance at member state level; (3)

monitoring of compliance with the regulations by transport enterprise managers; (4) updating of the regulations in line with the technical and socio-economic changes in Europe. Key factors affecting the process of road transport liberalization include (Scheele, 2010):

- The very diverse structure of the road transport sector, encompassing a substantial number of owner-drivers and/or small and medium-sized enterprises (SMEs) as well as larger companies.
- The tendency of the sector to engage in direct action on the streets (both staff and owners).
- The difficulties of controlling and enforcing effective implementation of major areas of the *acquis*, due to both the structure of the industry and the nature of the operations.
- A chronic lack of competitiveness of the EU industry compared with industry in third countries.
- The institutional reluctance of member states to cede control of external relations to the EU.
- The lack of any clear-cut economic arguments that would underpin a Commission legal initiative to force the situation.
- The possibility of using climate change policy (including the need to reduce CO_2 emissions) as an external factor justifying a change to the existing perceived balance of interests.

The extent of transposition of EU Directives into national legislation is documented on the European Commission website as 'Application of EU law'. Based on the information included in the 'Archives for the progress in notification of national directives implementing measures (all EU directives in force nationally)' it can be concluded that since 2007 some 160 Directives relating to the transport and energy sectors have been almost fully transposed (97 per cent) at the national level. However, this is a very high-level assessment that reflects whether the relevant national legislation exists. It is therefore necessary to look at more specific mechanisms to monitor compliance with Community law in the road freight transport sector. There are a substantial number of Directives and other legal measures relating to road freight transport, for which compliance is monitored by the EC. Monitoring and enforcement of the EU law related to road freight transport is realized in each member state by competent authorities (notably road inspections). Actually, at least 4 per cent of the transport operations should annually be subject to their controls according to EC requirements.[4]

The implementation of the *acquis communataire* in road sector is a difficult task due to a very large number of entities operating in the sector. The air, rail or waterborne transport regulations must be followed by some 20 000 existing firms, whereas in road freight transport more than 585 000 enterprises need to have an adequate knowledge of the legal framework. The road *acquis* is also much more complex (taking into account the number of Acts and level of detail of the legislation).

According to the opinion of Maurice Bernadet (former European Conference of Ministers of Transport expert dealing with the liberalization of road transport), within the EU simply holding a Community licence, issued under the authority of the country of establishment, is sufficient to authorize the holder to carry out transport between any two member states. In this way there is therefore free access to the market. This freedom is widely used and the statistics on market share for the various national carriers in the international transport sector show that creating competition between carriers is effective, since these shares have developed substantially. However, this does not mean that in practice there are no barriers designed to protect national markets from foreign carriers. No in-depth study has to date provided an overview of these barriers, for example practices of certain inspection officers whose attitudes are said to be clearly discriminatory against foreign vehicles (Bernadet, 2009).

One of the implementation problems concerns cabotage, where the interpretation of Article 1 of Regulation (EEC) No 3118/93 is not clear-cut. This Article states that: 'Any road haulage carrier for hire or reward who is a holder of the Community authorization . . . shall be entitled, under the conditions laid down in this Regulation, to operate on a temporary basis national road haulage services for hire-and-reward in another Member State.' The key issue relates to how 'on a temporary basis' should be interpreted. According to the findings of Bernadet, the Communication does not give a precise definition of what a 'temporary basis' does and does not mean. A number of member states (Greece, the United Kingdom, Italy and France), under pressure from their hauliers, went ahead and implemented restrictive measures without waiting for the Communication by the Commission (Bernadet, 2009).

Therefore, at present, gradual opening of the domestic road transport markets is considered as a key step towards the completion of the Single European Transport Area. In June 2011, a High Level Group of experts was mandated by the European Commission to draft a report on the situation of the EU road haulage market. In particular, the Group in its report published in June 2012 recommends that two different types of cabotage should be introduced (European Commission, 2012a): 'linked cabotage', limited to a short period of time and connected to an international carriage; and 'non-linked cabotage', which may take place for a longer time, independently of the existing international carriage, and which would be subject to a registration procedure to ensure that the drivers involved apply the labour law of their local competitor. The new set of measures would allow a step-by-step opening of the market, increasing flexibility of operations and competition in national markets, whilst ensuring fair competition and avoiding a 'race to the bottom' in social norms.

It should also be added that both the International Road Transport Union (IRU) and the European Commission in the last decade have been paying much attention to drawbacks in the implementation of the road *acquis* (e.g. IRU, 2006). This refers to issues such as the lack of uniformity in enforcement regimes resulting in the EU road transport market being segmented into many country-specific enforcement areas, with possible lengthy and duplicative control procedures and uncoordinated inspections of the same vehicle in different member states. Many specific national rules exist in the EU in the field of traffic, technical and road safety rules (diversity in fines imposed, driving bans, maximum authorized axle and total weights, different maximum speed limits). This highlights the need to develop guidance for best practice regarding road inspectors and inspections.

4.4   NEW STRUCTURES

The implementation of EU legislation has changed the structure of road freight transport. These changes are linked to a number of aspects which will be outlined below. One dimension of the regulatory reform is the role of regulators in the context of enforcement problems. Especially from the perspective of the international dimension of road freight transport, different enforcement practices can lead to distortion of competition between operators. It has to be noted that although the legislative framework is set out at the international level (EU), enforcement remains the responsibility of individual countries. For example, this is reflected in variation regarding practices on working and driving times in road freight transport (IRU, 2006). Therefore, it is important also to harmonize enforcement practices, to promote a uniform interpretation of infringements as well as the harmonization of controls, and not only harmonization of the rules and regulations.

As transport enterprises development is a crucial factor influencing road freight transport structure, this section presents comments on trends in the number of transport companies, their size (measured by the number of employees) and changes in own-account and hire-and-reward transport.

A characteristic feature of the road freight transport sector in the EU is the very large number of enterprises and their highly variable size. Regulations of the access to the profession and liberalization of the access to the market introduced in the years 1974–2011 have contributed to a slight increase in the number of firms (5 per cent) and a much larger increase in the number of employees (54 per cent). These changes are illustrated in detail in Table 4.2.

With almost 600 000 enterprises, road freight transport can be regarded as a sector of small entrepreneurs. None of the other transport modes can compared in respect of the fragmentation level of this mode. However, there are also significant differences in the structure of the market per country. The predominance of small entities is observed in Slovenia – 3168 hauliers per million inhabitants; Spain – 3039; the Czech Republic – 2702; and Poland – 2289. In countries such as France, the United Kingdom (UK), the Netherlands and Germany the corresponding figures are much lower (638, 547, 545 and 445 respectively). The EU-27 average is 1197 haulier per 1 million inhabitants (UNECE, 2011). However, a trend of concentration over recent years can be observed (see Eurostat data). The share of bigger hauliers has grown in the majority of the EU countries (e.g. in Poland, where there were 316 hauliers owning more than 20 vehicles in 2005; four years later there were 811 hauliers in this group).

It is likely that the liberalization measures have to some extent contributed to the increase in the number of enterprises. However, the intensification of competition in the liberalized markets has also contributed to consolidation of the sector, demonstrated by a significant increase in the number of medium-sized enterprises. The consolidation is also illustrated (see Figure 4.4) by the increase in average number of employees per company over the period 1990–2010 (from 3.5 employees per company in 1990 to 5.2 workers in 2010). In Figures 4.2–4.4 the data on employment size, the number of enterprises and persons employed per enterprise are presented. These figures show clear country variation. In Spain both the number of enterprises and the number of persons employed in road freight sector are the largest. It can be noticed that the first three countries with the largest number of enterprises are characterized by a high degree of fragmentation of the market (small enterprises dominate). The biggest transport enterprises have been established in Luxembourg, the Netherlands and Slovakia. As can be observed in Figure 4.4 the differentiation between countries in the number of persons employed per road freight enterprise has widened in the years 1990–2010. Consolidation is taking place in countries where hauliers have strong logistics competencies, while in other countries the market has remained fragmented, with small enterprises.

European logistics was formed in recent years largely due to the intensive development of road transport of goods. Large pan-European logistic companies strengthened their market position through mergers and alliances. Reinforcing the importance of large logistics providers is also

Table 4.2   Employment and enterprises in the road freight transport sector in the EU-27 (1990–2010)

Country	A. Number of persons employed						B. Number of enterprises					
	1990	1995	2000	2005	2010	2010: 1990 (%)	1990	1995	2000	2005	2010	2010: 1990 (%)
Austria	32 548	39 381	47 650	57 576	58 585	180	4 567	4 788	5 019	6 706	6 555	144
Belgium	44 805	52 717	62 026	63 191	64 641	144	6 735	7 011	7 298	7 602	7 641	113
Bulgaria	97 530	67 840	47 189	48 681	45 887	47	13 734	12 513	11 400	10 000	10 352	75
Cyprus	1 295	1 769	2 417	2 415	3 015	233	1 241	1 339	1 445	1 481	1 443	116
Czech Republic	48 979	68 872	96 845	102 569	110 480	226	12 883	15 920	17 734	26 538	29 133	226
Denmark	29 674	36 129	43 988	40 397	24 798	84	7 259	7 618	7 994	7 140	6 993	96
Estonia	11 060	9 867	8 802	13 218	13 801	125	1 187	1 153	1 120	1 763	2 618	221
Finland	27 554	32 370	38 027	39 569	46 178	168	10 940	11 383	11 843	10 935	11 195	102
France	243 002	272 286	305 100	341 268	363 510	150	41 891	43 084	44 311	42 643	35 259	84
Germany	176 836	236 015	315 000	289 918	361 155	204	28 561	30 647	32 885	33 472	34 773	122
Greece	25 638	33 012	42 506	40 000	42 239	165	16 832	17 907	19 050	19 400	20 647	123
Hungary	47 240	51 969	57 171	68 370	65 334	138	22 132	22 660	23 200	19 646	16 440	74
Ireland	5 938	8 712	12 782	16 200	20 622	347	2 424	2 660	2 919	3 800	4 115	170
Italy	240 589	272 497	308 637	339 770	336 173	140	105 409	108 738	112 173	101 813	78 850	75
Latvia	9 306	8 579	7 909	16 220	18 136	195	1 094	1 072	1 050	1 895	2 897	265
Lithuania	17 486	18 443	19 452	31 441	40 665	233	3 017	3 058	3 100	3 111	4 022	133
Luxembourg	2 588	3 779	5 517	7 613	8 768	339	398	436	478	443	527	132

Table 4.2 (continued)

Country	A. Number of persons employed						B. Number of enterprises					
	1990	1995	2000	2005	2010	2010: 1990 (%)	1990	1995	2000	2005	2010	2010: 1990 (%)
Malta	636	728	834	811	1063	167	323	334	345	346	386	120
Netherlands	94098	107181	122083	114843	121650	129	9650	9965	10290	9140	9033	94
Poland	121500	143596	207708	261621	258743	213	66374	70790	75500	76200	74013	112
Portugal	30060	37078	45735	62214	65637	218	5325	5608	5906	12237	9341	175
Romania	91590	70179	53773	68050	93150	102	11801	11025	10300	13555	24749	210
Slovakia	4461	6617	9813	10021	14556	326	475	522	575	824	1231	259
Slovenia	12189	14356	16908	17831	22704	186	8481	8833	9200	6143	6267	74
Spain	183076	234987	301618	390000	385891	211	115108	122394	130141	135549	133098	116
Sweden	42650	52036	63487	67730	72280	169	14356	14891	15447	14779	14743	103
United Kingdom	293621	310788	328959	308938	325045	111	35801	36306	36819	34734	30586	85
EU-27	1935949	2191783	2571935	2820475	2984704	154	547997	572655	597542	601895	576905	105
EU-15	1472677	1728969	2043115	2179227	2297172	156	405255	423435	442573	440393	403354	100
EU12	463272	462814	528820	641248	687532	148	142742	149219	154969	161502	173551	122
% EU-15	76.1	78.9	79.4	77.3	77.0		74.0	73.9	74.1	73.2	69.9	
% EU-12	23.9	21.1	20.6	22.7	23.0		26.0	26.1	25.9	26.8	30.1	

Source: Eurostat (2012), European Commission (2012b), national statistics of the EU member countries and own estimations.

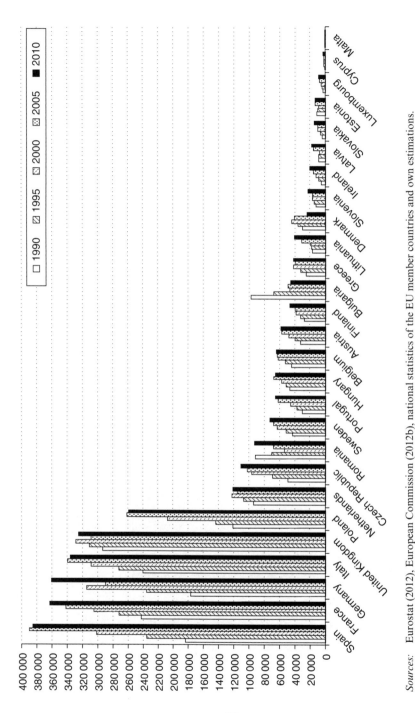

Sources: Eurostat (2012), European Commission (2012b), national statistics of the EU member countries and own estimations.

Figure 4.2   Number of persons employed in the road freight transport sector in the EU-27 (1990–2010)

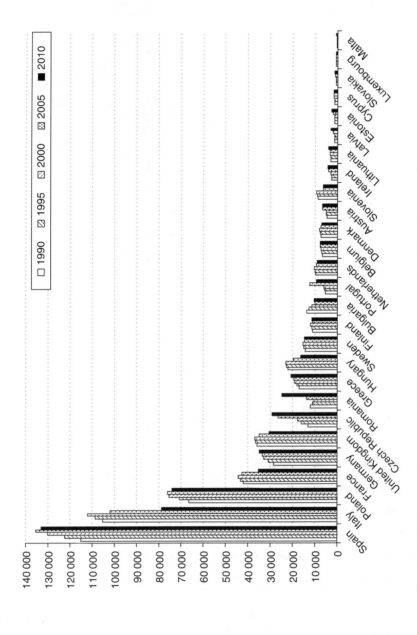

Sources: Eurostat (2012), European Commission (2012b), national statistics of the EU member countries and own estimations.

Figure 4.3 Number of enterprises in the road freight transport sector in the EU-27 (1990–2010)

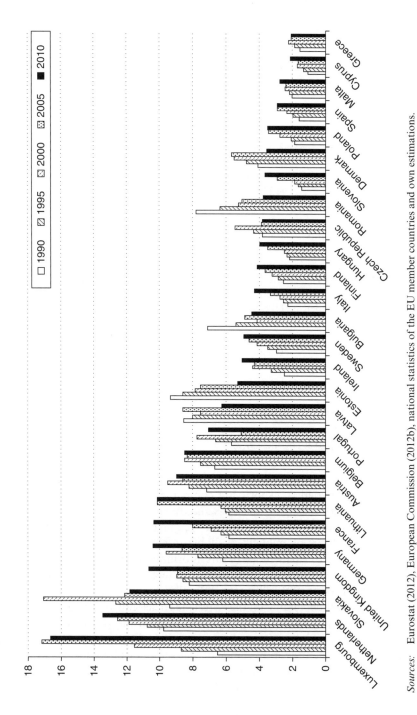

Sources: Eurostat (2012), European Commission (2012b), national statistics of the EU member countries and own estimations.

Figure 4.4   Number of persons employed per road freight enterprise in the EU-27 (1990–2010)

Table 4.3   Rankings of the ten largest logistics companies in the world (based on revenue in billion euros, by various sources)

L.p.	Forbes (2009 total sales)	SJ Consulting Group (2007, only 3PL)	DataMonitor (2008, logistics and transport)
1	Deutsche Post (75.87)	DHL Logistics (33.421)	Deutsche Post DHL (79.7)
2	United Parcel Service (51.49)	Kuehne & Nagel (17.535)	United Parcel Service, Inc. (51.5)
3	FedEx (38.81)	Schenker/ BAX Global (12.065)	Deutsche Bahn AG (49.0)
4	Nippon Express (19.05)	CEVA Logistics (7.800)	FedEx Corporation (37.9)
5	Kühne & Nagel Intl (16.86)	Logista (7.347)	Kuehne + Nagel International AG (16.6)
6	TNT ((15.30)	Panalpina (7.154)	TNT N.V. (16.3)
7	Yamato Holdings (12.28)	C.H. Robinson Worldwide (5.972)	CEVA Group (8.9)
8	Financière de l'Odet, Bolloré (9.34)	UPS Supply Chain Solutions (5.911)	C.H. Robinson Worldwide Inc. (8.6)
9	CH Robinson Worldwide (8.58)	Expeditors Int'l of Washington (5.235)	Panalpina World Transport (Holding) Ltd. (7.9)
10	Agility (6.11)	Dachser & Co (4.836)	Agility Logistics Co. (6.9)
	TOTAL (253.69)	TOTAL (107.276)	TOTAL (284.6)

Source: Global Transport & Logistics (2012).

associated with the fragmentation of the market and the large number of small businesses in road transport. Big companies often rely heavily on subcontracting work to small enterprises and owner-drivers.

In each EU country, the largest road freight carriers can easily be identified on the basis of publicly available information, often though logistics operators are also included in this information. Many institutions deal with the rankings of transport enterprises (e.g. Datamonitor, 2012; Research and Markets, 2012; Transport Intelligence, 2012). Obviously, these rankings differ depending on the criteria used, as shown in Table 4.3.

The market structure can be also considered from the point of view of hire-and-reward and own-account transport. The liberalization processes have strengthened the importance of transport for hire-and-reward transport relative to own-account transport. The volume of shipments in recent decades has increased more rapidly in this sector. In 2009, the hire-

and-reward businesses accounted for the vast majority of road freight in both national and international freight at the EU-12 and EU-15 levels. However, the hire-and-reward sector achieved relatively more importance in the international freight market, with a 94 per cent share in the EU-15 and a 95 per cent share in the EU-12 (European Commission, 2011). The largest market shares for own-account transport exist within the EU-12 for national freight, having on average a 35 per cent share of the total. This suggests that many of the EU-12 countries are still in a transition period towards a more modern logistics system.

Unfortunately data for own-account transport and hire-and-reward is not fully available. Figure 4.5 presents data for 1990 and 2007 accessible from Eurostat. For 11 countries among the EU-15 there is an increasing trend of hire-and-reward transport, with a strong dominance of this sector in Germany, Spain and France.

4.5   EFFECTS OF REFORMS

Regulatory reform of the road freight transport in the EU over the years 1990–2010 resulted in the deregulation of access to the carrier profession; full liberalization of market access (including cabotage); implementation of modern technical and environmental standards; improvement of the tax system (introduction of infrastructure charges for road usage and harmonization of fuel taxes); implementation of uniform standards of working time; and instruments to improve working conditions. This complex package of instruments could potentially lead to changes regarding: prices of the factors of production; unit costs and prices of transport services; production capacity of the sector (number of vehicles and road infrastructure network); and size and structure of road haulage companies. The reforms of the road regulatory system were not the only cause behind these changes: various macroeconomic and social trends in the European economy also influenced the road transport market, for example fuel taxes evolution, demographic trends, differences in the level of wages between countries, and so on. Despite a common EU transport policy, the character of the road regulatory reforms and their effects in various countries had quite a diverse nature. In particular, it is much more difficult to achieve the desired results in a situation of high unemployment, vulnerability to economic crises, political disturbances, and so on.

The regulatory reform aims at improving the road freight sector, increasing the quality of services and also reducing the distortionary impacts of regulations. Inappropriate regulations can impose substantial costs and inefficiencies on firms, sectors and the economy as a whole. The effects

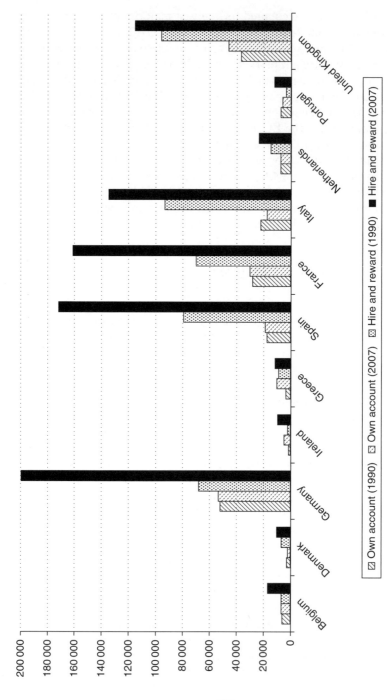

Legend: ⊠ Own account (1990) ▨ Own account (2007) ▧ Hire and reward (1990) ■ Hire and reward (2007)

Source: Eurostat (2012).

Figure 4.5 National own account and hire and reward transport in 1990 and 2007 in selected EU countries (million tkm)

of regulatory reform in road transport have generally been positive with regards to freight services. Following deregulation, services expanded and the efficiency of service providers increased substantially. By encouraging the road haulage companies to develop their services with regard to customer needs, it is likely that the reforms have contributed to achieve a better match between what the company is offering and what the customers demand. This is also a factor linked to the promotion of new logistic services (ECMT, 2001). Furthermore, destructive competition appears not to have emerged in countries that have reformed the regulations for this sector. In general, the fragmented nature of the sector and easy entry conditions have limited the emergence of market power (Blöndal and Pilat, 1997).

As for transport prices, it should be noted that transport policy has both a direct and an indirect impact on prices and costs. The direct impact concerns public transport fares and infrastructure charges as well as vehicle and fuel taxes. However, there is also an indirect impact from the measures to liberalize road transport resulting in increased competition and competitiveness, such that prices have fallen by 1 per cent per annum over the past 15 years (ECMT, 2001). This is due to the fact that competition forces the firms to improve their quality–price ratio, to offer services that better meet the needs of customers and to reduce their costs in order to retain their position in the market (ECMT, 2005).

Therefore, the regulatory reforms increased productivity, lowered prices and eliminated shortages. Examples of this are provided in various studies, for example Blöndal and Pilat (1997). According to this study the road haulage industries in the UK enjoyed increases in labour productivity of around 10 per cent after relaxation or elimination of outdated operational controls (while in France a 15 per cent increase was recorded, and in Germany 20 per cent). Capital productivity was also boosted; for instance France experienced a 25 per cent increase while the UK had a 10 per cent increase following liberalization. Reform of road freight transport may however increase road transport at the expense of rail freight. In this case it is important to address public concerns about the potential negative effects of regulatory reforms on safety, health and consumer protection (OECD, 1997, pp. 11–12).

In the period 1990–2010 the most noticeable effect of regulatory reforms in the transport of goods in the EU was the structural change regarding the four market segments: (1) domestic transport; (2) export and import haulage; (3) cross-trade; (4) cabotage. The liberalization of road freight transport in Europe has led to a higher degree of internationalization. Shippers make substantial savings in transportation costs by searching for the cheapest carriers, mainly located in EU-12 countries. As shown in Table 4.4, total freight road transport (tkm) increased annually by 2.8 per cent during the period 1990–2010 in the EU-27, while for the EU-15 the

Table 4.4 Evolution of the EU-27 road freight market segments (1990–2010)

TOTAL, mld tkm	1990	1992	1994	1996	1998	2000	2002	2004	2006	2008	2010	Rate 1990–2010 (%)
TOTAL, mld tkm												
EU-27	1021	1073	1175	1292	1381	1503	1596	1752	1855	1890	1768	2.8
EU-15	875	939	1034	1129	1201	1314	1374	1473	1497	1470	1333	2.1
EU-12	146	133	140	162	180	189	222	280	358	420	434	5.6
% EU-15	85.7	87.6	88.0	87.4	87.0	87.4	86.1	84.0	80.7	77.8	75.4	X
% EU-12	14.3	12.4	12.0	12.6	13.0	12.6	13.9	16.0	19.3	22.2	24.6	X
% of national	77.5	77.4	76.5	75.4	74.7	72.7	71.0	68.9	67.6	67.7	67.3	X
% of export + import	21.1	20.7	21.4	22.2	22.4	23.9	25.0	26.6	26.7	25.7	25.0	X
% of crosstrade	1.4	1.8	2.0	2.3	2.6	2.9	3.2	3.6	4.8	5.7	6.6	X
% of cabotage	0.1	0.1	0.1	0.2	0.3	0.6	0.7	0.8	0.8	0.9	1.2	X
National, mld tkm												
EU-27	791	830	899	973	1032	1093	1133	1207	1254	1279	1189	2.1
EU-15	681	732	800	867	915	987	1023	1078	1114	1121	1031	2.1
EU-12	110	98	98	106	117	106	111	129	140	158	158	1.8
% EU-15	86.2	88.1	89.1	89.1	88.7	90.3	90.2	89.3	88.8	87.7	86.7	X
% EU-12	13.8	11.9	10.9	10.9	11.3	9.7	9.8	10.7	11.2	12.3	13.3	X

Export+import, mld tkm

EU-27	215	222	251	286	309	359	400	467	496	486	442	3.7
EU-15	180	190	212	237	255	285	302	339	331	300	257	1.8
EU-12	35	33	39	49	54	73	97	128	165	187	184	8.7
% EU-15	83.7	85.3	84.6	82.9	82.6	79.6	75.6	72.6	66.7	61.6	58.2	X
% EU-12	16.3	14.7	15.4	17.1	17.4	20.4	24.4	27.4	33.3	38.4	41.8	X

Cross-trade, mld tkm

EU-27	14	19	24	30	36	43	51	64	89	108	116	11.1
EU-15	13	17	20	23	27	34	38	42	39	35	32	4.5
EU-12	1.2	2	3	7	9	9	13	22	51	73	85	23.7
% EU-15	91.6	90.4	85.9	76.9	74.9	78.5	73.8	66.0	43.3	32.3	27.2	X
% EU-12	8.4	9.6	14.1	23.1	25.1	21.5	26.2	34.0	56.7	67.7	72.8	X

Cabotage, mld tkm

EU-27	1	1	1	2	5	9	11	15	15	17	21	19.2
EU-15	1	1	1	2	4	9	11	14	13	15	13	16.7
EU-12	0.03	0.04	0.04	0.23	0.19	0.20	0.41	1	2	3	8	44.5
% EU-15	95.3	95.5	97.0	89.6	95.8	97.8	96.4	93.0	85.5	84.8	62.9	X
% EU-12	4.7	4.5	3.0	10.4	4.2	2.2	3.6	7.0	14.5	15.2	37.1	X

Source: Eurostat (2012), European Commission (2012b), national statistics of the EU member countries and own estimations.

growth was 2.1 per cent and for the EU-12, 5.6 per cent (over the same period).

During this period, the share of domestic transport (in total haulage) decreased from 77.5 per cent to 67.3 per cent; and international transport, including exports and imports, increased from 21.1 per cent to 25.0 per cent. The share of cross-trade increased from 1.4 per cent to 6.6 per cent and cabotage from 0.1 per cent to 1.2 per cent. A very important change caused by the regulatory reform was the increase of the share of new member states (EU-12) in the volume of transport: overall from 14.3 per cent to 24.6 per cent, in exports and imports from 16.3 per cent to 41.8 per cent, in cross-trade from 8.4 per cent to 72.8 per cent and cabotage from 4.7 per cent to 37.1 per cent. These changes were possible due to the persistent cost advantages of carriers in the EU-12. As an example, total operating costs (euros per hour) in 2008 were: in Romania €44.6, in Hungary €51.4, in Poland €52.05, in Italy €76.9, in Germany €79 and in France €80 (European Commission, 2009). The largest variation relates to labour costs. In the EU-15, the average personnel costs for 2005 (personnel costs per employee per annum) ranged from €16000 for Portugal to €43000 for the Netherlands. In contrast, for none of the 12 member states that entered EU in 2004 and 2007 (with the exception of Cyprus) did average personnel costs reach €10000. Hungary with €8000 had the highest personnel costs among the EU-12 countries, while Latvia and Romania with €2000 had the lowest (Eurostat, 2008).

Further opening of cabotage announced in the Report of the High Level Group on the Development of the EU Road Haulage Market in June 2012 (European Commission, 2012a) is seen as one of the means through which the vision of the Single European Transport Area will be achieved and will be probably gradually implemented during the next decade.

Cross-trade in 2006 was permanently dominated (almost 60 per cent) by carriers from the EU-12. The leaders of this market segment are represented by carriers from Poland (26.8 per cent), the Czech Republic (9.8 per cent), Slovakia (8.1 per cent), Hungary (7.1 per cent) and Lithuania (7.0 per cent). The the EU-12 carriers' share of total cabotage is not very large due to formal restrictions of cabotage; in 2010 it was 37.1 per cent, up from 2.2 per cent in 2000. It should be mentioned that cabotage is important from a social perspective and in some geographical areas; in Belgium and France, for instance, more than 2 per cent of the total domestic transport market is in the hands of foreign hauliers (ECORYS, 2006). From the perspective of active hauliers, road cabotage transport is also very important. This is especially true for hauliers from Luxembourg and carriers from the EU-12.

The role of carriers from the EU-12 in the transport of goods exported and imported was strengthened during the period 1990–2010, where their share increased from 16.3 per cent to 41.8 per cent. In 2010 the countries with the highest market shares were Poland (with 20 per cent), Spain (13.5 per cent), Germany (12 per cent) and the Netherlands (7 per cent).

The increase of road freight transport volume (in tkm) is associated with strong growth in market turnover from €137.6 billion in 1990 to €302.6 billion in 2007; followed by a decline to €278 billion in 2010 as a result of the recession. Across the EU-27 the average annual increase was 3.6 per cent, while in the EU-15 it was 3.3 per cent, and in the EU-12, −6.4 per cent. As a result, productivity measured in current prices was steadily increasing (average annual rate of 1.4 per cent), as shown in Table 4.5.

While in 1990 the average productivity of freight transport enterprises of the EU-12 was almost four times lower than that reached by companies from the EU-15, in 2010 it had already reached over 50 per cent of the EU-15 level. This is due to high productivity growth in the EU-12 (an average annual rate of 4.34 per cent), with relatively slow productivity growth in the EU-15 (an average annual rate of 0.99 per cent). Leaders in terms of productivity are enterprises from Denmark, the Netherlands, Belgium, Austria, Luxembourg, Finland, Italy, France and Sweden (€100 000–€200 000 per year per employee). Also, carriers from Germany achieve relatively high productivity, at a stable level of about €90 000–€100 000 per employee.

As a result of the liberalization regarding access to road transport markets, the empty running ratio has been reduced significantly. During the years 2004–11 it declined from 33.5 per cent to 31.8 per cent in domestic transport, and in international transport from 14.0 per cent to 13.0 per cent (based on Eurostat data), which resulted in significant cost savings.

A very positive (but less than expected) effect of reforms of technical and social regulations was a big improvement in road safety. In the period 1990–2010 the number of road accidents across the EU-27 decreased from 1.5 million to 1.1 million, and the number of road fatalities decreased from 76 000 to 31 000. As shown in Figure 4.6, for the majority of the EU countries the number of accidents involving personal injury in the years 1990–2010 was significantly reduced. Only five countries experienced an increase: Romania (+5 per cent), Slovenia (+2 per cent), Italy (+1.4 per cent), Ireland (+0.4 per cent) and Bulgaria (+0.1 per cent). For the remaining countries the rate was negative, and the strongest decrease in the number of accidents was reported in the Netherlands (−7 per cent).

The ratio of the number of road fatalities (persons killed) per 1000 accidents in the EU-15 decreased from 41.6 to 21.1, and in the EU-12 it decreased from 138 to 73. Still the most difficult objective to fulfil is to move towards the desired reduction in the number of victims of road accidents in the EU-12, especially in Bulgaria and Poland (more than 100 people killed in 1000 accidents). But as presented in Figure 4.7, in all

Table 4.5 Evolution of productivity of road freight enterprises in the EU-27, 1990–2010 (€1000 per employee), current prices

Country	1990	1992	1994	1996	1998	2000	2002	2004	2006	2008	2010	Rate 1990–2010 (%)
Denmark	84.5	75.5	67.5	69.9	83.8	100.8	120.1	125.6	142.8	155.8	211.7	4.70
Netherlands	64.7	66.6	68.6	70.6	72.7	90.1	116.2	129.2	143.7	143.8	155.3	4.47
Belgium	147.3	147.4	147.5	139.8	125.4	130.5	143.2	152.3	167.1	170.8	142.2	−0.18
Austria	88.6	84.9	81.5	83.6	91.7	112.4	116.0	123.5	133.8	138.3	142.0	2.39
Luxembourg	125.2	119.5	114.0	114.8	122.0	121.4	131.7	113.0	138.9	119.5	125.3	0.01
Finland	90.8	84.4	78.5	79.7	88.3	98.0	105.4	114.7	125.2	138.8	122.1	1.49
Italy	93.6	88.1	82.9	84.3	92.7	103.2	102.8	123.5	127.1	121.4	116.6	1.10
France	84.6	83.9	83.3	85.0	89.1	89.2	95.8	99.8	108.6	117.3	113.6	1.49
Sweden	113.7	99.2	86.5	86.5	99.1	115.8	111.3	108.5	117.8	112.5	112.7	−0.04
Ireland	80.5	77.9	75.5	75.9	79.3	118.0	125.9	124.3	177.0	100.5	105.3	1.35
Germany	89.6	97.6	106.3	109.2	105.7	74.5	85.3	87.1	91.2	84.0	89.9	0.02
United Kingdom	91.2	77.6	66.1	68.2	85.1	105.1	104.6	101.0	123.2	113.0	88.9	−0.13
Slovenia	45.3	45.3	45.4	46.1	47.5	47.9	57.0	68.9	84.1	80.4	87.8	3.36
Spain	66.2	58.0	50.8	52.2	62.8	70.8	78.9	81.9	92.5	86.0	85.1	1.26
Cyprus	22.0	22.7	23.5	24.3	25.1	24.4	26.6	29.4	35.2	59.6	71.7	6.08
Portugal	58.1	47.7	39.2	41.1	55.1	58.7	61.6	67.7	70.8	71.7	69.0	0.86

Greece	43.0	45.0	47.1	48.0	47.7	46.6	53.0	59.3	60.4	63.9	68.6	2.36
Czech Republic	22.9	23.5	24.1	25.1	26.4	26.8	32.3	42.2	59.1	58.0	67.3	5.54
Slovakia	25.3	26.2	27.2	28.3	29.6	29.6	36.6	40.0	48.2	46.3	62.0	4.58
Poland	13.2	14.1	14.6	15.2	15.7	17.4	21.7	28.2	43.1	55.0	57.9	7.66
Estonia	49.7	34.6	24.1	23.8	33.3	42.0	42.9	49.1	61.8	57.7	56.9	0.67
Hungary	36.2	36.5	36.8	37.0	37.3	39.4	40.9	46.2	53.5	52.8	51.9	1.81
Latvia	29.8	21.1	15.0	14.9	20.8	25.9	26.4	29.7	43.2	39.8	51.5	2.77
Lithuania	23.9	20.9	18.4	18.8	22.5	25.2	27.8	32.5	49.0	43.2	46.3	3.36
Malta	39.6	39.9	40.2	41.1	42.4	43.2	46.3	47.6	48.1	50.4	43.6	0.47
Bulgaria	24.1	20.1	16.7	15.7	16.5	19.3	20.8	28.9	32.7	36.2	41.7	2.79
Romania	21.6	21.1	20.5	19.1	17.1	18.2	20.7	26.8	39.1	38.6	29.9	1.63
EU-27	71.1	68.1	65.7	67.4	73.5	76.9	81.7	86.9	97.3	94.5	93.2	1.36
EU-15	86.1	81.5	77.9	79.5	86.5	90.7	96.9	102.3	112.1	108.3	104.8	0.99
EU-12	23.2	22.0	21.2	21.4	22.4	23.9	27.5	34.4	47.6	51.4	54.2	4.34

Source: Eurostat (2012), Statistical pocketbook of the DG Mobility & Transport, national statistics of the EU member countries and own estimations.

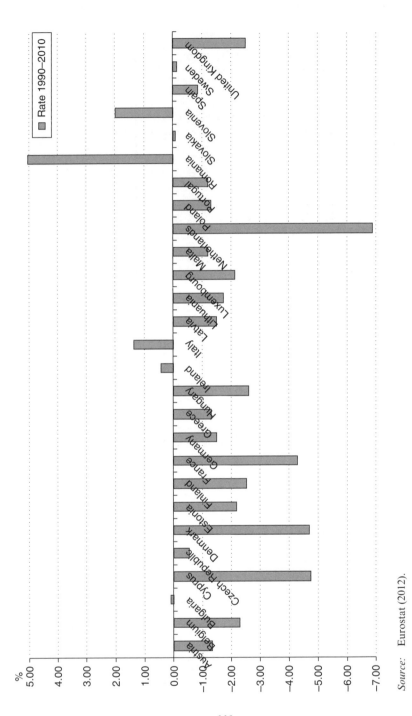

Source: Eurostat (2012).

Figure 4.6 Accidents involving personal injury in road transport, annual rate, 1990–2010 (in %)

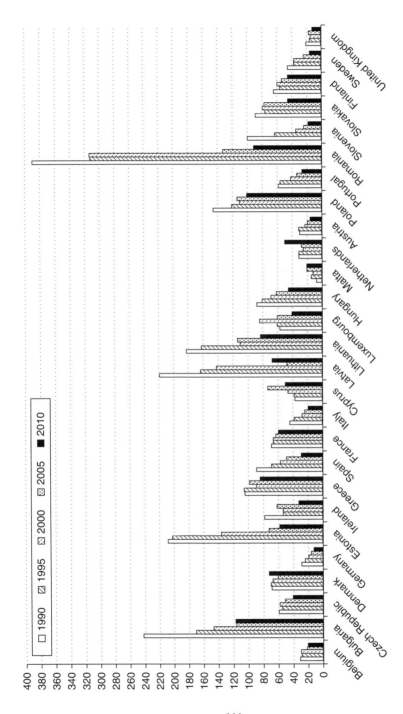

Source: Eurostat (2012).

Figure 4.7 Road fatalities (persons killed) per 1000 accidents

countries where road fatalities were at a very high level (e.g. in Romania 390 and in Bulgaria 240 persons killed per 1000 accidents in 1990) road safety has considerably improved during the past two decades.

4.6   CONCLUSIONS

EU transport policy and the regulations that implemented over 50 years have resulted in both expected and unexpected changes in the road freight sector. Restrictive traffic regulations throughout the period 1960–2012 (in the years 1960–1992 of a quantitative nature, and since 1993 of a qualitative nature) have not resulted in a reduction in traffic. On the contrary, the largest variation that occurred during that time is an increase in the volume of transportation (in the years 1990–2010 it was equal to +97 per cent).[5] The number of carriers and their activity was increasing and at the same time the price of their services dropped. This was achieved through higher utilization of assets, lowering costs and spatial availability of road transport services.

However, the increase in freight traffic volume also resulted in several negative effects, such as an increase in greenhouse gas emissions of more than 20 per cent in the years 1990–2009 (Eurostat, 2012), traffic congestion and the resulting increase in costs of time losses. Nevertheless, widespread availability of road transport services had some positive impact on the reduction of logistics costs in some sectors of the economy, and the decline in prices of goods and services.

To sum up, the implemented regulations have brought some noticeable results regarding important economic indicators of the road freight transport sector in Europe. In particular, these measures have contributed to enhance the functioning of the sector in terms of market, technology and ecology. However, maintaining this situation requires continuous monitoring of the sector, the uniform appointment of inspection bodies and the use of appropriate regulatory instruments. An unresolved issue remains whether and how the sector can cover the full infrastructure costs and damage to the environment and society.

NOTES

1. Regulation (EC) No 1071/2009 of the European Parliament and of the Council of 21 October 2009 establishing common rules concerning the conditions to be complied with to pursue the occupation of road transport operator and repealing Council Directive 96/26/EC, introduction, Whereas (2).
2. Regulation No 1072/2009 of the European Parliament and of the Council of 21 October 2009 on common rules for access to the international road haulage market.

3. The EU *acquis* (also referred to as the *acquis communataire*) refers to the total body of European Union law applicable in the EU member states.
4. The minimum percentage number of checks was set, as from 1 May 2006, at 1 per cent of days worked by drivers of vehicles falling within the scope of Regulations (EEC) No 3820/85 and (EEC) No 3821/85; this percentage was increased to at least 2 per cent from 1 January 2008 and to at least 3 per cent from 1 January 2010, and could be increased by the Commission to 4 per cent. See: http://ec.europa.eu/transport/road/social_provisions/ enforcement_en.htm.
5. According to Eurostat and DG MOVE statistics, in 1990–2010 road freight transport volume in the EU-27 increased from about 900 tkm to 1756 billion tkm.

REFERENCES

Bernadet, M. (2009), 'Report on the construction and operation of the road freight transport market in Europe', International Transport Forum Paper, Paris: OECD, available at http://www.internationaltransportforum.org/pub/ pdf/09FP01.pdf.

Blöndal, S. and D. Pilat (1997), 'The economic benefits of regulatory reform', OECD Economic Studies No. 28, 1997/I, available at http://78.41.128.130/ dataoecd/22/21/2733617.pdf.

Burnewicz, Jan (2005), *Sektor samochodowy Unii Europejskiej* (EU road sector), Warsaw: WKŁ.

Datamonitor (2012), available at http://www.datamonitor.com/store/Browse/? N tt=Logistic&N=4294853786.

ECMT (2001), 'Pan-European integration of transport: a baseline scenario for transport in Europe', ECMT, available at http://internationaltransportforum. org/IntOrg/ecmt/cm/pdf/CM200104e.pdf.

ECMT (2005), 'International road freight transport in Europe – market access and the future of the licence system (2005)', report of the 2005 Special Advisory Group to the ECMT (European Conference of Ministers of Transport), CEMT/ CM(2005)16, Paris, available at http://internationaltransportforum.org/IntOrg/ ecmt/cm/pdf/CM200516e.pdf.

ECORYS (2006), 'Study on road cabotage in the freight transport market', final report to the European Commission, DG TREN, available at http://ec.europa. eu/transport/road/studies/doc/2006_03_road_cabotage_study.pdf.

European Commission (2011), 'Road freight transport vademecum: market trends and structure of the road haulage sector in the EU in 2010', DG for Mobility and Transport, European Commission, available at http://ec.europa.eu/transport/ road/doc/2010-road-freight-vademecum.pdf.

European Commission (2012a), 'Report of the 2012 High Level Group on the Development of the EU Road Haulage Market', European Commission, DG for Mobility and Transport, Brussels, available at http://ec.europa.eu/transport/ road/doc/2012-06-high-level-group-report-final-report.pdf.

European Commission (2012b), 'EU transport in figures. Statistical pocket-book 2012', available at http://ec.europa.eu/transport/facts-fundings/statistics/ pocketbook-2012_en.htm.

Eurostat (2012), 'Environment, Statistics, Main tables', available at http://epp. eurostat.ec.europa.eu/portal/page/portal/environment/data/main_tables.

Global Transport & Logistics (2012), 'Financial ration analysis report'.

IRU (2006), 'The enforcement of European road transport rules', International Road Transport Union, Round Table, Brussels, 18 September, available at http://www.iru.org/cms-filesystem-action?file=en_News/IRU_paper_final_EN.pdf

OECD (1997), 'The OECD report on regulatory reform – synthesis', Paris: OECD, available at http://www.oecd.org/dataoecd/17/25/2391768.pdf.

Research and Markets (2012), 'European Road Freight 2010', Research and Markets report, summary available at http://www.researchandmarkets.com/reports/2238762/european_road_freight_transport_2012.

Scheele, J. (2010), 'Transport market integration at the pan-European level: lessons from the development of the internal market and enlargement', 3rd draft of paper (version 2, June 2010), available at http://scheejo.wordpress.com/transport-market-integration-at-the-pan-european-level-lessons-from-the-development-of-the-internal-market-and-enlargement/.

Transport Intelligence (2012), 'Global transport and logistics financial ratio analysis report 2012', available at http://www.transportintelligence.com/assets/files/Global_Transport_and_Logistics_Financial_Ratio_Analysis_2012_Brochure.pdf).

UNECE (2011), 'Openness of international road freight transport markets in the UNECE region', United Nations Economic Commission for Europe, Inland Transport Committee, Working Party on Road Transport, Geneva, available at http://www.unece.org/fileadmin/DAM/trans/doc/2012/sc1/Informal-SC1-2012-2e.pdf.

5. Long-distance coach services in Europe

Didier van de Velde

5.1 INTRODUCTION

While high-speed rail or airlines attract a lot of political and media attention, long-distance coach services tend to be much less visible. The coaching business also differs from the air and rail modes in that it mainly uses infrastructure that is already available for the general public (highways and motorways), requiring only smaller investments in suitable coach stations at attractive places in urban centres. Yet, long-distance (or 'express') coaches account for a substantial part of the mobility of Europe's less wealthy citizens, especially in those countries that have appropriately (de) regulated this activity.

Few international studies have been published on this topic. The report from the 114th Round Table organized by the European Conference of Ministers of Transport (ECMT) in 1999 (ECMT, 2001) was one such study, covering Britain, Poland, Sweden and the Eurolines organization. European National studies on the topic are scarce too, except perhaps in Britain, Sweden and Norway – three countries with a well-functioning deregulated coach market. Later, a paper written from the Organisation for Economic Co-operation and Development (OECD) and ITF (International Transport Forum) provided a review of the situation in the inter-urban passenger transport market by coach in Europe by 2009 (van de Velde, 2010).[1] The present chapter updates that study, adding some of the main developments that have taken place since then.

The chapter starts with a review of the potential regulatory background for this sector. For a number of selected countries it then describes the regulatory setting, the main market actors and some of the main developments that have taken place in the last decade or two. The chapter then summarizes some trends and challenges, especially in terms of regulation.

5.2   ORGANIZATIONAL FORMS IN LONG-DISTANCE PASSENGER TRANSPORT

The long-distance passenger transport services reviewed here are those open to everyone and operated according to a published timetable, that is, similar to local public transport, trains and airplanes. This means that the touristic coaching sector, private hire and organized package tours, are not covered.

The words 'long-distance coach services' need, perhaps, some further definition in view of the diversity that can be encountered across Europe. 'Long-distance coach services', also called 'express buses' or 'inter-urban coaches', have in common that they cater for transport needs outside urban agglomerations, usually from city to city, often also serving en route towns that are not well served by rail. Operations are generally done with coaches, not by buses, although the concepts 'coach' and 'bus' do not necessarily exist distinctly in the various European languages. The exact definition of long-distance coach services varies also from country to country, but these definitions determine the regulation under which services will fall. Distance is often a main criterion in order to fall under the regulatory regime applicable to long-distance coach services, but these distances can differ widely: over 15 miles in Britain, or over 100 km in Sweden at some point in time. Other countries often adopt an administrative distinction, where 'long distance' is defined as those services crossing the borders of the regional transport authorities, as in Italy or Norway, and earlier in Sweden.

There are two main families of organizational forms of passenger transport services. The first is 'market initiative' regimes where it is essentially transport operators that come up with ideas of the markets to be served (van de Velde, 1999). Operators are free, in such regimes, to suggest new services and request permission to operate them. In its pure form, the request for permission is a mere formality. Authorizations to operate (sometimes called 'licences', and sometimes confusingly called 'concessions') are then granted without further analysis by transport authorities of whether the market 'needs' the additional service, whether another operator already provides similar services, whether fares are appropriate, and so on. Such a regime can also be combined with various forms of regulatory interventions, limiting free access to the market by various requirements avoiding parallel services, requiring fare integrations, protecting railway rights, and so on. While the principle remains that of market initiative, such regulations can indeed become so tight as to effectively prevent entry, leading to incumbent or railway monopoly.

The alternative to market initiative regimes is a regime based upon 'authority initiative' (van de Velde, 1999). Here, a transport authority is charged with the creation of the transport services. The authority can then provide the services itself, with its own staff or company, or 'concede' these services to an operator of its choice, which usually takes place via competitive tendering. The essential difference from 'market initiative' regimes is that this regime prohibits any spontaneous initiative from market actors, as it grants all rights of service creation to the authority. If the authority does not take the initiative, nothing happens and nothing can (legally) happen. For the private sector to be involved, it requires the authority first to realize that a transport service is needed, then to specify its characteristics, and finally to organize a tendering procedure to award the service to an operator under a time-bound contract. Such contracts – called 'concessions' or sometimes confusingly 'franchises' – are often exclusive, although not necessarily so.

The overview of countries presented in the next section will show that most countries that have opened the long-distance coach market have opted for a regime based upon market initiative, with a large degree of deregulation. Authority initiative and competitive tendering are present too, but to a much lesser extent.

5.3 COUNTRY CASES

A few countries have been selected here to provide an illustration of the diversity and similarities in the inter-urban passenger coach market in Europe. The presentation of each country focuses on the national inter-urban coach operations, being for most countries the main part of the market. International coach services are another substantial part of the scheduled coaching business in Europe. This is presented in the section on Eurolines, as a main part of the international passenger coach services takes place under this brand.

5.3.1 United Kingdom

The British coach market was fully deregulated by the 1980 Transport Act. The only requirement (besides licencing requirements) to create services was that an authorization was to be requested 28 days before starting the operations. This 28-day prior authorization was scrapped under the 1985 Transport Act; hence no prior notice is now needed for operation of an express route.

Today, National Express is the main supplier of express coach services. National Express was privatized in the 1980s and was the former monopolist of the express coach market as part of the former NBC (National Bus Company). Most services are operated by local contractors under the National Express brand rather than directly by National Express with its own staff.

The deregulation provided intense competition in the 1980s on some routes. A company called British Coachways, grouping six existing operators, attempted to establish a network to compete with National Express, but this failed as early as 1983 (Robbins, 2007). By the middle of the 1980s, most competitors of National Express stopped their services, as innovations such as lower fares or more comfort had been copied by National Express. Additionally, National Express initially had access to most of the coach stations and refused access to other operators. An important issue at the time was control of Victoria Coach Station in central London. The coach station was subsequently transferred to the control of the London transport authority (now Transport for London).

The decline of competition in the 1980s after a strong competitive period resulted in a de facto monopoly by National Express. This disappeared in 2003 with the arrival of Megabus.com as a no-frills, low-cost coach brand provided by the Stagecoach group, another main player in local public transport and passenger rail in the UK. Megabus strives to differ from National Express by concentrating on low-income target groups such as students, young people without driving licences and elderly people. Its network is less extensive, has lower frequencies and focuses on routes between London and other major cities. Since 2012 it has also expanded to Paris, Brussels and Amsterdam. It uses pre-booking with yield management in its pricing strategy, copying the success observed in the low-cost airline business and to some extent by National Express. Megabus also tries to get closer to its target groups by remaining outside the coach stations used by National Express and by stopping closer to where its target groups are located, on the curbside or on university campuses. A high propensity of the target groups to use the internet, and the strategy of Megabus to sell tickets via the internet, meant that access to a coach station as a central information and access point to the coach network became less essential (Robbins, 2007); furthermore, it contributed to save costs.

Coach travel in Great Britain represents a substantial share of mobility, but a clear accounting of the market share of the coach sector is difficult, as statistics tend to combine (local) bus services in the accounts. National Express remains dominant in this market, despite the entry of Megabus. A study of the competition between National Express and Megabus on the London–Bournemouth route (which also showed that car ownership and access to car usage is about 50 per cent lower for Megabus users), calculated a market share on this route of 79 per cent for National Express and 21 per cent for Megabus (Robbins, 2007).

One of the main challenges for new entrants to the British coach market was to find a niche that National Express had not yet occupied. Another challenge was the implementation of appropriate channels for ticket sales. The increasing usage of the internet was a chance for Megabus as it facilitated market access for the company as it did not have to rely on the access to existing travel agents where National Express already had an advantage. Most of the ticket sales of Megabus.com is now done through the internet (Robbins, 2007).

5.3.2 Sweden

Deregulation of the long-distance coach market in Sweden took place in three steps, where the first step involved a reversal of the 'burden of proof'. From 1993 onwards, the national railway carriers SJ had to prove that the opening of a coach line would seriously damage the railway business, or counties had to prove that it would seriously damage county bus routes (contracted and subsidized), rather than the entrant having to prove that it would damage neither the railway nor the regional bus services. Although this first step was neutral from an aggregate welfare point of view, it also led to gains for low-income (low value of time) customers, while the railways lost a little revenue (SIKA, 1997; Jansson et al., 1997). The second deregulation step took place in 1999 with a full deregulation of the coach market with, however, a continued possibility for the country passenger transport authority to prevent coaches from picking up and setting down passengers in certain cases when these travel only within their area of authority. The third step took place in January 2012 with the abolition of that last barrier to open market competition.

Long-distance coach services were defined in Sweden as those running for at least 100 km and crossing at least one county border. That market was already completely deregulated and non-subsidized. With the enactment of the new passenger transport law on 1 January 2012, the above definition has vanished as all markets for passenger transport services (both long and short distance, whether crossing county borders or not) have now been opened to competition on the road. This also means that the local public transport services (that are competitively tendered and subsidized by county transport authorities) have lost their exclusivity rights.

Three main players dominated the Swedish market in 2007, providing 79 per cent of the total supply in coach-km; while 32 operators provided long-distance coach services in Sweden in 2011. The main player currently is Nobina, the largest bus operator in all Nordic countries, through its subsidiary Swebus, with a self-reported market share above 50 per cent in the express coach market. Svenska Buss is a cooperative company owned by regional Swedish bus and coach operators. GoByBus and Bus4you are now owned by the Norwegian group Nettbuss, itself part of NSB (the national Norwegian rail operator). Ybuss is a smaller Swedish privately owned operator that exists besides several other regional operators.

As in other countries, passengers are mainly students, the elderly and low-income population groups. Most of the Swedish long-distance coach services are run on a commercial basis, with only a few per cent run under contract from a transport authority. Coach services represented in 2005–06 about 5 per cent of the number of long-distance trips and 6 per cent of the passenger-km. The train (about 15 per cent in passenger-km in 2005–06) has a larger market share in trips and in mobility, as do airplanes (11 per cent in passenger-km in 2005–06) in terms of kilometres only as few people use buses for very long distances (above 600 km) (SIKA, 2008). The relative share of collective means of transport increased in the period 1993–98, in line with the deregulation of both inland air traffic and long-distance coach services. While mobility increased by 9 per cent during this period, collective transport grew by 13 per cent. This evolution was reversed between 1998 and 2004 (growth of 9 per cent for collective means of transport while total mobility grew by 13 per cent), but bus travel remained stable during that period, illustrating a shift from air to rail (Banverket, 2006). Although supply of services measured in bus-km recently decreased by about 14 per cent between 2008 and 2011, usage simultaneously grew by about 18 per cent (Trafikanalys, 2012).

Long-distance coach services are often included in regional fare integration schemes managed by the county passenger transport authorities, allowing local customers to use the long-distance buses as part of the total regional network and under the same fare conditions. This constitutes an interesting additional source of revenue for the coach operators, and an interesting additional service for the customers of the county passenger transport authority. It remains to be seen, however, what influence the new legislation will have on these practices.

The results of the deregulation started in 1993 and fulfilled in 1999 are perceived to be positive. Coach services are seen in Sweden as a welcome addition to the rest of the public transport system. Deregulation has become a part of the Swedish passenger transport system, with the subsequent deregulation of the national railway system (full open access since October 2010) and the abolition of the exclusive right of tendered local passenger transport services in January 2012.

5.3.3 Norway

The current express coach services have evolved from the old authorization regime, and the pre-existing local public transport services. These local public transport services were and are regulated by the counties, and appeared historically on the basis of route authorizations initiated by operators. Many of these routes are subsidized by local authorities. Competitive tendering has also been used since the end of the 1990s for unprofitable area or route-based contracts.

The current regulatory regime for long-distance coach services has been in place since 2003 and represents almost complete deregulation. It is the result of a gradual liberalization that started in the 1990s after new initiatives for route cooperation by existing operators started at the end of the 1980s. The express services developed from existing transport companies initiating new and faster transport services, crossing the boundaries of their traditional (county) areas to provide more attractive bus connections. The extension of services mostly happened in partnerships between the transport companies involved in the areas served. Other routes resulted from the extension to Oslo of the former long-distance rail feeder routes.

Initially, these initiatives led to some resistance from the authorities, who feared the weakening of local public transport, and from the national Norwegian railway company Norges Statsbaner (NSB) which also wanted to avoid competition. However, the introduction of inter-urban express coach services through this market initiative led to high popularity amongst users (Leiren and Fearnley, 2008) and the fears of excessive competition between coach and rail appeared unfounded (Hjellnes COWI, 1999).

Today, most inter-urban coach services in Norway are organized via NOR-WAY Bussekspress, which is a marketing organization owned by 25 member companies (40 in 2009) running the different coach lines, some of which are run in cooperation with one another. The members are each responsible for the design of the services regarding timetables and fares. The main competitor to NOR-WAY Bussekspress is Nettbuss TIMEkspress in Southern Norway. The services are run by Nettbuss, the coach operator of NSB, which also offers further coach brands such as Bus4you, GoByBus (to Sweden and Denmark) and Flybussen (airport express brand). It should be noted that Nettbuss also runs further inter-urban services for NOR-WAY Bussekspress. Other competitors are Lavprisexpressen en Konkurrenten.

The main part of the express coach services is run commercially and market access is de facto free. The current express coach network is seen more as a useful complement than as a competitor to the rest of the public transport services. It caters for 6 per cent of the trips above 100 km, which is rather constant through time, though it loses market share to air on distances above 300 km (Aarhaug et al., 2011). Policy documents, such as the National Transport Plan 2010–2019, reiterate that these services are welcome additions to the public transport system as they service areas that would otherwise not benefit from public transport; also they are seen to contribute to a better environment and to fewer accidents by reducing car traffic.

Studies conducted in Norway showed that most passengers are new or attracted from the car rather than from train and airplane services (see Hjellnes COWI, 1999; Strand, 1991). Studies also showed that public transport usage has, on the whole, increased on the corridors with train–coach competition. In total, ridership has more than doubled between 2002 and 2007 while productivity has reached levels significantly higher than in neighbouring Sweden which has also deregulated its market but with less possibility for cooperation between operators (Alexandersson et al., 2009). Ridership seems to have stagnated since 2008, while the number of operators has been halved by mergers and takeovers (Aarhaug et al., 2011).

Whereas route authorizations used to be issued by the national government, this competence was decentralized to the counties, and in practice all requests for authorizations are granted for as much as quality standards of operations are fulfilled. The counties can, however, impose regulations to protect subsidized local public transport services. However, it seems that in many cases counties have adapted the local services to the existence of the express services and choose to 'buy' specific additions to the express services to fulfil local needs (school transport, lengthening routes, and so on), though this represented only 3 per cent of the total turnover of long-distances buses in 2010 (Aarhaug et al., 2011). While it was feared earlier on that European rules could force the use of competitive tendering in all cases of subsidization – which would effectively have constituted a threat to the free-market nature and drive of the industry, replacing it with a more centrally planned system – it now seems that fare compensation can easily be allowed as part of the so-called 'general rules' allowed by EC Regulation 1370/2007 on public services obligations (PSOs). Interestingly, transport authorities report that such arrangements with commercial long-distance operators prove to be cheaper than organizing a separate local contract (competitively tendered) (Leiren and Fearnley, 2008; Aarhaug et al., 2011).

Cooperation between operators, although sometimes looked upon critically by competition authorities, is perceived to be beneficial. A study by the Norwegian Transport Economic Institute (Leiren et al., 2007) showed that the coach network, including the routes with cooperation within that network, led to substantial welfare gains (NOK 1.5 billion per year).

5.3.4 Poland

Public transport in Poland was, prior to 1990, organized in a similar fashion to that in other former communist countries. The State Road Transport (PKS) was the main carrier of passengers and goods by road. Before 1988 passenger transport operations in more than one region (*voivodship*) required a permit from the Ministry of Transport. Permanent permits were only given to state carriers. Other road operators' access to the market was limited to single or periodic permits. It was the Act on Economic Activity (1988) that liberated many fields of activity, including road transport (Taylor and Ciechanski, 2008).

PKS was split into four state-owned firms in the early 1980s: one national PKS and three regional companies. The organizational structure of PKS counted numerous local branches receiving subsidies from the state budget. In 1990 the four firms were disbanded and all 233 branches became individual enterprises (Taylor and Ciechanski, 2008). There was little interest from foreign investors. Less than half of all firms were subsequently privatized, the most popular form taken involving a privatization to the company's employees. The only main international concern interested was Veolia, which had taken control of 11 PKS companies as of mid-2006 (Taylor and Ciechanski, 2008). The limited interest in privatization by foreign investors could be linked to the rapid decline in ridership. By 2005, public transport ridership was only one-third of the 1989 figure due to the extensive development of individual motoring (Taylor and Ciechanski, 2008)

Little competition appeared at the national level. A new company started in 1994: Polski Express, a subsidiary of Britain's National Express Group, and mainly targeting connections not well served by rail. This company experienced serious economic difficulties later on (Taylor and Ciechanski, 2008).

In the late 1990s, real competition came from private 'independent' operators having small numbers of buses, usually of a lower standard, serving the most profitable routes. These activities led to a worsening of the economic situation of local PKS companies (more involved in local and regional transport). In some areas, local PKS companies went out of business. PKS remained dominant, however, accounting for 92 per cent of passengers and 95 per cent of scheduled bus and coach services in Poland (Taylor and Ciechanski, 2008).

Also, Polbus-PKS was created in 1995 as a reaction to Polski Express.

Polbus PKS was set up by 21 PKS companies and a couple of private companies as a marketing company, inspired by the example of NOR-WAY Bussekspress. It aimed at providing a modern coach network for domestic services with a unified sales and information system for the services of its member companies across Poland. The company started providing long-distance services, especially where rail links were unattractive (Taylor and Ciechanski, 2008). Pekaes Bus, set up in 1996 as spin-off of PKS, also provided long-distance services. It was subsequently taken over by Veolia Eurolines Polska.

The Polish market remains turbulent, with the latest development being the appearance of a substantial bus network meant to serve over 20 cities across Poland and Central and Eastern Europe, provided by PolskiBus.com, a company created by Brian Souter who is also the owner of Stagecoach (Great Britain).

Komornicki (2001) reported a substantial supply of semi-legal and illegal bus connections between Poland and neighbouring countries at the beginning of the 1990s. He reported that this problem (lack of quality certification, accidents, etc.) was considerably reduced from 80 to 20 per cent of the market by 1998. It would be interested to know whether the issue has completely vanished now that Poland has become a member of the European Union (EU), and whether the issue has reappeared further East.

5.3.5   Spain

Long-distance concessions are granted by the national government on an exclusive basis. The length of those concessions varies between eight and 20 years. Regional inter-urban bus concessions are awarded by regional governments. In both cases, contracts are now mainly granted by means of competitive tendering, although direct contracting is possible in some circumstances but mainly in urban transport. Until 1990, both long-distance and inter-urban services were under state control and concessions were awarded directly, without tendering. Reform was introduced with the decentralization to the Autonomous Communities (Regions) and reform of the passenger transport legislation (in 1987 and 1990). As a result of this, the 113 existing concessions for long-distance services (none of them subject to tendering) could be extended until at least 2007; most were extended until 2013 and some until 2018. New concessions for the provision of services on routes insufficiently served or replacing illegal lines have to be awarded through public tendering.

Numerous coach operators exist on the Spanish market. In 1988 ENATCAR was created as a public company taking over all coach services of the national railway carrier RENFE. This operator was subsequently privatized to ALSA, which is the main supplier of long-distance coach services with nearly 10 per cent of the market and offering a wide range of differentiated services. The company is privately owned, a member of Eurolines. In 2005 it was sold to British National Express Group. Since then ALSA has expanded its influence in the Spanish bus sector, for example integrating the second national transport operator Continental Auto in 2007.

Coaches traditionally have a strong position in Spain's long-distance public transport market. Reliable statistics seem to be absent, but the coach market is believed to be four times larger than that of the train when measured in passenger-km (García-Pastor et al., 2003). The further development of the Spanish high-speed network may bring a change in this situation, however, as did low-cost airlines. The 2008 annual report of National Express mentions these competitive pressures and its response to the entry of low-cost airlines and the development of high-speed rail by varying service frequency, adapting prices and altering its network to provide complementary services. Furthermore, it also announced the launch of new services with revised on-board catering and on-board WiFi, being the first transport mode in Spain to offer this facility.

Despite the usage of competitive tendering, Spain's long-distance coach services are all profitable, in the sense that they do not receive public subsidy. García-Pastor et al. (2003) report that, according to a study for the Spanish Ministry of Development (Consultrans, 1999), the competitive tendering initiated in the 1990s did, however, have positive effects on service quality and ticket prices for these concessions. According to this study, extended concessions appeared to have 46 per cent higher passenger-km fares than tendered concessions.

5.3.6 Italy

The Italian inter-urban coach market can be divided into national and regional services. National inter-urban coach services (*linee extraurbane statali*) operate commercially on routes of 200–1200 km between the larger cities located in different regions. The legal regime applicable to those services has recently been modified with a decree from November 2005 aimed at opening the market. Services do not receive any subsidy. Coach operators now have to apply for an authorization at the Ministry before starting new services. While the former regime did not allow competition, the new authorization regime is supposed to make competition on the road possible. However, existing exclusive rights can be kept until 31 December 2013, explaining why little competition has taken place until now.

Regional inter-urban coach services (*linee extraurbane regionali*) serve routes of 30–300 km between larger cities located within the same region. Most regional routes are still directly awarded concessions, are subsidized and have regulated routes and fares. Some deregulation is also planned here, as some regions have developed regional legislation that follows the national decree. However, this competition often seems restricted to those services that do not interfere with existing subsidized regional services operating under concession contracts.

Operators differ significantly in size. No national operator dominates the market at the moment. Busitalia – Sita Nord, as a large operator, is owned by the national train operator Trenitalia. Arriva Italy is one of the largest wholly privately owned operators, having entered the market by taking over 11 regional companies, many of which operate in the inter-urban market. The rest of the market is highly fragmented with a large number of local operators, often owned by regions and municipalities, but privately owned operators exist too. Most operators are based in one region and offer, in addition to regional services, connections with Rome or other main Italian cities. Few companies offer nationwide services.

Some services are supplied as a complement to the existing high-speed trains of Trenitalia. Busitalia, as a subsidiary of Trenitalia, is a main supplier of such services. Some services include high-quality seats and on-board internet facilities. Other services are directly competing with long-distance train services. Fares on those routes are comparable to the (highly subsidized) railway fares on those routes from the north to the south of the country. These fares are generally lower than domestic air fares.

In 2008, Ibus was initiated, a cooperation between nine operators integrating marketing and ticketing activities, and also a member of Eurolines.

5.3.7 France

There were until recently essentially no long-distance express coach services in France. The regulation of public transport is allocated to the state for interregional passenger transport services and these are the monopoly of the national railway company SNCF. Regional and local transport services are organized by the *départements* (to be compared with counties) and by (cooperation of) municipalities. The services are run publicly or (mostly) submitted to competitive tendering. Express services exist at the scale of the *départements*, when ordered by the respective transport authority, but not at the national scale on very long distances.

As a result of this, and although some competition exists between SNCF's train services – in particular its TGV (Train à Grande Vitesse) high-speed train services – and the airline business, there was until recently no competition between rail and road. Market entry by market initiative by individual transport operators is not foreseen in the current transport legislation (dating back to 1982) which explicitly prevents direct competition to SNCF services. As a result, entry seemed de facto impossible as gaining the agreement of SNCF seemed illusory.

However, the right-wing government in place until 2012 announced in July 2009 its intention to introduce a number of amendments to the current legislation to allow international coach services some degree of cabotage on French territory (this was introduced in 2012 on 230 international routes now operated by Eurolines, though with apparently little effect yet) and, more importantly, to allow a full liberalization and deregulation of the long-distance coach business at the national level (but this was postponed for the next government to consider). However, the liberalization of the international railway services has been enacted, in line with European rules, and it is expected that national long-distance (TGV) services within France will later on be submitted to open-access competition.

It is unclear whether the current left-wing government will move forward with coach deregulation or rather choose a concession tendering regime, more in line with the organization of local public transport in France, following the example of its Spanish neighbour. The expectation is that, as in other countries, students, less wealthy customers and people with a lower value of time would be the main beneficiaries of such liberalization. One could also conjecture that SNCF may in the long run benefit from replacing some of its loss-making interregional train services by more profitable coach services (Kramarz, 2009). It seems, however, that direct competition between coach and train will not rally a political majority, which could tip the balance towards a Spanish-style concession regime.

In the meantime, and with these evolutions in mind, SNCF started changing its attitude, perhaps seeing opportunities for its subsidiary Keolis that is currently expending its activities not only in France but also in the rest of Europe. In 2012, SNCF launched its international iDBUS network, following the low-cost iDTGV brand it had introduced earlier on its high-speed train services. iDBUS is currently positioned only as an international coach network serving Paris, London, Amsterdam, Brussels, Turin and Milan, with two hubs in Lille and Lyons, as the national long-distance market is not (yet) opened in France. A bit earlier a private competitor (Starshipper) had opened a line from Lyon to Turin, showing that the French market is starting to evolve towards a more competitive organization.

5.3.8 Germany

The basic regulatory principle of the German express coach market is that of free-market initiative by transport operators. The market is, however, strongly regulated by the national law on public transport. That law restricts direct on-route competition between transport operators and provides some protection to incumbent operators. Supplying new more or less parallel services has only been allowed when these represent a significant improvement over existing services. However, a recent change in the legislation may well introduce substantial changes in the functioning of these markets. As of 1 January 2013, the long-distance coach market has been liberalized and competition with the railways has been allowed. Further changes to the interpretation of the level of exclusivity in local passenger transport may also have implications for these markets.

Today, there is an extensive inter-urban coach network with Berlin as its hub. Most of those services are relics of the division of Germany. West Berlin as part of the Federal Republic of Germany was located inside the territory of the German Democratic Republic; the bus services provided connections between West Berlin and other cities in the Federal Republic. These connections are operated by Berlin Linien Bus, a joint venture of various coach operators, partly owned by DB. Most connections are served once a day. Every journey must have Berlin as starting point or destination. Services starting in Berlin cannot be boarded at other stops, and buses to Berlin can only be left in Berlin (Maertens, 2008).

Other providers are Touring and Public Express. Touring, owned by Eurosur (a joint venture of the Spanish and Portuguese bus operators Alsa, Linebus and Socitransa), operates a night service from Hamburg via Kassel, Frankfurt and Darmstadt to Mannheim. Other services mostly go to the other European countries. These represent most of the services performed by Touring. Touring runs these services under the flag of Eurolines. Further national services are provided by Public Express which offers coach services between Berlin, Bremen, Oldenburg and Groningen in the Netherlands, and also between Bremen and Aurich. Another segment of regular coach services is airport express buses. Many regional airports are served by such coach services (Maertens, 2008).

The evaluation of the potential of inter-urban coach services shows that inter-urban coaches would provide travel possibilities for people with lower incomes (Maertens, 2008). The services of current suppliers such as Touring and Public Express confirm this, with Public Express focusing on students and families, with many rebates for these groups, and Touring attracting travellers through low fares for those who book the journey well in advance.

Suppliers as Touring and Public Express show that there are market parties which want to expand but were hindered by the law until 2012. The lack of clarity of regulation (interpretation of quality improvement), and the resistance coming from the established operators, caused long court trials between operators of new services and incumbents. A case was the attempt by Touring to open a coach service competing with DB on the Frankfurt–Cologne route (Köhler, 2009). However, one can also observe that a new company called AutobahnExpress had managed in 2009 to obtain a number of authorizations for routes linking Potsdam, Dresden, Leipzig, Halle, Kassel and Göttingen via motorways, with interchange at the Leipzig/Halle airport. Yet, services were stopped again in February 2012 due to disappointing ridership figures.

Two political parties (the liberal democratic FDP and the Green Party) tried to promote the idea of a deregulation for inter-urban coach services in 2005 and 2006, but the Parliamentary Committee on Transport, Building and Urban Affairs rejected both requests (Maertens, 2008). However, deregulation of inter-urban coaches went ahead in January 2013, following the plans set out in the coalition agreement of the federal government (CDU, CSU and FDP) published in autumn 2009. It will be interesting to see whether the deregulation of this market will lead to developments similar to what could be witnessed earlier on in Britain and Sweden.

5.3.9 International Coach Services

Eurolines is a joint venture of European coach operators which organizes most of the international coach services inside Europe under the brand name 'Eurolines' group. Twenty-eight independent coach companies providing, together, Europe's largest regular coach network. Eurolines developed common quality standards for all its members and harmonized the sales and travel conditions. The network currently connects over 500 destinations, covering the whole of the Continent and Morocco.

Eurolines was founded in 1985 as a competitor to Europabus, which had been created by several European rail companies in 1965 to prevent other coach operators from competing with their rail services. While the transport services of Europabus remained limited, Eurolines developed its market by providing services on international routes with significant demand, starting with the travel needs of migrant and guest workers coming from Spain and Portugal. Various initiatives in the various countries, such as Budget Bus in the Netherlands (and many more examples in other countries), were eventually bundled together under the common flag of Eurolines as a marketing brand for regular international services.

The Eurolines Organization is an 'international non-profit organization' according Belgian law. Membership is open to (groups of) companies operating international scheduled passenger services by coach. Decisions concerning Eurolines Services, a commercial daughter of the Eurolines Organization, are made by a council of directors of all Eurolines member companies. An executive committee consisting of nine directors of the member companies guides the implementation of new product developments. A main challenge for Eurolines has been the differences in national legislation pertaining to the operation of passenger coach services, as differences in fuel taxes and rules for value-added taxation, for example, caused a lot of bureaucracy (Bochar, 2001).

It is interesting to note that Veolia has acquired a significant position in Eurolines as it owns the brand in Belgium, France, the Netherlands and Portugal, and it operates the brand in partnership in the Czech Republic, Poland and Spain.

5.4   MAIN TRENDS AND CHALLENGES

Let us summarize some main facts, trends and challenges that emerge from the countries reviewed above.

5.4.1   Evolution of Organizational Forms

In the countries presented, and as can be seen in Table 5.1, the deregulated market initiative is clearly dominant. Germany is the most recent country moving in this direction. Existing market actors had pressed in that direction, and a few routes already existed as the existing legislation was in principle based upon the market initiative principle, making it a relatively simple move – though it required a very long time before all actors agreed. The opening of the railways markets (internationally in 2012 and nationally earlier on) is probably also a factor that facilitated a shift in position by DB, itself interested in the coach business (as can be seen by its cooperation with a Czech company in the market to Prague) and a total liberalization of all markets.

The situation in France is bound to evolve soon, although the outcome is still uncertain. As France has organized the rest of its local and regional passenger transport system on the basis of a strict authority initiative and competitive tendering regime, this seems to leave little space for the free market, which seems 'foreign' to this setting and would require quite a fundamental change to the legal setting. However, the international rail liberalization and expectation of a national liberalization as fostered by the European Commission, and the steps taken by SNCF on the international coach market, may influence this position.

As a result, Spain appears to be the only country in the sample (and apparently also in the rest of Europe) that bases its regime not on free market principles, but on a regime of concessions awarded by competi-

Table 5.1   Organizational forms in long-distance coach transport in Europe (2012)

Authority initiative		Market initiative	
Public sector	Private concessions	Regulated	Deregulated
• France: long-distance monopoly for rail (SNCF), no long-distance coach services except for some cabotage rights, competitively tendered coach services at the local/regional level	• Spain: exclusive concessions awarded increasingly by competitive tendering to private operators, both at the national and regional level	• Germany (until 2012): market initiative in theory but almost no possibility of entry in practice to due protection of railway monopoly, deregulation to be implemented in 2013	• Great Britain: open market, free competition, no railway protection • Sweden: open market with some regulatory rights for regional transport authorities, no railway protection • Norway: open markets with some regulatory rights for regional transport authorities, no railway protection • Italy: open market, but still in a transition stage • Poland: open market but still many state-owned operators present

tive tendering. It should be noted, however, that the current concessions are more the result of historical rights that were probably initiated by the market and not the authority at their origin. Some of the existing concessions have already been submitted to tendering, but the bulk is still to come in the next years.

At the level of the operators, the organizational form is characterized by a diversity of arrangements, many of which are hybrid. Operators provide services with own vehicles and staff, but often also make use of subcontractors (such as National Express in Great Britain). This can be observed in most countries analysed. This, incidentally, allows smaller family-based operators to participate in larger networks of services. But smaller operators are also present individually in the market, as can be seen, for example, in Sweden and Italy.

An indirect influence resulted from the opening of the international passenger rail market for competition in 2010. The European Parliament forced this unexpected move and the European Commission is pushing towards a liberalization of the national markets. It is still unclear how this will evolve, but open-access passenger rail services have started to appear – though more at the national than at the international level, as can be seen in Italy, Austria, Sweden and even Germany. This could be the starting point of a new approach of the coaching business, as is now expected in Germany. However, existing national public service concessions will benefit from some protection, though this will be interpreted differently in the various countries. While further rail deregulation may have some effect on the international coaching business, it is likely that here too – just as for the deregulation of the national coach markets – coach and train will hunt for customers with different values of time.

Another dominant feature of this market is the 'marketing cooperation'. Individual operators, conscious of the existence of demand-side network effects present in this industry, bundle their products under an attractive brand name, allowing them to realize a wider service coverage and higher product attractiveness together than would be the case as isolated providers. Eurolines is the best example of this at the European level. NOR-WAY Bussexpress is another example at the country scale. Further examples can be found in Sweden. At the extreme, the marketing cooperation, which is a kind of commercial franchise (contrary to the usage of the word 'franchise' in the context of competitively tendered concessions), approximates the model of the main operator subcontracting most of its operations to local operators. Yet, main differences exist and lie in the balance of power and attribution of risks between the small contractors and the main contractor, or the assembly of operators in the case of the cooperation.

5.4.2 Performance

As can be read in the cases presented, the liberalization and deregulation of the coach sector is perceived to be a success in those countries that have implemented it. Some countries went for a 'big bang' approach, such as the United Kingdom (UK) in 1980. Others, very much in their tradition, went for a more gradual approach, as such Sweden; or a pragmatic approach, such as Norway; or an incomplete approach, such as Italy. It remains to be seen how France and Germany will tackle their current reluctance to deregulate.

The competitive tendering alternative to the market, as used in Spain, also delivered good results according to the studies reported in the case study. Tendered concessions proved to have lower fares than extended (negotiated) concessions. This does not allow us to draw a conclusion on the relative advantage of tendering above deregulated markets, as one has to remember that the Spanish concessions are exclusive and therefore lack the competitive pressure present in countries such as Norway, Sweden, Poland or the UK. An international comparison of service levels, quality and fares would be needed to be able to make a judgement about this.

Contrary to most of the rest of public transport, long-distance coaches are operated on a commercial basis, in the sense that subsidization is almost non-existent. The railway sector, on the contrary, even protected from competition from the coach sector, mostly requires subsidization, if not directly in operations then at least through part of the infrastructure expenses.

Another attractive aspect of the coach sector can be found in the fact that coaches produce little pollution per passenger-km and reach a safety level in terms of accidents that is comparable to that of the train and airplanes, which is substantially lower than the car system (see, e.g., ECMT, 2001). The proponents of deregulation then combine this argument with the observation that in countries that have removed railway protection and deregulated the coach sector, coaches tend to capture more passengers from cars than from rail, leading to the conclusion that coach deregulation would be beneficial from an overall transport policy point of view.

It would be nice to be able to compare the size, modal shares and modal shift in inter-urban passenger travel in Europe. Unfortunately, statistics of national and international inter-urban passenger transport are difficult to compile. Numerous differences in definition exist from country to country, making international comparisons hazardous. Census data for travel surveys often do not include trips made by foreign nationals. Local and regional buses are often aggregated with coach statistics, making this data rather useless for the purpose of the analysis presented here. Differences in the definition of 'inter-urban' make international comparison of modal shares unreliable. Table 5.2 should therefore only be seen as a mere illustration of the limited size of mobility by bus and coach compared to the share of mobility by car. It is also striking to see the similarity of the modal shares for bus (and coach) and train. However, 'bus' includes here urban buses, regional buses and inter-urban coaches. While the share of inter-urban coaches could be 50 per cent or more of the total of the category 'bus' – this is probably the case in Spain with its extensive coach network and relatively limited rail services – this percentage can however be much lower in other countries.

Table 5.2   Modal shares (in passenger-km)

Country	Year	BUS	CAR	TRAIN
EU-15	2010	8.3	84.4	7.4
EU-25	2010	8.8	84.1	7.1
Germany	2010	6.1	85.9	8.0
Spain	2010	12.3	82.3	5.4
France	2010	5.8	84.4	9.9
Italy	2010	12.2	82.3	5.5
Norway	2010	6.8	88.4	4.8
Poland	2010	6.4	88.4	5.2
Sweden	2010	7.2	83.4	9.4
UK	2010	5.1	87.4	7.5

Source: Eurostat (2012).

5.4.3   Markets Served

Providers of long-distance coach services focus rather clearly on specific target groups: students, the elderly, people with no access to cars, and poorer people in general. Swedish and UK studies have shown the advantage of a deregulation for these groups, while showing at the same time the limited impact on the rail system in terms of passengers captured. Rail and coach seem to cater for people with different values of time in terms of long-distance travelling. Some studies even show that direct competition between both modes in one corridor tends to result in a growing market for both at the expense of the car.

In addition to this, coach also tends to serve quite successfully routes that are not available by rail, in particular by providing direct links between airports and various areas.

Eurolines is obviously the main player for international services in Europe. Clear statistics do not exist, making the presentation of clear observations on this market difficult. Poland, and probably also the Czech Republic and other former communist countries not reviewed here, appear to be main players in term of the European network of coach services. This has much to do with the current propensity of some workers from Poland and other Central and Eastern European countries to seek job opportunities elsewhere in (Western) Europe. Family visits, tourism and further exchanges are responsible for the growth of these markets since the fall of the Iron Curtain. As such, this development is very similar to market developments that could be observed several decades ago and that were responsible for the development of the coaching business at that time, especially in relation to the transport flows between Spain and Portugal and the rest of Europe.

Two main European countries still have only very limited coach services, except for the international Eurolines services: France and Germany. Changes are clearly overdue here and political momentum is now building up for change in France after the recent deregulation decision taken in Germany.

Smaller European countries have, in view of their sheer size, limited or no long-distance coach services. This is the case in the Netherlands, Belgium and Switzerland. Denmark does have a few long-distance coach routes from Copenhagen to Jutland. It should be noted that the railway services are excellent in these countries for the distances considered. These countries are of course also well served by the Eurolines services.

5.4.4 Network Effects, Monopolies, Barriers to Entry and Regulatory Needs

Network effects need to be recognized in this industry. The marketing cooperations presented above appear out of the market process in a profitable, competitive and open market. This is an indication of their desirability. But it is also an indicator of their questionability from a regulatory point of view. The British, Norwegian and Eurolines cases show the attractiveness of this concept for the passengers (information, ticketing, image, attractiveness, etc.) The sheer existence of a cooperation between providers in a competitive market is prone to attract suspicion from the competition authorities, as can be seen in the Norwegian case reported earlier, or in the acquisition of the Scottish Citylink by National Express at the end of the 1990s (followed by a forced divesture), as reported by White (2008).

Yet, as already stated by the 1998 Round Table on Interurban coaches (ECMT, 2001), these cooperations and the resulting conglomerates of operators do not seem to lead to the abuse of dominant positions. This is due to the strength of the intermodal competition with (mainly) the car, low-cost airlines and, to a lesser extent, rail. Furthermore, as exemplified by the Megabus entry in Britain, the market seems to remain sufficiently contestable in terms of intramodal competition. It is important to stress that this lack of worry can only be true as far as entry barriers are appropriately removed. This relates to non-discriminatory access to coach stations, fair licencing requirements and fair authorization procedures. This also requires non-exclusive route authorizations, or a very clever authorization-issuing authority (which is perhaps too much to ask for in many cases). Last but not least, it requires the enforcement of fair access to existing marketing organizations when these have a dominant position on some markets. Indeed, competing marketing organizations could also exist, but their viability will be very much dependent upon the size of the market to be served.

Fair access to coach stations seemed to be more of a problem in the 1980s than it appears to be nowadays. None of the studies accounted for in this research mentioned coach station access as a main issue. Stations can be owned either by the public sector or by a main operator, but need and seem to be accessible at fair rates. Furthermore the relevance of stations as places to find information and buy tickets has lost much of its relevance with the advances reached in internet sales in this sector.

While coaches are often operated by numerous local, small, family operators, one can also observe the continuous expansion of a few main European-wide operators. While the traditional model of small operators as subcontractors of larger brand-holders or members of market associations does not yet seem to be threatened, it will also be interesting to see whether this model will lose its importance and be gradually replaced by larger operators. The expansion of Veolia, as the main French group, is currently very visible all across Europe. The British National Express is a second example, although less prominent. Earlier expansions of international groups, such as Stagecoach, have been witnessed in Sweden, but events showed that these expansions could be very volatile. The future will tell, but a point for further study, in terms of regulatory preoccupations, is whether expanding large conglomerates poses a larger competitive threat to the coaching market rather than to the cooperations per se.

The European Union adopted in 2007 a new regulation on public service obligations in the passenger transport sector (Regulation 1370/2007) that has been applicable since the end of 2009. In short, services granted exclusive rights or financial support must be submitted to competitive tendering. There are a number of (complex) exceptions to this, however (see van de Velde, 2008 for more details). Deregulated markets without exclusive rights are not directly affected by the regulation. Furthermore, compensation for fare rebates can continue to exist, when accessible to all operators. This means that the long-distance coach sector is not affected by the measure, as it operates without subsidy and without exclusivity. The main exception is Spain, but as competitive tendering has been chosen as awarding mechanism in that country, it seems compatible with the regulation. However, as could be seen in Sweden and Norway for instance, long-distance coaches do not exist in isolation from other public transport services. As it happens, regional transport authorities in countries with low densities of population and under whose responsibility local public transport falls have many times discovered the mutual benefits that may exist between local buses and long-distance coaches. Integrating coach services with regular local services can realize service improvements (speed) for local customers, and can allow serving remote areas that would otherwise not be served if a long-distance bus did not stop on its way to the next remote main city. Combining both types of services often requires subsidization of the long-distance coach. A problem could appear here if this amount or the size of the contract exceeded some threshold, forcing or pushing the authority to use competitive tendering, which would only be counterproductive in this case. There is no clear view on the extent of this problem, but it could constitute a (probably minor) challenge in the years to come if pragmatism cannot be used.

5.5 CHALLENGES FOR THE NEAR FUTURE

The points of view and opinions in markets that are currently closed, such as France and Germany, have much in common with what could be heard in countries such as Sweden and Norway before their own deregulation: the railways needed to be protected against coach competition as the opening up of that market would result in losses of attractiveness for the rail system by substantial losses in passengers. The facts proved different in those countries: rail hardly suffered and coaches opened up new markets with people that could not afford the train anyway. Major opportunities are certainly present in these two countries as well.

The next challenges will consist of the real opening of the Italian market when current exclusive rights expire, and of the renewal of the Spanish (tendered) concessions when the existing contracts expire. Largely uncovered in this chapter, the evolutions in countries such as the Czech Republic, Hungary and Romania should also be studied in more detail. Attractive services are being developed here, though perhaps more in competition with rail than in Western Europe, due to the worrying condition of the underfunded railway networks in some of these countries. The development of true international networks, perhaps in competition with one another, is another interesting development (see Eurolines, Megabus and iDBUS).

The review has illustrated that the clear choice of most countries is for the free market, and not for a system of competitively tendered concession, nor for a regime of exclusive rights. Those countries that have not (yet) opened up their market are also more likely to move to a deregulated regime rather than a system of tendering concessions. Deregulation has shown that it can work and that markets seem to remain sufficiently competitive, both in an intermodal and an intramodal sense.

NOTE

1. I would like to thank the OECD for kind permission to use and expand upon this earlier work in this book.

REFERENCES

Aarhaug, J., P. Christiansen and N. Fearnley (2011), 'Statusrapport for ekspress-bussnæringen', TØI rapport 1167/2011, Oslo: Transportøkonomisk institutt.
Alexandersson, G., N. Fearnley, S. Hultén and F. Longva (2009), 'Impact of regulation on the performances of long-distance transport services: a comparison of the different approaches in Sweden and Norway', 11th International Conference on Competition and Ownership in Land Passenger Transport, Delft, 20–25 September.
Banverket (2006), 'Järnvägens roll i transportförsörjningen', Stockholm: Banverket.
Bochar, D. (2001), 'Eurolines or the pan-European coach network of regular lines services: an introduction', in *Regular Interurban Coach Services in Europe*, Economic Research Centre – Round Table, Vol. 114, pp. 7–44, European Conference of Ministers of Transport, Paris.
Consultrans (1999), 'Present and future situation of the concession system of road passenger transportation under the control of the general administration of the state', Report for the Spanish Ministry of Development, Madrid.
ECMT (2001), *Regular Interurban Coach Services in Europe, Round Table 114*, Economic Research Centre, European Conference of Ministers of Transport, Paris.
Eurostat (2012), 'Passenger transport statistics', Eurostat data from September 2012, available at http://epp.eurostat.ec.europa.eu/statistics_explained/index.php/Passenger_transport_statistics.
García-Pastor, A., C. Cristóbal-Pinto, J.-D. González and M. López-Lambas (2003), 'The Spanish situation of road public transport competition', European Transport Conference, Strasbourg, 8–10 October.
Hjellnes COWI (1999), 'Evaluering v konkurranseflater for ekspressbussruter. Endelig rapport for empiriske undersøkelser', Oslo: COWI.
Jansson, K., I. Vierth and J. McDaniel (1997), 'Economic analysis of the deregulation of coach services in Sweden through model simulations of historic and hypothetical competitive situations', European Transport Conference, Association for European Transport.
Köhler, M. (2009), 'Vier Jahre Rechtsstreit um einen Linienbus nach Köln', *Frankfurter Allgemeine Zeitung*, 11 March.
Komornicki, T. (2001), 'The development of international bus transport in central Europe: the case of Poland', in *Regular Interurban Coach Services in Europe*, Economic Research Centre – Round Table, Vol. 114, pp. 47–76, European Conference of Ministers of Transport, Paris.
Kramarz, F. (2009), 'Pour des bus Greyhound à la française', *Les Echos – Blogs*, 8 July.
Leiren, M.D. and N. Fearnley (2008), 'Express coaches – the story behind a public

transport success', European Transport Conference, Leeuwenhorst Conference Centre, Netherlands, 6–8 October.

Leiren, M.D., H. Samstad, N. Fearnley and H. Minken (2007), 'Ekspressbusruter – ett samensatt marked', 904/2007, Oslo: Transportøkonomisk Institutt.

Maertens, S. (2008), 'Intercity-Busverkehr in Deutschland – Notwendigkeit und Perspektiven einer Liberalisierung', *Fachgespräch Potentiale des Fernlinienverkehrs in Deutschland*, Münster, 2 June, Institut für Verkehrswissenschaft.

Robbins, D. (2007), 'Competition in the UK express coach market 25 years after deregulation: the arrival of Megabus.com', European Transport Conference, Leeuwenhorst, Netherlands, 17–19 October, Association for European Transport.

SIKA (1997), 'Effekter av avreglering av långväge busstrafik', 1997:6, Stockholm: SIKA.

SIKA (2008), 'Långväga buss 2007', SIKA Statistik 2008:21, Stockholm: SIKA.

Strand, S. (1991), 'Konkurransen mellom tog og ekspressbuss', 0078-1991, Oslo: Transportøkonomisk Institutt.

Taylor, Z. and A. Ciechanski (2008), 'What happened to the national road carrier in a post-communist country? The case of Poland's state road transport', *Transport Reviews*, **28**, 619–640.

Trafikanalys (2012), 'Långväga buss 2011', Statistik 2012:8, Stockholm: Trafikanalys.

van de Velde, D.M. (1999), 'Organisational forms and entrepreneurship in public transport (Part 1: classifying organisational forms)', *Transport Policy*, **6**, 147–157.

van de Velde, D.M. (2008), 'A new regulation for the European public transport', *Research in Transportation Economics*, **22**, 78–84.

van de Velde, D.M. (2010), 'Long-distance bus services in Europe: concessions or free market?', in *The Future for Interurban Passenger Transport – Bringing Citizens Closer Together*, Paris: OECD/ITF.

White, P.R. (2008), *Public Transport: Its Planning, Management and Operations*, 5th edition, Abingdon: Routledge.

6. Urban public transport

Rosário Macário

6.1 INTRODUCTION

The challenges and related options for regulatory intervention in urban transport have been the subject of extensive studies and discussions during the past two decades. This discussion is also reflected in a number of policy papers issued by the European Commission (EC). However, the subsidiarity principle prevents the European Commission from imposing top-down solutions which are considered unlikely to be appropriate for the diversity of local situations that can be found in Europe. The role of the EC is thus to disseminate good practice, harmonize technical standards, provide research funds and adapt legislation.

In this context Regulation 1191/69 set rules for the structure and content of public service contracts that incorporated public service obligations and respective financial compensation. However, this regulation did not advance any solutions for the way contracts should be awarded, and public procurement Directives (92/50 and 93/38) allowed public transport to be exempted from competitive tendering.

It is worth mentioning that in 1990 an overview of European countries by Gwilliam and van de Velde reported the following state of the art in the bus industry:

> local bus services are operated under monopoly franchises in most countries we have examined: only Denmark, Sweden and Portugal appear to be to any significant degree competitive. Moreover, all those local monopolies have been in existence for many years: so the a priori expectation would be that regulatory capture has occurred (Gwilliam and van de Velde, 1990)

Indeed the European public transport sector was characterized by a strong dominance of state monopolies providing services of relatively low quality and extremely high cost. Everywhere in Europe the financial situation was reaching a bottleneck and this was the main driver for the European Commission to start approaching the problem, which was initiated with a first European survey commissioned to William Tyson in 1994[1] (ISOTOPE Consortium, TIS.PT, 1997).

In very broad terms this was the legal European context for urban public transport until a proposal of the European Commission was put forward for a new regulation replacing 1191/69. The main step forward was to open competition to the majority of urban public transport services with exception of routes and networks without the potential to be profitable, that is, routes where public service obligations were required to ensure minimum services. There was much resistance from local authorities in different member states (in particular in cities where monopolistic public operators existed) to this proposal, and the amount of revisions done to the original text can easily constitute a European regulatory benchmark.

The regulatory process was leapfrogged in 2003 by a decision of the European Court of Justice (the Altmark case) stating that whenever public service obligations are clearly defined, subsidies can be paid without breaking competition rules. In 2007 the EU finally adopted a new regulation (1370/2007) mainly with a twofold purpose: determining levels of competency for authorities; and setting the conditions and rules to compensate operators when contracting public service obligations. In brief, it can be said that the new regulation enforced more transparency and accountability in urban public transport services in Europe.

This regulation establishes that any grant of an exclusive right, and/or any other compensation given to an operator by the competent authority in return for delivering public service obligations of whatever nature, can only be awarded within the framework of a public service contract. Contracts are here defined in a very flexible way, it may be one or more legally binding Acts confirming the agreement between a competent authority and a public service operator to entrust to that public service operator the management and operation of services subject to public service obligations. Contracts are very dependent on the law of the member states.

The relevant legal framework for the award of public transport contracts consists of (INNO-V et al., 2008):

- EU secondary legislation: the Public Service Obligations Regulation applicable to public transport (Regulation 1370/2007/EC on public passenger transport services by rail and by road, repealing Regulations 1191/69/EEC and 1107/70/EEC);
- EU secondary legislation: public procurement Directives;
- EU primary law: treaty principles;
- national (regional/local) rules for the award of public transport contracts
- existing European and national jurisprudence with regard to in-house awards and concessions.

- Commission interpretative communication on the Community law applicable to contract awards not or not fully subject to the provisions of the public procurement Directives (2006/C 179/02).

In the face of these changes the different countries and cities adopted various approaches regarding organization and regulation of urban public transport which are marked by the degree and type of competition allowed. Some countries have introduced wide-ranging reforms that typically evolved around deregulation in order to enable private entry in the provision of public transport; in some cases institutional design was questioned and changed (Macário, 2005b). Procurement procedures and design of contracts have been the main element to distinguish the approaches adopted. But there are also countries where only limited change occurred.

This chapter presents an overview of the various choices made. The background theories behind and their advantages and disadvantages show that different instruments are required if the same level of performance is to be attained under distinct regulatory regimes. The chapter also shows that no regulatory regime is doomed to underperform, as is often, and wrongly, pointed out. Finally, a way forward for regulatory interventions in urban public transport is proposed.

6.2   COMPLEXITY: MAIN DIFFICULTY IN ORGANIZING AND REGULATING URBAN PUBLIC TRANSPORT

By way of a systematic observation of European cities in the past two decades, the period 1994–2012, we have found a chain of decisions taken by different actors that, despite being taken before the moment of production and consumption of the services, are an integral part of the process of conceiving, developing and implementing mobility services. That is, they are part of the mobility supply chain. As described below, those decisions can be allocated to three decision levels.

Firstly, at the strategic level, the main concerns relate to long-term decisions, such as: definition of mobility policy, market shares, level of cost coverage by revenues, definition of areas of intervention for the mobility system, defining the levels of accessibility to be provided to different areas at different times, delimiting the public service character of the services to be provided and the means to be allocated to the production of those services, and establishing the degree of intermodality provided by the system. In brief, the strategic level provides a long-term vision of where we want the system to be, or what we want to achieve.

Secondly, at the tactical level, the main concerns are medium-term decisions largely related to the configuration of system supply, individual service definition to match the different market segments and detailed specifications, such as: type of vehicles, routes, timetables, different fares, additional services, definition of performance standards, and definition of contractual basis for engagement of service providers. In brief, the tactical level provides the plan that defines how the system must be organized to reach the strategic objectives.

Thirdly, at the operational level, the concerns are mostly short term and related to the management of services and resources. This is the action level, at which the service is carried out but also performance monitoring is undertaken. Production scheduling can extend from infrastructure management to vehicle and staff rostering. Depending on the degree of integration of activities, all these functions can be allocated to one or several entities, through different ways as defined in the regulatory framework. In brief, the operational system is where field action takes place and where we can establish whether the strategic vision and the plan have provided adequate results, outcomes and impacts over time.

The complexity of any urban mobility system is thus largely dependent on the number of entities at each level of decision (or planning) conditioning the adequacy of mechanisms meant to induce a concerted action among these agents. The diversity and disparity of agents is also essential for the characterization of interdependencies that can be typified along the following categories:[2]

- Bilateral interdependence exists whenever the object of relation affects two parties in any interaction process. This is typically the case between transport and land-use authorities within a municipality. This is a common case in Europe.
- Multilateral (or transversal) interdependence exists whenever any agent taking part in the system creates more than one bilateral dependence relationship with other entities, as long as there is no relation of subordination between the parties. This is typically the case of financing authorities in relation to other bodies.
- Vertical interdependence exists whenever the relation between entities is bounded by a subordinate status of one regarding the other, both entities having specific roles within the same domain of intervention. This is the case of federal hierarchies or subordination of regional entities to state entities.
- Oblique interdependence is the equivalent of vertical interdependence in the case when the entities bounded by subordination status belong to a different domain of intervention (e.g. urban and

suburban operators). It is worth mentioning that one of the most difficult aspects in managing urban mobility systems lies in the conflicts originated by this type of interdependencies.

- Longitudinal interdependence exists whenever dependency is irreversibly based on previously taken decisions, that is, a sequential relation exists between decisions taken in different time moments. These time-related dependencies might be due to decisions of one or more entities. This is a typical case of labour-related issues.

Furthermore, we have seen that interdependence can be established by formal or informal instruments: the former can vary from simple partnerships (e.g. quality partnerships) up to contractual frameworks and other legally established obligations, while the latter may even be more complex since interdependence can exist without any direct relation. For indirect relations the informal institutional link can be established through third parties or even by simply sharing a common resource without any protocol. Examples of these interdependencies without formal direct relationship are wage revisions in one entity that may induce workers of another agent to have analogous behaviour, or as an example, a municipal decision of revision of traffic space assigned for parking, without any consultation with the public transport company.

Several authors relate degree of interdependency with complexity of coordination mechanisms and the corresponding framework (Macário, 2005a, 2011). As suggested by Scott (1981), higher levels of interdependence need more extensive and complicated coordination mechanisms. As a corollary to this note, Chisholm (1989) suggests that 'by increasing the requirements for successful coordination, the level of interdependence among the components of the system may be artificially increased as an unintended consequence. Under these conditions, coordination requires greater agreement across a broader range of values and the solution of cognitively more complex problems.'

Indeed, from our empirical observation we conclude that unless some degree of vertical (or oblique) interdependency exists, the key function in order to bring a complex system to good performance levels is not coordination, but instead we need concertation of decisions,[3] which is a form of leadership mostly based on inducement of actions and decisions instead of direct hierarchical command.[4]

For these purposes a wide spectrum of institutional settings can be found across Europe. In some countries and cities it is for the authorities to develop all functions, whereas in others private agents carry out significant elements. Whatever the solutions adopted, it is through the definition of their function in the whole mobility system that these entities have their departure point to move in a certain direction and to define purpose and values to guide their characteristic actions and reactions, that is, to establish the patterns of their institutional behaviour.

Regulatory frameworks, contracts and prices are the main instruments to steer these behaviours in favour of system performance. As Hayek notes: 'In a system where the knowledge of the relevant facts is dispersed among many people, prices can act to co-ordinate the separate actions of different people in the same way as subjective values help the individual to co-ordinate the parts of his plan' (Hayek, 1945).

Agents' own interests or goals play an essential role in principal–agent mechanisms, in which the agent should pursue the interests of the principal. In urban mobility systems there are several levels of nested principal–agent relations, the topmost level being between the government (principal) and the regulator (agent); the second level being between the regulator (principal) and the organizing authorities (agent); and the third level being between each organizing authority (principal) and the several agents acting at the operational level upon which the individual citizen, who has the capacity to use common mobility facilities on a self-service basis, is also one of those agents. Moreover, even the operator of mobility services can play the role of principal whenever part or the totality of productive services is subcontracted in order to enhance efficiency.

Indeed, we can observe that agents are often confronted with playing a double role, where they have to act both as principal and as agent; this is often the case with municipal transport. Being so, it is important to come up with a systematic definition for the structure of these organizations, which is defined along five main aspects (Macário, 2005a, 2011):

- Domain of intervention: a set of values, principles, axioms and rules, based upon which intervention is made for system ruling and control, at different decision or planning levels. In an urban mobility system we can categorize the existing domains of intervention as three main types: framework-related, process-related and resource-related;
- framework-related domain: entails the definition of the underlying structure of an urban mobility system, entailing policy definition in the several related fields of intervention such as land-use, traffic and environment, but also the identification of the type of actors involved in the system; most of the strategic decisions are located in this domain;
- process-related domain: entails the definition of the management rational leading to the production of services in the most efficient and effective way; and

Table 6.1   Nature and roles of entities interacting in an urban mobility system (authorities)

	Type of entity
Political authorities	• national government • regional government • local government
Regulating authorities	• transport authorities (e.g. Passenger Transport Authorities) • economic authorities • fiscal authorities
Technical authorities	• transport authority (e.g. Passenger Transport Executive) • traffic authorities • land-use authorities • environmental authorities • safety authorities • security authorities

Source: Macário (2005a).

- resources-related domain: concerned with supply of resources.
- Ownership: capital ownership that formally means the financial resource to establish the agent as an economic or social unit.
- Nature: a set of attributes that characterize institutional behaviour allowing an institution to be recognized by their actions and reactions to external stimulus. Typical natures in a mobility system are indicated in Tables 6.1 and 6.2.
- Institutional (legal) statute: the statutory form adopted by the agent that determines some of the legal procedures followed in the management of the entity, and to a certain extent its degrees of freedom as a collective entity.
- Roles: functions and mission developed by an agent which is best represented by the set of activities performed. Typical roles are: regulator, organizing authority, auditors, planner, operator, infrastructure manager, supplier of services or materials.

The synergetic combination of these categories of aspects means that each agent will be in a unique institutional setting that it will try to alter and adjust to the most adequate configuration in the process of pursuing its own objectives, occasionally leading to progressive segregation. This diversity and evolutionary process provides a degree of uniqueness[5]

Table 6.2   Nature and roles of entities interacting in an urban mobility system (operators and other stakeholders)

	Type of entity
Operators	• transport operator (e.g., train operating company) • developers (i.e., land use 'operators') • other service operators • emergency services
Suppliers of productive resources	• vehicle industry • staff (e.g. man power firms for crew members, public attendance, etc.) • management information systems (e.g. radio, TV, etc) • consumables.
Clients	• transport user/consumer group (e.g. cyclist association, commuter group) • specific local residents (e.g. as property owners, threatened parties) • specific local businesses (e.g. as employers, as threatened parties)
Other interested parties	• non-governmental organizations • community groups (i.e., meaning here a group based on a particular local area) • other interest groups / activist groups (e.g., green lobby etc.)

Source: Macário (2005a).

to each urban mobility system that cannot be directly reproduced to fit another system without going through careful transferability analysis (Macário and Marques, 2010).

6.3   BALANCING POLITICAL CONSISTENCY WITH STAKEHOLDER REQUIREMENTS AND EXPECTATIONS

The territorial definition of the urban mobility system is indispensable to define the boundaries within which the power of institutions that are in charge of its governance is defined (Sanjum, 2005; Viegas, 2005). Three issues must be considered for an efficient territorial definition: (1) the systemic reality; (2) the need to compare and transfer solutions; (3) the financial manageability of the system. The concept of a system is by itself required to ensure that the relevant analysis considers the reality observed as part of a set in which the whole must be referred.

Urban mobility systems are nested in an upper system, which is the respective urban agglomeration, as defined by their land-use pattern and the jurisdiction of political-administrative institutions. Since the size of an urban agglomeration is a consequence of its economic organization and of the opportunities for social relations, we may conclude that there is a relation between the dimension of the urban area and the factors influencing the need for mobility.

The need for comparability and assessment of potential for transferability of solutions is a serious handicap felt by both communities of research and practitioners. In fact, we can observe in our set of cities that comparability and any further performance assessment of mobility systems are hindered, and sometimes even unfeasible, due to a wide diversity of base concepts for the administrative definition of urban boundaries, thus lacking a common reference unit.

For mobility management purposes the basic concept should be the urban region, or urban basin served by the same mobility system. However the concept is missing in the administrative organization of most countries, which precludes effective management of any financial process due to the absence of institutions with a jurisdictional capacity adjusted to the territorial insertion of the mobility services.

Along the above-defined relational perspective of the territorial dimension we also have a formal institutional territory, complementary to the previous one, and represented by the land occupancy of countries, regions and municipalities. Some authors (e.g. Sack, 1986) consider institutional territory as no more than an imperfect arrangement due to the following main reasons:

- the rigidity in which it is organized;
- difficulties in establishing optimum scales (e.g. financing services and infrastructures shared by a number of communes, cantons or even countries; or the opposite, i.e. one citizen 'belonging' to several jurisdictional units[6]);
- the fuzziness in defining institutional and legal engagements for tackling cross-border problems.

These arguments support the conclusion that the static concept of institutional territory is necessary but clearly insufficient to deal with the dynamics of modern societies. A relational territorial dimension is required to deal with the network dynamics of urban communities. Observation of the evolution of urban areas enabled us to understand that the 'predict and provide' paradigm performed rather well whenever spatial and environmental resources were far from their limits. Unfortunately these conditions have become rarer, and the result is three major weaknesses emerging in several cities:

- planning processes are developed without considering the existence of those limits;
- new supply is projected and decided with poor forecasting of induced demand;
- non-articulated decisions on land-use, road network development and public transport development.

In brief, strategic decisions are pushed by those taken at tactical level (planning) without being explicitly assumed and reflected with transparency and rigour in the corresponding allocation of resources and respective limits. Moreover, fragmentation of authorities by mode has led to a clear dilution of responsibility. Changing this paradigm implies first and foremost accepting that the territorial definition of the urban mobility system requires the use of variable institutional geometry so that the interaction between land-use and mobility can be effectively achieved. Institutional design should thus be guided by a network logic providing service-related (and associated decision-making) continuity in the administrative and jurisdictional setting of the institution holding responsibility for the territorial management of urban mobility.

Much has been discussed across Europe, and also on other continents, about different methods and intensities of the existence and intervention of the public sector in the markets. Irrespective of the opinions taken regarding direct state intervention in the provision of services or products, public policy is generally recognized as necessary to guide, correct and influence market behaviours, mostly due to the following circumstances that despite being general market requisites are much visible in the urban mobility sector:

- The claim that market mechanisms lead to efficient use of resources is based on the condition that competitive factors and product markets do exist. This logic entails the implicit assumptions that market entry is easy, and both consumers and producers have full market knowledge. These conditions fall in the policy–business interaction area but can only be secured by regulation.
- Similar assurance is required whenever decreasing costs patterns give room to inefficient competition.

- A regulatory and legal structure is needed to protect and enforce contractual arrangements and exchanges required by market operations. This structure can only be secured by political institutions.
- Even if all the previous conditions are met, there are still problems arising from 'externalities' caused by the production and consumption of some goods and services, and requiring compensatory mechanisms that can only be activated through public sector action.
- In addition, there are other social and economic objectives, such as employment and rate of economic growth, which cannot be assured by market systems, and again public policy is required to intervene in securing these objectives.

Four government branches can be envisaged to answer these needs, each of them consisting of various agencies, departments or activities (depending on the government structure) charged with preserving certain social and economic conditions. These branches are to be understood as having different functions: allocation; distribution; stabilization; and finally the concertation, coordination and conflict management between the previous functions (Musgrave and Musgrave, 1984). Although these divisions have no match with the government organizational setting it is desirable to consider the essence of these functions in the configuration of the network of policy institutions.

The allocation branch has the responsibility to keep price mechanisms within the principles of competition and to prevent an upsurge of unreasonable market powers. As Musgrave and Musgrave (1984) observes: 'the benefits from social goods are not vested in the property rights of certain individuals, and the market cannot function'. Urban public transport is one such case where the signalling system between producers and consumers does not work properly, not only because social exclusion is undesirable but also because it is frequently impossible or very expensive to apply. So this branch is responsible for the identification and correction of efficiency deviations.

The distribution branch is responsible for preserving justice in the distributive shares by means of taxation and often also through adjustments in property rights. Within this stream of action, levies and regulation are applied with twofold objectives: the first is to correct the distribution of wealth, envisaging the provision of fair opportunities; and the second is to withhold revenues that will later be applied as financing sources to secure provision of public goods and services. Taxation techniques provide a wide diversity of solutions which will lead to differentiated effects that are addressed in questions of political judgment and analysis which will not be discussed here as they largely are outside the scope of this work.

The stabilization branch is meant to solve some of the additional problems left from market mechanisms, such as balanced employment and steady growth rates. This branch always acts in synchronized partnership with all the others. Together with the allocation branch it maintains the general efficiency of market economy. Together with the distributive branch, a transfer function is developed where social needs are taken into account and priorities are assigned with respect to other competing claims. In these, attention must be paid not only to active claims from different sectors of economic and social activity, but also to time-related effects of implemented policies, in particular issues of equity between generations.

Finally, it is through policy concertation and coordination of planned actions of the different economic sectors that priorities are defined and the concept of public service is made operational for the different sectors. Despite the autonomy of these sectors, each country tends to adopt a common philosophical approach to the concept of public service, transversal to all economic sectors. In this respect, we can observe two main political streams in what concerns the public service character of the transport sector (Hensher and Macário, 2002), these are the so-called 'Code Napoleon' and the Anglo-Saxon philosophy.

The 'Code Napoleon' approach, best exemplified by the French reality, takes transport as an input into a wider socio-economic and political framework, in which case the sector should have strong state intervention and thus the full application of public service obligation, usually materialized in the obligation to operate, the obligation to carry and the tariff obligation.

In all countries observed where this philosophy holds (NEA, TIS.PT, 1998; INNO-V et al., 2008), it was possible to conclude in general terms that these obligations are meant to ensure an obligation of providing a service that is expected to satisfy fixed standards in terms of continuity, regularity and capacity, as well as to accept and carry passengers, and in some cases also goods (e.g. transport to islands, as in the case of the Portuguese archipelagos of the Azores and Madeira, or the Spanish archipelago of the Canaries), as well as to respect predefined limitation regarding fares, sometimes with price levels set politically. The basic rationale behind this approach is that public service obligations guarantee the satisfaction of the population's mobility needs that otherwise would not be properly provided by the market.

The Anglo-Saxon philosophy, best represented by the United Kingdom (UK) experience, takes the opposite rationale: that is, that transport is like any other sector in the economy and as such should be provided as efficiently as possible; thus private participation and commercial approaches are the dominant orientation, and markets are thought to provide better performance of the transport systems than that obtained though government intervention.

In practical terms most countries found a mixed solution in-between these two philosophical streams and we can find several different ways of applying the public service concept to the transport sector. Each different solution requires different instruments to achieve similar aims. That is, the revised paradigm should evolve from 'predict and provide' to 'aim and manage',[7] choosing appropriate instruments and resources, and activating the strategic level of decision.

6.4   ALTERNATIVE ORGANIZATIONAL FORMS AND THEIR EVOLUTION

Satisfying mobility needs in an urban area involves the provision of several different complementary services that result in a chain able to ensure safe and fluid movement of citizens between a range of possible origins and destinations. This means that mobility represents the outcome of an articulated effort that intertwines pedestrian movements, movements with private individual motorized transport, and movements with public collective and individual transport. That is, the supply side of the mobility systems gathers mobility services provided directly or indirectly by the state, by the market, and also self-provision, for all of which there is the need to ensure adequate infrastructure. The balance between the utilization (or consumption) of these different means represents a key element of the sustainability of urban areas and as such must be subject to careful thought.

From the four networks that form the urban mobility system – walking, cycling, private motorized transport and public transport, with associated infrastructure – the public transport network is one of the components of the system where the market access regimes represent an instrument of articulation between agents and where regulatory issues gain prominence. Another element where market access issues can be raised is in the access to infrastructure (e.g. limits to circulation of some vehicles on certain roads), although here the constraints to market access are not related to reasons of competition or market contestability.

Depending on the regulatory option, public transport services can be performed directly by the transport authority, contracted out to an operator (private or public) by direct negotiation or through a tendering procedure, or directly in the market by an operator under a deregulated regime. The system design (that is, the planning) is also a service on its own and can be outsourced with or without tendering, although it is usually seen as a separate market from the provision of transport services.

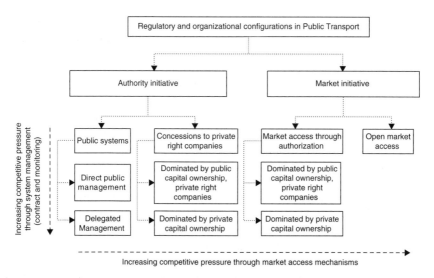

Source: Adapted from van de Velde (1999).

Figure 6.1 Regulatory and organizational configurations

In ISOTOPE research a global classification of regulatory and organizational frameworks for public transport was consolidated, and further refined in MARETOPE. Figure 6.1 is based on the findings and formulations in these research projects and illustrates the global classification of these regimes in what concerns the supply of public transport services.

The main distinction is given by the entrepreneurship variable, that is, the dichotomy between authority-initiated or market-initiated regimes. In the first, authorities have the exclusive right to initiate services and any direct attempt of market entry is deemed to be illegal according to the legal and regulatory framework that rules the way services are allowed to be provided. Consequently, in these cases all service supply results from a planning initiative from the authorities, which is the current situation with urban public transport in France, Belgium and also, formally but not yet in practice, in Portugal.

In market-initiated regimes, service supply is based on spontaneous market entry of operators, which results from a normal market process subject to some regulatory evaluations at the moment of entry, such as technical, legal and economic ability to perform the operation, based on legally pre-established principles and criteria. This is the current situation in Great Britain, Germany and the Netherlands, although each of these countries has opted for different categories and processes for verification of professional and social capability of service provision. In these cases the authorities are still entitled to develop planning functions, but operators are legally allowed to enter the market with new services as long as the relevant criteria for acceptance (by the authority) are fulfilled.

In both cases, with the exception of the pure open market regime, it is possible to maintain competitive tendering for parts of the services since, as van de Velde (1999) stresses, competitive tendering is merely a selection mechanism in the context of outsourcing. Indeed it is simply a method of organization of production available to any service supplier whatever the regulatory regime and organizational form used. Therefore, the alternative regimes to consider are public production systems, limited access (also known as controlled competition) and open entry (subject only to demonstration of professional capability), as represented in Figure 6.1.

This sequence also corresponds to a spectrum of market openness which is embedded with an increased competitive pressure to enter the market that can be observed when we move from public control regimes to open-entry ones. However, market access is not the only way of imposing competitive pressure, as this can also be achieved in all regimes through contracts and monitoring dispositions. In this respect we may also observe that when moving from public to private capital ownership the competitive pressure also increases by way of those management tools.

Within the authority-initiated regimes it is possible to distinguish two categories of regimes: the publicly owned regime and the concession to a private or public company. Publicly owned regimes can be divided into two forms: public management, where vehicles and other installations are directly run by the public administration, which is common in small cities such as Carcassone in France and Barreiro in Portugal; or delegated management, where the authority makes the assets available to a private operator company to which the management of the network is delegated through contractual arrangements that can be very diversified according to the way commercial and operational risks are shared, and the degree of freedom that can be given in the service design. As we have observed in ISOTOPE, QUATTRO and MARETOPE research, NEA, TIS.PT (1998) and INNO-V et al. (2008), France is the country where more of these types of contract have been identified.

The alternative category for authority-initiated systems is the concession. Here the authority selects a private company to operate public transport services on a route, in an area or in a network, and the concessionaire is normally responsible for the vehicles and installations through ownership or leasing. Depending on the legal framework in place this company is selected either directly (no longer allowed in the European Union, but still a practice in other places), or through negotiations after a shortlisting procedure, or through competitive tendering.

Market-initiated regimes are largely divided into two categories: open-entry regimes, where the so-called on-street competition exists, of which the best example is urban transport in Great Britain outside London (very often incorrectly designated as 'deregulated regimes'); and restricted authorization regimes,[8] where licensed operators are given the right to apply for an authorization to exploit a certain service with some degree of exclusivity, which varies enormously from one country to another, and even within the same country from one city to another, or between services of different type, although in all of them the operator is, for the period of time of the authorization, at least partly protected from competition. One of the main drawbacks of this regime that has been pointed out by some authors (e.g. Van de Velde, 1999, among others) is the risk that this protection, if extensively applied, will eliminate market contestability and develop regulatory capture.

Open-entry regimes in turn have been associated with some degradation of service quality, despite their efficiency advantage (TIS.PT, 1998). The need to address this problem was at the root of the development of quality partnerships in Great Britain. Through these agreements, seen as 'light touch regulation' (Carr, 1997), a number of rules committing both authorities and operators can be established, such as provisions for service coordination, integrated ticketing, obligations to use vehicles accessible for the handicapped, bus priority lanes, and so on. However, these agreements have also been condemned by the advocates of free competition regimes, given their potential to raise barriers to new entrants, whenever the quality partnership is restricted to existing operators. Indeed, risks exist that collusion might build up if the partnership is allowed to be closed to new entrants.

The organizational forms and respective regulatory regimes described represent the pure conceptual options. In practical terms what we find in the real world are mostly intermediate forms and also the coexistence of different regimes for the multiple services provided in an urban area or network. All regimes and forms present advantages and disadvantages and no universally best solution has been identified. Market-initiated regimes enable the active participation of the operator in the service design, providing the stimulus for the improvement of the service and consequently a stronger willingness to share the planning and revenue risks with the authorities. The latter is mostly related to patronage and fares, and the former is highly influenced by the quality and appropriateness of the service to the customer needs, which is the reason why the involvement of the operator in the design of the services is so important.

Where the creation of the services is left to the authorities – that is, authority-initiated systems – the compliance with requirements established in accordance with the strategic goals can be, at least theoretically, more easily achieved, and consequently enforcement should be made at a lower cost than in other regimes. The main advantage of these regimes is that they give structural priority to integration and stability of supply, while seeking cost-efficiency through other instruments.

Despite the consensual awareness of the positive and negative aspects inherent to each pure regulatory option, the mix of regimes for each specific mobility system has considerable variation from one country to the other. However, the following key variables can be identified as being present in all decisions regarding the structural configuration of the system:

- Variables external to the mobility system:
  – political-administrative organization of the country or region;
  – regulation emanating at a higher level but applicable to the urban mobility system in question (e.g. the case of the European Union or federal states such as Brazil).
- Variables internal to the mobility system:
  – legal possibility of having a plurality of initiatives on the market (i.e. degrees of freedom) and entrepreneurship for those initiatives (i.e. who takes the initiative);
  – degree of competitive pressure and incentives in the system;
  – level of technical competence of the interacting agents in planning complex networks.

A number of different solutions have been implemented across Europe and worldwide, and there is strong evidence that the trend has been to replicate the political-administrative division of the countries (i.e. national, regional and local division) into the organizational framework of the transport system. One of the main reasons for this almost systematic option is the need to match fiscal and financial autonomies with the organizational responsibilities in order to facilitate the handling of the funding sources and mechanisms that support the management of the urban mobility system.

Additionally, the varieties of organizational forms that can be identified are the result of variations in the functions to be performed at the different planning and decision levels with the regulatory regime. In this way the following organizational solutions in the surveys done for ISOTOPE research and later confirmed in MARETOPE could be found.[9]

Firstly, central planning and tendering of the operations: the transport authority determines the policy goals that represent the planning framework for the planning department or agency, which in turn is obliged to contract-out part or the whole of the planned services to private operators under competitive tendering. This organizational option is known as the 'Scandinavian model', which is found in the Copenhagen region, among other places, where a set of regional and local governments cooperate to form a transport authority (MOVIA). An alternative to this form is to have a management contract between the transport authority and the planning company that obliges the latter to contract-out the realization of all or part of the planned services to a private company through tendering procedures. This organizational form was used in the Malmö region,[10] although it is no longer in force.

The second solution is similar to the previous one, but allowing the operator to redesign the services in its areas of operation as an incentive, although this freedom is limited in order to preserve system integration. The planning company sets fares, bears the revenue risk and induces the operator's choices by setting minimum standards and paying a passenger-kilometre-based fee; that is, sharing the commercial risk with the operator. This organizational form is known as the 'Adelaide model' since the real case that inspired this specification was Adelaide in South Australia (Radbone, 1997, pp. 1–18)

Thirdly, tendering planning and operations – normally designated by concession, where the authority can also establish the minimum standards and set the public service obligations. It is worth clarifying this is also the organizational form adopted in the case of British Rail, in my opinion wrongly designated as 'franchising', since the objective was to give more freedom to the operator for service definition and marketing, which is precisely the opposite to what happens with the commercial franchises in the retail sector (product specification is rigid and marketing is centralized by the franchising entity). Concessions are common in many European countries, for example Portugal and France. A derivation of this form can be the tendering of the planning function at a different procurement process than the one used for the operations. This option was conceptually recommended in the conclusions of the ISOTOPE report (ISOTOPE Consortium, TIS.PT, 1997) and currently its discussion is again gaining prominence within practitioners, although no effective successful implementation was yet reported.

And finally, the free competition form, with or without light-touch regulation, as already explained above.

6.5   THE RELATIONSHIP BETWEEN AUTHORITY AND OPERATOR: CONTRACTUAL INSTRUMENTS

Theoretically, several methods exist for the selection of agents and these are conditioned by the regulatory frameworks in place that determine the available options for market access. The selection of agents is thus a function of the way the tactical level of planning and control is organized whenever outsourcing of the whole or parts of service production is done. However, it should be made clear that outsourcing is simply a 'method of production available to any initiator of services', irrespective of the organizational form or the regulatory regime (van de Velde, 1999). In fact, in the INNO-V et al. (2008) study it is concluded that several items determine the relationship between authority and operator. These are:

- roles and tasks of the parties;
- ownership of infrastructure and ownership of the transport operator;
- risk level for the operator;
- planning and design of public transport services;
- control of performance.

As already mentioned, competition is seen as an important mechanism to improve service performance, in particular efficiency; quality being imposed through regulation. In a more economic perspective, competition is considered by many authors as the most important mechanism for the maximization of consumer benefits and to limit monopolistic power, with the underlying intent of improving industry performance by increasing the role of market forces. The main pillars of this rationale are rivalry and freedom to enter the market, and the most relevant game instrument between actors is the competitive threat from potential as well as existing competitors.

As noticed by Beesley (1997), in relation to British Airways, the simple announcement of the intention to privatize the company helped to increase efficiency, thus providing more evidence that the issue at stake is the ability to keep competitive pressure over the market agents, as also concluded in the ISOTOPE research project (ISOTOPE Consortium, TIS. PT, 1997), regarding urban public transport. The privatization threat has also been an effective instrument for efficiency in Portugal with the incumbent companies of Lisbon and Oporto, respectively CARRIS and STCP.

In fact, a number of studies have been dedicated to the analysis of the efficiency effects accruing from the introduction of competition. In ISOTOPE, based on information obtained from 207 operators from 108 cities across Europe for the period between 1993 to 1996, it was concluded that 'Deregulated markets have theoretical and empirical advantages in terms of efficiency of production. Regulated markets have theoretical and empirical advantages in terms of efficiency in consumption. Limited competition markets may have advantages of both' (ISOTOPE Consortium, TIS.PT, 1997). In fact in the limited competition or controlled competition markets, an operator competes for the award of exclusive rights of an operation but once the contract is signed stability is achieved, hopefully during the whole of its duration.

In a study commissioned by the European Commission to Colin Buchanan & Partners for a 'Study on Good Practices in Contracts' (Buchanan & Partners, 2002) using information from a sample of 43 European cities with a population of at least 500000 inhabitants (29 with no competition, 10 with controlled competition, and 4 with deregulated market access), all of them with at least six years of data available and for a similar period, between 1991 and 1996, found that:

- In cities with no competition there was a small average annual decrease in passenger numbers of 0.2 per cent; for cities with limited competition there was an annual increase of 1.7 per cent; and in the cities with free competition (so-called deregulation) a drop of 2.6 per cent per year was reported.
- The fare coverage ratio increased at a rate of 1.2 per cent for cities with limited competition while in the ones with no competition this rate was 0.5 per cent. For free competition cities a low increase of 0.1 per cent was found, but in these cases fares tend to cover most, if not all, of the operating costs, since they are not regulated.
- The number of employees in public transport companies reveals an average annual decrease of 2.1 per cent in cities with no competition, and an increase of 1.2 per cent in cities with limited competition. In cities with free competition this data was not available for the period covered.

Despite the impact caused by the above-reported figures, none of these studies was able to prove a causal relation between the regulatory and contractual practices and the productive efficiency of the urban mobility system in general, or the public transport operation in particular. Looking at the last 18 years of studies done on regulatory and organizational issues and contractual analysis,[11] all the evidence collected only reinforces the statement that competitive pressure contributes to the enhancement of efficiency and other elements of performance. In addition, the study by Buchanan & Partners lacks rigour in the constitution of the sample of cities, since it brings together a group of cities which cannot be considered in the same cluster, such as Paris, Porto, Lille and Rotterdam, to name a few examples only, and applies statistical averages over it on basis of the assumed similarity of the regulatory system.

The clustering pitfall is mostly related to the fact that in the group of cities selected[12] there are several cases of non-comparability in the domains of city dimension, mix of modes offered, rate of change in the process of introduction of competition, degree of participation of the state in operating companies, and so on. It is only fair to mention that the lack of consistent series of data was a major problem in all the studies cited, which is also clearly recognized by Buchanan & Partners (2001).

The legal feature that governs the relation between transport authorities and operators is much diversified. Within the instruments used we could find licences, authorizations, concessions, contracts and so on. Besides, in all the studies mentioned there is strong evidence that the meanings of the terms 'licence', 'concession', 'authorization', and so on have different interpretations when one looks at the different legal regime worldwide. This diversity largely justifies the wide-open definition adopted by the EC Regulation[13] (art 2 (i)):

> 'Public service contract' means one or more legally binding acts confirming the agreement between a competent authority and a public service operator to entrust to that public service operator the management and operation of services subject to public service obligations; depending on the law of the member states, the contract may also consist of a decision adopted by the competent authority:
>
> - taking the form of an individual legislative or regulatory act, or
> - containing conditions under which the competent authority itself provides the services or entrusts the provision of such services to an internal operator.

The most recent study, (INNO-V et al., 2008) based on the cross-cutting transversal analysis, comparing European practices on contractualization of public service obligations in public transport identified the most critical relevant dimensions, as seen from the perspective of the European legal context, to be risk allocation and award procedures. It is worth noting that these findings of the 2008 study confirmed what was previously found in the ISOTOPE study (1995–97). The risk allocation element distinguishes a spectrum of risk allocation to the operators: no risk, only production cost risk, production cost and revenue risk. For the award procedure there are two options: direct awarding, or awarding based on competitive procedure, in which case it is negotiation-based or multicriteria-based (INNO-V et al., 2008).

In the real world we can find an endless diversity of variations from the pure contractual forms as these are almost always covered by incentives mechanisms of different types.[14] But a common element is the fact that public transport contracts are often funded by public funds to a certain extent, which gives room for the application of European rules on state aid. According to these rules, compensation is not allowed to exceed the costs which would have to be borne by a typical service provider.

6.6 OUTCOMES OF REGULATORY CHANGE: ADJUSTING INSTITUTIONS AND GOVERNANCE

As recognized by Viegas (2003), the definition of the contemporary city is ambiguous and complex; ambiguous because it depends on relations of 'belonging', regarding territory, people and even institutions. Complexity, in turn, grows from the spread to peri-urban areas which imposes a diversity of spatial relations, with each citizen very often relating with two or more urban areas, or having stronger links to other cities than the one where they formally (i.e. administratively) have their residence. The territorial definition of the urban mobility system is indispensable to define the boundaries within which the power of institutions that are in charge of its governance is exercised. But we may often observe a mismatch between the spatial insertion of the urban mobility services and the administrative organization of the institutions with responsibilities over the system. In fact this is a major source of underperformance for institutions and systems.

The system boundary is indeed a rather unstable definition, dependent on too many factors, such as: the judgement of the observer on what they take as being the system; and legal and technological competencies that underpin, respectively, the actors' territorial and spatial competences (authorities and operators), and the actors' technical capabilities. Besides, in reality there are two sets of decision-makers: one set on the supply side, which even where there is a good organizational framework, only rarely addresses the decision at system level; and the other on the demand side, which is characterized by hundreds of disorganized decisions.

Transport is one policy area where there is a greater split of competencies across levels of the administration than in other policy areas. This decentralization is largely related to the recognition that mobility problems are better identified and dealt with if the decision-maker is closer to the source of problem. In this case there is also a strong motivation in the domain of fiscal responsibility, leading local and regional administrations to take the hard and publicly accountable decisions regarding the allocation of public money.

It is also possible to advance the preliminary conclusion that voluntary binding agreements of variable geometry entail considerable appeal to politicians and local governments, and their acceptability seems to be based on the following attributes:

- Voluntary binding agreements do not require permanent structures with associated powers, so they have a high degree of reversibility and consequently are perceived to have a lower risk of imposing unwanted change.
- These agreements entail power sharing but they do not touch the rigid structure of power, only that directly related to the initiative; that is, the variable one.
- Leadership can be exercised without establishing permanent hierarchies.

For the society in general, these new forms of governance also seem to bring some benefits, such as:

- Accountability is high but rewarding.
- Partnership search entails some competitive behaviour towards good performance in public management.

Voluntary binding agreements are agreements between two or more agencies for the provision of a common public utility (e.g. transport, water, sewage). These can be found in metropolitan areas in Europe, or simply in sets of conurbations (e.g. Portugal, Spain), and also in the United States with the Metropolitan Planning Organizations (MPOs) (Plumeau, 2005). The motivation for these agreements is largely driven by the economies of scale and scope that can be offered (Frey and Spear, 1995). As in any initiative there are also costs to consider, such as:

- Decision-making processes tend to be longer and can generate considerable opportunity costs.
- In situations of lack of consensus the system can easily be blocked since all members of the 'consensus assembly' have similar power.
- Voluntary partnership may promote the use of smaller planning units with a consequent loss of synergies.
- Voluntary partnerships may be too fragile, and susceptible to demolition as a consequence of misunderstandings between politicians

and other stakeholders for some reason unrelated to the matters they address.

Different countries have come up with different constitutional solutions for this problem in its more general dimension, and institutional design and organizational solutions for the urban mobility problems have to adapt to those frameworks. But some general guiding principles can be pointed out, that can be applied throughout for the promotion of consistency in policy and action, and through it to more efficient and sustainable urban mobility.

Possibly the first such principle is that, even if urban public transport (UPT) is mostly a matter for local responsibility, there is an important role for national governments to play in the organization of those systems, namely at the levels of policy definition and of the setting-up of the administrative organization of the country (including geographical contours and recommended procedures for inter-agency cooperation), as well as in specific decisions in areas of national government intervention that more directly influence decisions with an impact on urban mobility and on its sustainability (namely the regulatory framework, taxation and some parts of physical planning). For the European Commission the main role is to influence by inducement, through dissemination of good practice, pilot projects and so on (e.g. Civitas).

When a regional or state level is present, some organizational matters will be located there, with the advantage that the level of diversity within the region will be smaller than at the national level. The competencies delegated to regions frequently include that of financial support for public transport, and sometimes also the choice about the production model (direct production, contracting to the private sector, and in what regime: meaning authority initiative versus market initiative). Land-use is also an area where a strong role for regions is frequently found.

In almost all countries today it is the local level of the administration (sometimes the municipal, sometimes the metropolitan) that has the responsibility of organizing UPT. But in spite of all the local specificities there is enough commonality across regions and countries to have allowed a general diagnostics framework to evolve and to gather significant consensus regarding relevant measures to address current difficulties. The same cannot be said about the policies and strategies being applied in practice in the various countries: the palette of instruments available is rather wide, some of the measures may face political difficulties, and the result frequently is a piecemeal approach that lacks the coverage and the consistency to produce the intended improvements in favour of sustainability.

6.7 CONCLUSIONS

There are very different financial situations of UPT operations in European Organisation for Economic Co-operation and Development (OECD) member countries and cities, with levels of cost coverage of operational costs (including rolling-stock-related costs) by operational revenues varying between little more than 15 per cent to in some cases close to 100 per cent. The definition of cost categories[15] is not uniform across countries, which makes comparisons risky without going into detailed definitions, but probably the majority of operations have cost coverage levels between one-third and two-thirds. In the majority of countries, the part of revenue not coming from operations is largely dominated by public subsidy.

However, the main problem of UPT financing is associated with coverage of operational costs, and the engagement of private funds for investments increases the dimension of that problem, because that investment has to be paid back instead of just being considered as a sunk cost, as is the usual case with public investments. This raises the issue of economic feasibility of public transport, a main concern in most of our cities. There is today a rather large consensus that we need to articulate funding and financing needs with the capacity to capture value from other activities benefiting from the existence of public transport.

But this corresponds to a very in-depth change regarding principles, policies and processes. Change is inevitably a difficult undertaking whenever institutions are related to territorial sources and expressions of power. Understanding change is first and foremost a matter of understanding interactions between the entities that form a specific organizational field and its environment (MARETOPE et al., 2003). Political networks and communities work on the basis of influence, domination and also a considerable degree of implicit and voluntary trust with unofficial rules of appropriateness. Trusting behaviours can be defined following Lorenz (1989, in Gambetta, 1989, pp. 194–210), who settled on these as a sort of behavior that 'consists in action that (1) increases one's vulnerability to another whose behavior is not under one's control, and (2) takes place in a situation where the penalty suffered if the trust is abused would lead one to regret the action'.

Europe has experienced significant political and administrative changes. In Central and Eastern Europe, transition to democratic regimes has been accompanied in several cases by decentralization of responsibilities for public transport, but this has frequently not been accompanied by budget reform, leading to a situation of underfunding, ageing fleets and poor service. Given the high percentage of captive users of public transport in these countries, these difficulties may easily generate significant political tension.

In Western Europe, a similar trend towards decentralization of public transport can also be observed, some of the stronger examples being France, Italy and Holland. As local budgets are frequently tight, this may cause strains in the process of the search for stable financing solutions, in favour of public transport systems of good quality.

The observation of institutional behaviour in different sectors of activity led Macário (2005a) to ascertain that change is more likely to occur when institutions possess no rules binding their usual behaviour or defining the appropriateness of their behaviour: the 'no-rules arena', is often used in policy participatory processes as a powerful instrument to boost change processes.

NOTES

1. Bill Tyson, former Chairman and Managing Director of the Greater Manchester Passenger Transport Executive (GMPTE).
2. In his analysis of the San Francisco Bay area Chisholm, (1989, pp. 40–63) also defines bilateral and multilateral interdependencies but ignores the existence of hierarchical and longitudinal ones, which seems to be a strange conclusion, even considering the United States urban mobility framework.
3. Coordination entails direct hierarchical command which in reality does not exist in most relations between agents.
4. I define 'command' as the capacity to exercise authority without allowing stakeholders in a subordinate position to participate in the decision process. 'Authority', in turn, represents the capacity of one entity to guide the decisions of another, without giving the latter the opportunity to independently assess the merits of those decisions.
5. Often raising serious difficulties in comparability exercises, as experienced in several European Union (EU) research projects dedicated to these topics, such as ISOTOPE, MARETOPE and TRANSPLUS.
6. Cost 332 research reports that the Swiss national census carried out in 1990 showed that one person in every two works in a different commune from that of their residence, besides the possible additional mobility element related to the consumption of goods and services (EC, Cost 332, intermediate report).
7. This dichotomy was first discussed in Viegas and Macário in a workshop on Urban Transport Regulation, 14 October 2011, organized by the Florence School of Regulation, European University Institute, Italy.
8. It is worth mentioning that the concepts of 'licence' and 'authorization' are often used with different meanings. In this work I consider 'licence' as referring to the professional qualification (including creditworthiness and reliability), and 'authorization' as the right to the commercial exploitation of the service.
9. Also reported in van de Velde (1997).
10. Reported in ISOTOPE research (ISOTOPE Consortium, TIS.PT, 1997).
11. The main studies in this field in Europe in the domain of regulatory and organizational issues in urban mobility were: Tyson (1994); ISOTOPE, 1995–97 (ISOTOPE Consortium, TIS.PT, 1997); QUATTRO, 1997–98 (OGM (1998); Public Service Obligations, 1998 (European Commission, 1998); Buchanan & Partners (2001);

Integration, 2003 (NEA, 2003); MARETOPE, 2000–2002 (MARETOPE Research Consortium, TIS.PT, 2003); and INNO-V (2008).
12. Amsterdam, Barcelona, Berlin, Birmingham, Bochum, Bologna, Bordeaux, Brussels, Cologne, Copenhagen, Dortmund, Dresden, Dublin, Dusseldorf, Essen, Frankfurt, Genoa, Gothenburg, The Hague, Hamburg, Hanover, Helsinki, Lille, Lisbon, Liverpool, London, Lyon, Stockholm, Manchester, Marseille, Milan, Munich, Nancy, Newcastle, Nuremberg, Paris, Porto, Rotterdam, Strasbourg, Stuttgart, Valencia, Venice and Vienna.
13. Regulation (EC) No 1370/2007 of the European Parliament and of the Council of 23 October 2007 on public passenger transport services by rail and by road.
14. Authority interference has been identified in this study as negatively affecting the power of incentives (INNO-V et al., 2008).
15. CEMT/CS/URB(2005)2/REV5.

REFERENCES

Beesley, M. (1997), *Privatization, Regulation and Deregulation*, London: Routledge.
Buchanan, C. & Partners (2001), 'Study of good practice in contracts for public passenger transport – Final report', commissioned by the European Commission, Belgium.
Carr, J. (1997), 'Light touch regulation for the privatised bus industry', Fifth International Conference on Competition and Ownership in Land Passenger Transport, Leeds.
Chisholm, D. (1989), *Coordination without Hierarchy: Informal Structures in Multiorganisational Systems*, Berkeley and Los Angeles, CA, USA and London, UK: California University Press.
European Commission (1998), 'Examination of community law relating to the public services obligations and contracts in the field of inland passenger transport', NEA, DGVII, European Commission, Belgium.
Frey, W.H. and A. Spear, Jr (1995), 'Metropolitan areas as functional communities', in Donald C. Dahamann and James D. Fitzimmons (eds), 'Metropolitan and Non metropolitan areas: new approaches to geographical definition', Working Paper No. 12, Washington, DC: US Bureau of the Census, Population Division.
Gambetta, D. (ed.) (1989), *Trust: Making and Breaking of Cooperative Relations*, Oxford: Blackwell.
Gwilliam, K.M. and D.M. van de Velde (1990), 'The potential for regulatory change in European bus markets', *Journal of Transport Economics and Policy*, **24**, 333–350.
Hayek, F.A. (1945), 'The use of knowledge in society', *American Economic Review*, **35** (4), 519–530.
Hensher, D.A. and R. Macário (2002), 'Organisation and ownership of public transport services', *Transport Reviews*, **22** (3), 349–357.
INNO-V , KCW, RebelGroup, NEA, TØI, SDG and TIS (2008), 'Contracting in urban public transport', study developed for the European Commission, DG Energy and Transport (DG MOVE), Brussels.
ISOTOPE Consortium, TIS.PT (1997), *Improved Structure and Organization for Urban Transport Operations of Passengers in Europe*, Transport Research

Fourth Framework Programme Urban Transport, 51, Luxembourg: Office for Official Publications of the European Communities.

Macário, R. (2005a), 'Quality management in urban mobility systems: an integrated approach', PhD dissertation, Instituto Superior Técnico, Universidade Técnica de Lisboa.

Macário, R. (2005b), 'Restructuring, regulation and institutional design: a fitness problem', in R. Macário, J.M. Viegas and D. Hensher (eds), *Competition and Ownership in Land Transport*, Proceedings of the 9th Conference, Lisbon: Elsevier.

Macário, R. (2011), *Managing Urban Mobility Systems*, Bingley: Emerald Group Publishing.

Macário, R. and C. Marques (2010), 'Transferability of sustainable urban mobility measures', *Research in Transportation Economics*, **22** (1), 146–156.

MARETOPE Research Consortium, TIS.PT (2003), 'MARETOPE – Managing and Assessing Regulatory Evolution in Local Public Transport Operations in Europe, final report', Fifth Framework Programme, Urban Transport, DG TREN.

Musgrave, R.A. and P.B. Musgrave (1984), *Public Finance in Theory and Practice*, 4th edition, New York: McGraw-Hill.

NEA, TIS.PT (1998), 'Examination of community law relating to the public services obligations and contracts in the field of inland passenger transport', Final report to DGVII, European Commission, Brussels.

NEA (2003), 'Integration and regulatory structures in public transport – final report', DG TREN, European Commission, Belgium.

OGM (1998), 'Dissemination report confidential', QUATTRO – Quality Approach in Tendering Urban Public Transport Operations, Transport Research, Fourth Framework Programme, Urban Transport, DGVII, European Commission, Belgium.

Plumeau, P. (2005), 'Metropolitan planning organizations in the United States: issues and challenges', in R. Macário, J.M. Viegas and D. Hensher (eds), *Competition and Ownership in Land Transport*, Proceedings of the 9th Conference, Lisbon: Elsevier.

Radbone I. (1997), 'The competitive tendering of public transport in Adelaide', in J. Preston (ed.), *Proceedings of the Fifth International Conference on Competition and Ownership in Land Transport*, May, Leeds.

Sack, R. (1986), *Human Territoriality: Its Theory and History*, Cambridge: Cambridge University Press.

Sanjum, K. (2005), 'The reflexive consensus system: a new governance model', 6th Global Forum on Reinventing Government, Seoul, 24–27 May.

Scott, W.R. (1981), 'Developments in organization theory, 1960–1980', *American Behavioral Scientist*, **24**, 407–422.

TIS.PT (1998), 'Report on methodological framework to assess financial schemes – Deliverable D1', FISCUS – Cost Evaluation and Financing Schemes for Urban Transport Systems, Fourth Framework Programme, Urban Transport, DGVII, European Commission, Belgium.

Tyson, W. (1994), 'Organizational frameworks for urban public transport in Europe', Study developed for the European Commission, DGVII (unpublished), GMPTE, Manchester.

van de Velde, D.M. (1999), 'Organizational forms and entrepreneurship in public transport, Part 1: classifying organisational forms', *Transport Policy*, **6**, 147–157.

Viegas, J.M. (2003), 'Competition and regulation in the transport sector: a recurrent game and some pending issues', European Conference of Ministers of Transport, ECMT Symposium, Budapest.

Viegas, J.M. (2005), 'Transport and governance: co-decision and power sharing', in R. Macário, J.M. Viegas and D. Hensher (eds), *Competition and Ownership in Land Transport, Proceedings of the 9th Conference*, Lisbon: Elsevier.

7. Inland waterways

Tilman Erich Platz and Kees Ruijgrok

7.1 BACKGROUND

Inland navigation is a specific mode of transport that is perfectly suitable for bulk transport and container transport, especially on medium and long distances (more than 100 km). In particular, the large rivers in Europe and the canals, which for the large part were built in the nineteenth century, are perfectly fitted for this mode of transport. In Figure 7.1 the freight volumes in European Union (EU) member countries in 2009 are indicated by country of origin, demonstrating that the vast majority of inland navigation in Europe takes place in four countries – the Netherlands, Germany, Belgium and France.

This picture shows that the Rhine Scheldt estuary is especially popular for inland navigation. Almost 30 per cent of the containers and the majority of coal and ore that is shipped from Rotterdam to the hinterland use this mode of transport.

Another peculiarity of inland navigation is the age of its fleet.

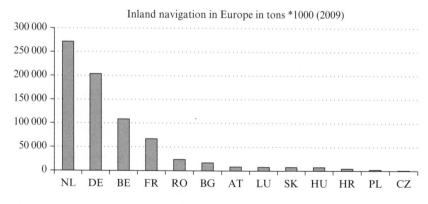

Inland navigation in Europe in tons *1000 (2009)

Source: Eurostat (2011).

Figure 7.1   Inland waterway transport volume in EU member countries in 2009

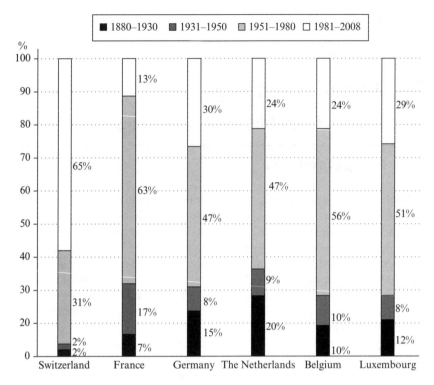

Source: IVR in De Vries (2009, p. 45).

Figure 7.2 *The age composition of the inland navigation fleet per country of domicile*

Figure 7.2 shows that a high proportion of the fleet stems from the nineteenth and twentieth centuries, but also that new ships have been added to the fleet.

Inland navigation has experienced regulation and deregulation in various ways, and in varying intensity, according to region since its early start in the Middle Ages up to the present market situation within the European Union.

When it was decided to realize the European single market, effective by 1 January 1993 as a logical outcome of the original decision to create a common European market with free transport of persons and goods, this implied deregulation for the transport market. As far as inland waterway transport was concerned, in the Rhine navigation area there had already been a liberal market regime for about 120 years. But for the other navigation areas, the regulatory situation used to be different and was far from being deregulated. For example, there was limited market access for foreign shipping companies along the German, French and Dutch canal network, and there were fixed tariffs for domestic inland waterway transport in Germany. Furthermore, in the Netherlands, Belgium and France, the system of chartering by rotation (*tour de rôle*) was applied to allocate shipments to transport operators and ships, in some cases also involving fixed tariffs. As a consequence, some deregulation measures had to be taken by transport policy on the European level, and implemented accordingly. As a consequence, by January 2000, in the EU the inland waterway transport sector had become completely liberalized with open market access and prices being freely negotiated along with increased competition.

The deregulation of the market was no easy process and had to overcome some resistance, however. The resistance came especially from those parties that were protected by a regulated environment. During the deregulation process, a challenge had been the market structure, which was characterized by overcapacity in terms of the number of inland ships available, and because of the inelasticity of this supply. The conservative powers of the inland waterway transport sector aimed at the protection of employment within the sector. The modernization of the fleet was blocked because of these barriers.

In addition to that, variations in speed in deregulation of inland transport markets in the various European countries could be observed. Some of the EC member states wanted the deregulation to be complemented by harmonization, but the 1985 judgment of the European Court (European Court, 1985) had clearly stated that there would be no link between market liberalization and the harmonization of competitive conditions. This became another challenge for the deregulation process, because there were different policies with regard to the context of harmonization and deregulation.

Besides the deregulation of the market function of inland transport itself, in this chapter attention is given to regulation with regard to safety and labour conditions. Also, taxation for usage of the infrastructure will be discussed, as well as the need and possibilities for an internalization of external costs. All these aspects are related to the main subject of this chapter: the development of regulating the usage of inland waterways for freight transport in Europe. With the term 'Europe' we mean all countries and waterways involved in the present EU context, but including the countries and waterways that are directly connected to that territory (so we include Switzerland and the Danube delta countries).

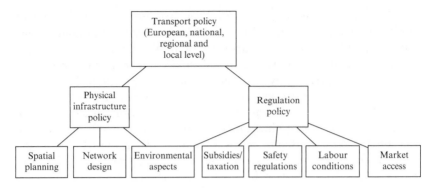

Source: Platz (2009, p. 78).

Figure 7.3 Fields of policy attention

7.2 LEGAL FRAMEWORK FOR INLAND WATERWAY TRANSPORT

There are different policy areas that influence inland waterway transport. These are shown in Figure 7.3. While physical infrastructure policy comprises the planning, construction, operation, maintenance and classification of inland waterways, regulation policy deals with the certification and licensing of companies and their staff, working time rules, safety rules (sailing speed limits, traffic regulation, harmonization of navigational instruments), competition law and environmental regulations. Regarding the regulatory aspects for inland waterway transport, here the emphasis is on the right-hand side of the figure.

The following institutions play a role in the regulatory framework of inland waterway transport:

- The European Commission (EC) (http://eur-lex.europa.eu). The EC develops Directives and regulations governing inland waterway transport, for instance on the implementation of River Information Services (RIS).
- The International Transport Forum (ITF) (formerly known as European Conference of Ministers of Transport CEMT/ECMT), http://www.internationaltransportforum.org). The ITF publishes declarations and resolutions and other information on certain topics which are relevant for the inland waterway sector.
- The United Nations Economic Commission for Europe (http://www.unece.org). The UNECE takes care of the harmonization of

technical requirements and safety in inland shipping and published the classification of European navigable inland waterways.
- The commissions for European rivers of international importance. The Central Commission for the Navigation of the Rhine (CCNR, http://www.ccr-zkr.org) and the Danube Commission (DC, http://www.danubecommission.org) police the freedom of shipping, the equal treatment of flags and the free use of these large rivers. Moreover, these organizations develop common police regulations for inland navigation, and aim at the removal of all technical and administrative obstacles impeding inland shipping. There is also a Moselle Commission (http://www.moselkommission.org) established to develop Moselle navigation.

The most important European navigation area is the River Rhine with its adjacent waterways (de Vries, 2009, p. 32), and all European transport by inland waterways is dominated by international transport. The European Economic Community (EEC) was founded on the basis of the Treaty of Rome (1957), whereas the CCNR had developed a framework for international inland waterway transport a long time before, stemming from the nineteenth century. This led to a situation where the Rhine navigation regime played the leading role in the development in European inland waterway transport, at least as long as the EC did not follow its own propositions for such a framework. So it makes sense to have a closer look at the framework for Rhine navigation across the borders.

The legal basis of international shipping on the River Rhine is the Convention of Mannheim (Revised Convention for Rhine Navigation) signed in 1868. It was signed by Belgium, France, Germany, the Netherlands and Switzerland. In the Convention of Mannheim it is stated that all the countries neighboring the Rhine should have free and unlimited access to the River Rhine. Also, pricing of waterborne transport services is free. Furthermore, the Convention of Mannheim laid down that navigation on the Rhine is free of charge, and that no customs duties may be levied. The Convention for Rhine Navigation originated in 1831. The latter is also called the Convention of Mainz.

The Convention of Mannheim represented one of the most important outcomes of the activities of the Central Commission for the Navigation on the Rhine (CCNR) which was founded in 1815–16 and is located in Strasbourg (France). The CCNR has since then been responsible for the Rhine regime. CCNR member countries are the signatories of the Convention of Mannheim. Of course, Belgium is not a Rhine riparian state, but has been an important country for inland navigation in Western Europe. Its inland waterway network is interconnected with the Dutch and the French networks, and the Flemish port of Antwerp is an important gateway for German foreign trade. Belgium became a member of the CCNR in 1920.

In 1963, the Convention was amended in Strasbourg. The amendment concerned the status of the non-riparian member countries (the United Kingdom, the United States) that later on left the CCNR, and the enforcement of the Convention's regulations in Switzerland – a member country that originally had not signed the Convention of Mannheim. Moreover, the amendment affected the internal organization of the CCNR and led to a change in the higher courts of justice in charge of Rhine navigation.

The regulations agreed on at the CCNR level are applicable to all waterways of its member countries. Its member countries also accommodate the most important inland waterways in Western Europe, so it made sense to use the regulations as a basis for the legal framework of inland navigation in the former EC. The liberal regime of the Convention of Mannheim was incorporated into the rules of the EEC (e.g. Regulations 1356/96/EC, 3921/91/EC, 2919/85/EEC), after some conflicts between the EC and the CCNR were resolved. Historically, the EU (or former EC/EEC) did not play a role in the regulatory framework of inland shipping. It gradually gained importance in the deregulation process, in the 1980s. Initially, it had paid little attention to this sector, and when it started to intervene in the inland waterway transport sector, conflicts arose in the 1960s and 1970s. It took some time until the work of the CCNR and the EC was streamlined, but this succeeded in the end. There is a mutual allowance for the participation in meetings of the other organization and an exchange of relevant documents and information. But the EU has gained in power, as there has been the chance to apply the principle of subsidiarity when CCNR member countries could not agree on certain issues such as the removal of structural overcapacity in the market. Another aspect was the enlargement of the EU, making formerly agreed bilateral treaties with Central and Eastern European countries redundant. In the end, the CCNR took over the relevant European regulations.

In questions tackling Rhine navigation, today's European Union considers the interests of the CCNR, and for the rest of the inland waterways of the EU, the EU, as well as national bodies, often relies on the experience of that organization. For instance, all rules elaborated by the CCNR were expanded to all German inland waterways by the German government (for example, the regulations on the inspection of vessels on the Rhine which is applicable for the Rhine navigation area contain the same requirements as the *Binnenschiffuntersuchungsordnung* which is applicable along the River Weser).

The Danube Commission, located in Budapest, represents the governments of its member states (Danube riparian states plus Russia) and deals with questions of navigation regulation and Danube infrastructure needs.[1] The Convention regarding the Regime of Navigation on the Danube, signed in Belgrade on 18 August 1948, represents the international legal instrument governing navigation on the Danube. The so-called Belgrade Convention provides for free navigation on the Danube in accordance with the interests and sovereign rights of the contracting parties of the Convention, aiming thereby at strengthening the economic and cultural relationships among themselves and other nations. According to the Danube Convention, Danube navigation is free of charge, free of contingencies and free of permits, except for cabotage traffic, which is regulated by national laws. Moreover, freight rates can be negotiated by the market parties – there are no fixed tariffs. Another convention which is relevant for Danube navigation is the Bratislava Convention, regulating the design of freight documents, the loading and unloading of the ships, factoring procedures and liability issues in the Danube navigation area.

The Moselle Commission was established in 1962 and is based in Trier (Germany). Like the Rhine and Danube regimes, the Moselle navigation follows the principle that ships of all flags are allowed to use this international inland waterway. The Moselle police regulations are connected to the police regulations developed by the CCNR in order to have a common sailing regime. Generally, the CCNR and Moselle Commission cooperate intensely. A basic difference to the Rhine regime is that, for sailing on the Moselle, user charges are set by the Moselle Commission. The income is partly used to upgrade the Moselle waterway. Merging the CCNR and the Moselle Commission has been considered, but this would have to be decided by the Moselle treaty signatories, France, Germany and Luxembourg.

These intergovernmental organizations are to a great extent responsible for the safety, effectiveness, efficiency, working conditions and environmental questions of European inland navigation. For example, the CCNR specifies the technical requirements for the admission of inland vessels in the Rhine Vessels Inspection Regulations, which form the basis for the construction of Rhine vessels and the final application for a ship's certificate. Another subject that the CCNR deals with is the 'Rhine Patent'. This is a document that proves that an inland ship navigator is allowed to navigate on the Rhine. Of high importance are the police regulations, determining the maximum dimensions and draught as well as the stability requirements of ships. There are separate police regulations for the Rhine, the Danube, the Moselle and for the other inland waterways on a national basis (e.g. *Binnenvaartpolitiereglement BPR* in the Netherlands; *Binnenschifffahrtsstraßen-Ordnung*, BinSchStrO, in Germany). For

Table 7.1   Important legal documents for Rhine navigation

Legal document	Content
Rheinschifffsuntersuchungsordnung (RheinSchUO)/ Règlement de visite des bateaux du Rhin/ Reglement Onderzoek Schepen op de Rijn	Rules on ship stability, constructional strength, maneuverability, safety regulations for manning
Rheinschifffahrtspolizeiverordnung (RheinSchPV)/ Règlement de police pour la navigation du Rhin/ Rijnvaartpolitiereglement	Traffic regulations, rules on maximum allowable ship dimensions etc.
Schiffspersonalverordnung-Rhein (RheinSchPersV)/ Règlement relatif au personnel de la navigation sur le Rhin/ Reglement betreffende het scheepvaartpersoneel op de Rijn	Regulations on boatmaster's certificates, on-duty time, rest periods, manning
Revised Convention for Rhine Navigation (originating in 1868, amended in 1963, additional protocols of 1972, 1979, 1989)	Free and unrestricted market access to the Rhine, no waterway user charges
Strasbourg Convention on the Limitation of Liability in Inland Navigation (CLNI)	Harmonization of the limitation of contractual and non-contractual liability of the shipowner and the salvor in the field of inland navigation on the Rhine and the Mosel
European agreement concerning the international carriage of dangerous goods by inland waterways (ADN)	Requirements for the inland waterway transport of dangerous goods (hazardous material)
Projet d'Accord européen relatif au transport international des marchandises Dangereuses par voie de Navigation intérieure sur le Rhin (ADNR)	Requirements for the inland waterway transport of dangerous goods (hazardous material)

Notes: All legal documents listed here are developed by CCNR with the exception of the European agreement concerning the international carriage of dangerous goods by inland waterways (ADN); this document was put forward by UNECE. Some legal documents of CCNR are only published in German, French and Dutch.

international navigation on the Rhine, the most important relevant legal documents are set out in Table 7.1.

One of the most important documents created by the CCNR was the ADNR, which deals with the carriage of dangerous goods (hazardous material) on the Rhine (ADNR = *Projet d'Accord européen relatif au transport international des marchandises Dangereuses par voie de*

Navigation intérieure sur le Rhin). It contains rules on packaging, combined loads, technical devices required for the ships, and rules for sailing and loading/unloading of the ships. It came into force in 1972 and was revised in 1995. The 1995 version provided a harmonization with the regulations for dangerous goods transport by road and rail (ADR/RID, e.g. by using the same classification of dangerous goods). The CCNR decided that following a period of transition, a pan-European legal framework applicable to all movements of dangerous goods on inland waterways in Europe, ADN (European Agreement concerning the International Carriage of Dangerous Goods by Inland Waterways), would replace the ADNR. This took effect on 1 January 2011.

The United Nations Economic Commission for Europe (UNECE) – and not the European Union – is responsible for the harmonization of technical, professional, safety and infrastructure matters of inland navigation in the whole of Europe, and therefore develops and provides corresponding legal and technical measures. This stems from the former separation of Western Europe (including all EC member states) with its liberal market economy, and socialism-oriented Eastern Europe. Examples are the common classification of European inland waterways, traffic signs and navigation rules. ADN as a European agreement on the international carriage of dangerous goods by inland waterways was established in 2000 and adopted by a diplomatic conference jointly organized by UNECE and the CCNR that took place in Geneva 22–26 May 2000. Both international organizations officially cooperate in the development of the regulatory framework for inland navigation in Europe.

7.3 (DE)REGULATION OF THE INLAND WATERWAY TRANSPORT MARKET

After the Rome Treaty (1957), the following interventions by the regulatory framework set by transport policy could be found in the field of European inland waterway transport:

- Prices set by the state (fixed tariffs): this occurred in inland waterway transport to allow all suppliers of inland waterway transport services – even the ones operating inefficiently – to make a living, primarily considering social aspects.
- Limitations to cabotage (domestic transportation by a foreign transport company).
- Distribution of cargo: a shippers' exchange was established in the sea ports to assign cargo to certain ships.

- Actions to reduce ships' capacity: there were ship scrap actions during the period 1969–92 involving scrap premiums being paid on a national level by scrap funds where dedicated surcharges on freight rates were collected, and later on there was the 'old-for-new' regulation of the EU. This was more a harmonization issue than a deregulation issue (see the next section where we indicate how both concepts are interlinked).

Apart from the international shipping on the Rhine and the Danube, in other parts of the European inland waterway network, market conditions until 1993 were mostly regulated. While pricing for international transport was unrestricted, in domestic inland waterway transport in Germany, fixed tariffs were mandatory till the end of 1993.[2] Just as it used to be for road transport, certain committees (called *Frachtenausschüsse*) were in charge of certain inland navigation areas or certain goods, and developed and continuously revised a set of tariffs for all transport relations. As a consequence, the carriage of a certain cargo across the borders was sometimes charged lower than the carriage of the same cargo on a national transport relation, even if the transport distance was much longer. For example, the transportation between Rotterdam and Mannheim (580 km) used to be cheaper than the transportation between Duisburg and Mannheim (355 km). Another problem was considered to be the disadvantage of inland waterway transport in intermodal competition against rail freight transport: too high a freight rate in inland waterway transport prevents shippers and freight forwarding companies from using this mode. A third problem that was discussed in those days (before effectively opening up the European market for freight transport) was the influence on the competition among the sea ports along the north-western European coast (ranging from Hamburg, Germany to Le Havre, France). The hinterland carriage by inland waterway from for example Duisburg or Dortmund to the port of Antwerp was much lower priced than the hinterland carriage to Bremen, in spite of a similar sailing distance. From a macroeconomic point of view, taking economic theory in consideration, fixed tariffs should be questioned because the state is not assumed to calculate better prices than the transport industry itself. Moreover, losses in welfare might result from less efficient transport operation, because at a lower market price, more transportation volume would be demanded by the cargo owners. This German domestic fixed rate system was abolished as of 1994.

Germany, the Netherlands and France also made use of their right to limit cabotage on the canals until the end of 1994. In the Rhine navigation area, though, Germany had already in 1974 renounced its right to limit cabotage, and later on, Belgian, Dutch and French inland navigation companies were also allowed to offer transport services on all intra-German transport relations in the Northern German canal network (north-east of Dortmund). As nearly all transport on inland waterways involved international traffic to and from the sea ports of Rotterdam and Antwerp, this carriage was not affected anyway. This limitation to cabotage became abolished by the Council of the European Union (Council Regulation (EEC) No 3921/91 of 16 December 1991).

The system of chartering by rotation (in French, *tour-de-rôle*; in Dutch, *Evenredige Vrachtverdeling*) was applied in Belgium, the Netherlands and France and covered the allocation of cargo to inland ships according to their notice, normally at fixed tariffs, to calm down competition between transport companies. This sort of transport market regulation in the sea port arranged an allocation of cargo according to the 'first come, first serve' principle. The next available cargo was to be loaded onto the first inland vessel on the notification list. In practice, the sequence of unloading of ships determined the position in the queue. Container traffic was excluded, so it covered first and foremost dry bulk shipments. Disadvantages resulting from this system were a high number of empty trips, an often poor capacity usage of the ships, and high costs for refitting the ships because the cargo was not assigned appropriately to the ships from a technical point of view. Price and quality competition was halted. An optimal load for a certain type of ship could hardly be achieved with this system, because the cargo requirements did often not meet the features of the vessel which was chosen according to the list of available ships. Council Directive 96/75/EC of 19 November 1996 on the systems of chartering and pricing in national and international inland waterway transport in the Community addressed these issues. The *tour-de-rôle* system was discussed for many years and was finally withdrawn in 1998. According to Aberle (2009, p. 174), in 1994, 8 per cent of the cargo carried on inland waterways of the EU was handled according to this procedure.

The regulation of the inland waterway transport market in the former EC was the result of the attempts of national governments to: (1) protect the national railway companies from intermodal competition of inland shipping; and (2) avoid the risk of overcapacities and ruinous competition. By the term 'ruinous competition' is meant that owner-operators (small inland shipping operators owning up to three ships, living aboard) might operate their business in spite of the fact that they do not cover their full costs. It results from so-called 'inverse market behaviour': while normally a reduced demand or price level makes suppliers reduce their available capacity, inverse market behavior is characterized by an increase of the available capacity when there is a fall in demand or transport price. In doing so, the suppliers aim at achieving contribution margins, in order to cover part of their fixed costs. Inverse market behaviour occurs when:

- there is operation at a low level of marginal costs;
- there is an information deficit about the future demand situation;
- there are barriers to exit the market (such as sunk costs);
- there is an individual commitment to the profession as a transport operator.

These features can be found in the business of the owner-operators engaged in inland shipping. They live aboard their ships, and many of them have a family tradition as skippers. The ships are furnished according to their needs, and are expensive to purchase. The ships have a period of use of up to 80 years, and the average life-span of an inland ship is reported to be 40 years (information on the dates of construction of the ships sailing under different European flags can be found in Figure 7.2). It is not that easy for the ship owners to simply and immediately sell their ships after a slump in demand. Naturally, the second-hand market for inland ships in Europe is limited, and normally all inland shipping companies are affected by the same market development. The cost structure of inland waterway transport is characterized by high fixed costs (depreciation, interest, maintenance and repair of ships, fixed salaries), and quite low variable costs (mainly fuel and lubricants, plus variable personnel costs). This leads to a situation where the average costs (ACs) exceed the marginal costs (MCs) at every level of output (Figure 7.4). There is operation at low marginal costs. In the short term, in a competitive environment, according to eco-

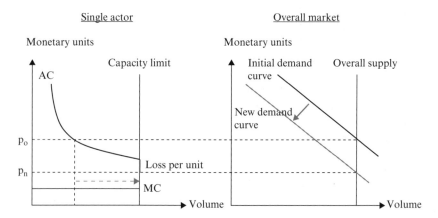

Figure 7.4   Ruinous competition in inland waterway transport

nomic theory on pricing strategies, the price for a single product or service has to cover the marginal cost for its production or provision; whereas in the longer term, full costs (average costs) must be covered by the revenues. The low level of marginal costs for inland waterway transport operation then allows the operators to set low prices to gain market share in a situation when market volume decreases. In doing so, they hope they can increase the price again later on. While in many markets an interim decline in demand or market price can be survived by the suppliers by temporarily reducing their prices, for the owner-operators it is not easy to see how the future business will develop. As a consequence, they show a tendency to exploit themselves economically in ruinous competition. In this ruinous competition, transport services are offered at prices even well below the marginal or variable costs (which are already low in inland shipping). The situation may last over a longer period of time with high losses incurred without any ship capacity being withdrawn from the market. The worst thing is that this affects not only the inefficient suppliers, but also all of their competitors that normally would survive in the market if the inefficient suppliers gave up.

Theoretical deliberations may question the need for intervening regulations by transport policy. It may be the case that it is less costly to take old capacities (where the depreciation in cost accounting is zero as the residual value in the balance sheet has already reached zero) from the market than is assumed by the inland waterway transport companies. In that case, the barriers to exit the market would be smaller than expected. Furthermore, the increase in oil prices has increased the fuel costs for inland shipping (which represent variable costs), so the marginal costs of inland waterway transport are not so small today. So operation at a low level of marginal costs cannot be assumed any more. Additionally, market intelligence could anticipate future seasonal variations in demand. And, lastly, it should be possible to cross-subsidize the transport operations business throughout the year, as many transport companies from other transport modes use cross-subsidies to survive in their markets (the liner shipping industry has the same challenge: there, periods of losses are compensated for by periods of profits).

Normally, inland waterway transport operation should succeed without any subsidies. There are some exceptions: whenever inland navigation becomes impossible, and a waterway is closed, the transport operator incurs great financial losses. This results from the need to organize alternative transportation in the short term, since a transport guarantee is regarded as necessary by the shippers, and part of the transport contracts. Thus, in some European countries, public insurance against navigational interruptions is offered. For France, there is a government regulation that foresees financial compensation whenever an inland waterway is blocked due to an accident. One prerequisite is that the inland navigation companies pay a premium (as for insurance). But no compensation is paid for high water levels, low water levels or blockages due to maintenance work. The Czech Republic has been paying inland shipping companies compensation in the case of losses owing to cancelled transportation at low water levels on the Elbe (European Commission, 2006). The government aid covers up to 60 per cent of the eligible losses that can be attributed to the low water levels.

Many experts indicate the lack of entrepreneurship in the sector with regard to logistical innovation, to gain a larger share in the transport market, which is said to be the reason for the lack of investment in specialized equipment and new transport systems. The reluctance of the owner-operators to innovate occurs because future gains and losses are difficult to anticipate. Breakeven periods for investments in ships are long, and rates of return are usually relatively low. This might make many entrepreneurs refrain from such investment. Furthermore, financial institutions are generally risk-averse for long-term projects and the internal models used by banks to assess risk do not fit easily with the typical capital structure of an inland shipping operator. Normally, inland navigation companies are small, and because of intense competition they have not had the chance to earmark part of their revenues for investment, so there is little investment taking place. A solution to this problem might be the provision of venture funds, as already proposed by the European Commission. The public capital would be repaid when the investment becomes a success. Such an innovation fund could make investments such as in low-emission engines or innovative vessel types. An example of this type of funding is given by the Marco Polo Programme. This 'Marco Polo II' programme of the European Commission (Regulation (EC) 1692/2006) promotes shifting freight traffic off the roads to other transport modes and financially supports related innovation and modal shift.

Alternatively, the state can make a financial contribution to investment. Since 2005, the Belgian region of Wallonia has paid a premium of up to €100 000 per ship for the technical adaptation and modernization of the domestic fleet (ECMT, 2006). Another example is Austria where the NAP (Nationaler Aktionsplan zur Förderung der Donauschifffahrt) contains the provision of financial means for the promotion of an environmentally friendly, and market-oriented, Austrian fleet (via donau 2006, p. 23). In the Netherlands in the period 2006–10, in total circa €10 million was available for innovation in the Dutch inland waterway transport sector (Kolkman, 2009, p. 69). This amount of money was partly used to build up an innovation centre for inland shipping (Expertise and Innovation Centre

Inland Shipping, EICB), and partly available for inland waterway transport operators for innovative projects. In Germany, a fleet modernization programme expired in 2011.

NAIADES (Navigation and Inland Waterway Action and Development in Europe; communication by the European Commission COM(2006) 6 final) is an inland waterways transport (IWT) sector-specific programme of the European Commission covering the years 2006–13. One of the strategic areas defined in NAIADES is the modernization of the inland shipping fleet. NAIADES also includes the development of state aid guidelines for support schemes and *de minimis* rules for IWT (smaller subsidies paid by national bodies that do not require permission by the EC). In 2006, the EC decided that the 'de minimis' rule also applies to the transport sector, so state aid may be granted to an undertaking up to €200 000 over a period of three years without further authorization at EU level (Regulation (EC) 1998/2006). Moreover, a funding database and handbook for the IWT sector was composed in the context of NAIADES.

7.4 IMPLEMENTATION OF THE MARKET LIBERALIZATION AND HARMONIZATION

Prior to the 1985 judgment of the European Court demanding market liberalization in the transport sector in Europe, the EC member states could not agree on the harmonization of competitive conditions in the European transport market. When the deregulation of the EU inland waterway transport market was implemented, not all parties and countries agreed on the ambitions and policies. Moreover, there were significant country variations. This means that a level playing field had not been achieved and that some carriers operating in some economic environments had advantages against their competitors. While some of the harmonization issues have been solved in the meantime, some have not, such as the harmonization of infrastructure costs and infrastructure user charges in intermodal competition between rail and inland waterway transport. There seemed to be a lack of coordination in the deregulation process. The deregulation of the market was no easy process and had to overcome some resistance, especially from those parties that thought they were protected by a regulated environment. In other words, there was a demand for regulation.

One example is the treatment of the inelastic supply of ship capacity resulting from market regulation that became an eminent problem as a result of a generally higher productivity of the inland navigation industry (the latter was the consequence of a technological switch from towing to pushing in the mid-1950s, plus the deployment of larger vessels on major inland waterways such as the Rhine). Some older ship capacities had to be broken up with public (national and EU-wide) support, in vessel scrapping and 'old-for-new' programmes, linked with penalties. Either money was paid to operators withdrawing capacity from the market by scrapping it, or for every new tonnage introduced in the market a certain amount of older tonnage had to be withdrawn.

In Germany, such a scrapping scheme ran from 1969 until 1992. There was a surcharge on all freight rates paid in inland waterway transport provided by German inland shipping companies. The surcharges were collected in a scrap fund and used to reward a premium for the scrapping of inland ships of the German fleet. This led to a reduction of the German fleet (vessels sailing under the German flag) from 7489 inland ships in 1960 to 2990 in 1990. In the end, the clients of the German inland waterway transport sector had to pay for this. From 1969 till 1992, in total, 4781 self-propelled motor vessels with a load-carrying capacity of 2161 million tonnes, 377 motor tank vessels with a load-carrying capacity of 0.361 million tonnes and more than 1200 barges were scrapped (Aberle, 2009, p. 103). €109 million was paid from the national scrap fund, plus €11.3 million funded by the Federal Republic of Germany. On the other hand, there was the modernization of the German fleet: new ships that had higher productivity and capacity appeared on the market. This reduced the impact of the scrapping action.

This led to a European regulation: in 1989, Council Regulation (EEC) No 1101/89 regulated a European-wide roll-out of this scheme that was also joined by Switzerland (not being an EC member country), in order to achieve structural improvements in IWT. It was concluded that due to the short duration of the programme, there was limited success. Thus, with Regulation 3690/92 EEC, a second European scrapping action was agreed upon, that had a longer duration. It was linked with an old-for-new rule requiring that for every tonne of a newly built inland ship a corresponding tonne of capacity of an old inland ship had to be withdrawn from the market. If this withdrawal did not take place, a penalty would have to be paid, collected in a European scrap fund, which was co-funded by the EC. This, in theory, should have ensured that the overall EU fleet could not grow (De Vries 2000, pp. 51–53). Problems encountered during the implementation of these programmes where that there was still an incentive for an investment in new ship capacity, as well as differing regulations in different countries (e.g. Germany, France, the Netherlands) prior to the European action. These differing regulations had caused a market situation where the fleet capacity of one country was reduced by regulation over a certain period, while the fleet capacity of another country grew. The problem was aggravated by the low prices for new tonnage delivered by Eastern European shipyards. Thus, with effect from the autumn of 1994, the relationship between older and newer tonnage was changed to 1.5:1. An additional European scrap action followed (1996–98), leading to a reduction of the European fleet (in the EU) by 15 per cent. The difference was that this one was mainly publicly financed (totalling €200 million, with only €32 million being paid by the sector). It expired slowly in the period 1999–2003. Aberle (2009, p.103) reports that between 1990 and 1998, €335 million was allocated to the European scrap action, of which 43.6 per cent was paid by the inland waterways transport sector, 48.9 per cent by the EU member states and 7.5 per cent by the European Commission. It was decided to have the measure of regulated capacity reduction via old-for-new rule up one's sleeve and to accrue an IWT sector fund (Inland Waterway Reserve Fund, created under Council Regulation (EC) 718/1999) as an EU crisis management mechanism that can be activated in case of future overcapacities.

After the end of the Cold War, discussions had started over who would be responsible for the harmonization of the two inland waterway transport regimes in Western and Eastern Europe. One central question from the Western European perspective was whether the EC/EU, the national governments or the CCNR would have the mandate to negotiate the harmonization procedure. Considering the principle of subsidiarity laid down by the Treaty of Maastricht in 1991, the European Commission would only be allowed to act if the aims of the measures proposed could not be reached by the national bodies of the member states. But the national governments of the EC member states had already signed mutual and bilateral conventions with the relevant Central and Eastern European (CEE) countries. In addition to that, for a long time the EU did not pay any attention to Danube transportation. So the role of the EC was questioned. Since the accession of Poland, the Czech Republic, Slovakia and Hungary to the EU in 2004, the corresponding mutual conventions have no longer been applicable, so this problem was solved by an enlargement of the EU.

A topic that was intensely discussed at the time the market was liberalized was the enlargement of the EU (from the EU-15 to the EU-25, later on to the EU-27), not only increasing the EU inland waterway network, but also implying further harmonization challenges. Because of the lack of privatization of the Eastern European inland navigation business, the Western European inland shipping industry feared that competitive disadvantages for Western European inland shipping companies would occur, because the cost structure of the Eastern European suppliers leads to a lower cost price. The reasons were: (1) the vertical integration of inland waterway transport companies, shipyards and inland ports; (2) lower wages; (3) in part, no harbour dues. Price dumping by the East European fleet was already feared when the Iron Curtain was still in place. The problem for the parties that aimed at harmonized conditions for all suppliers, such as the navigation associations and the transport politicians who wanted to protect the inland shipping companies from the EC/EU, was the integration of the Eastern European inland waterway transport business into the Western European (EC) transport market. It is discussed in detail in Sengspiel (1993).

In the end, the extension of the EU from the EU-15 to the EU-25 in 2004 led to an increase in the EU fleet of only 1161 ships, having a capacity of 881000 tonnes, giving a total of 12000 ships with a capacity of 12.8 million tonnes (Bellack, 2006, p. 24), so the impact was not as substantial as had been feared. Inland navigation companies from Western Europe have better knowhow, and inland ships with a higher technical efficiency, so that the transport market conditions compensate for the disadvantages resulting from different cost structures (Buck Consultants et al., 2004, p. 11). While in the new EU member countries pushed convoys dominate, the inland ships of the former EU-15 are mainly self-propelled motor vessels that have a higher sailing speed and are more flexible with regard to the shippers' demand. For example, the self-propelled motor vessels are designed for certain types of cargo and purposes and are available in many sizes to sail along the European inland waterway network, whereas the pushed convoys were mainly built to carry different types of dry bulk cargo in certain navigation areas (the River Elbe and River Danube), and are still deployed in these areas (de Vries, 2009, p. 47).

Even if this process of integrating the different countries of Western and Central and Eastern Europe in one market has shown good progress, another problem has been the different legal regimes for European inland navigation. There are countries that fall under the regime of the Convention of Mannheim and the CCNR (including countries to which the EU regulative framework is applicable), and countries that depend on the Convention of Belgrade and the Danube Commission. While the regulatory framework of the CCNR and EU is mandatory (and some countries fall under both regimes), the application of the regulatory framework of the Danube Commission is only voluntary (i.e. not legally binding for the member states).

A basic declaration was signed by the participants of an official conference taking place in Rotterdam, 5–6 September 2001, in which the representatives of European governments and the international organizations of the CCNR and Danube Commission took part. The declaration also covered important harmonization issues (technical rules, safety rules, dangerous goods transport, manning, a common competitive market regime, employment, liability and environmental standards).

Meanwhile, some concrete harmonization of the regulatory framework for inland navigation in Europe has already taken place as will be outlined below. The EU adopted a new Directive on technical requirements for inland vessels (Directive 2006/87/EC), being harmonized with the RheinSchUO of CCNR, containing the same requirements for the River Rhine and other inland waterways with similar features (e.g. the Danube). It creates harmonized modern requirements for inland waterway vessels on the entire Community waterway network, including the Rhine.

Non-CCNR countries may now apply for acceptance of their boat masters' certificates at the CCNR. The acceptance may be based upon Directive 96/50/EC, on the harmonization of conditions for obtaining national boatmasters' certificates. In addition, the CCNR and the Danube Commission are discussing harmonizing the testing of knowledge of the boatmasters on waterways. In 2010, CCNR signed an administrative arrangement on the mutual recognition of service record books with the national administrations (Ministries of Transport) of Austria, Bulgaria, Hungary, Poland, Romania, the Slovak Republic and the Czech Republic, to enter into force by 1 July 2011. In 2011, the CCNR decided to initiate a joint working group concerning the mutual recognition and modernization of the qualification of onboard personnel, involving experts from CCNR member states as well as other countries whose boatmasters' certificates and service record books are approved on the Rhine. The European Commission as well as other inland navigation organizations and CCNR observer states are invited to participate in this group as well. Nonetheless, there are still no European minimum standards defined for IWT training and education, hampering the mutual recognition of boatmasters' certificates. Concerning onboard personnel, there is also a lack of harmonization for the manning requirements (minimum number of crew members and their minimum qualifications) (CE Delft et al., 2011, p. 165).

Regarding the carriage of dangerous goods, CCNR's ADNR formed the basis for ADN (see the previous section), which has just come into force, and which is relevant for the whole of Europe. The content of both regulations is congruent. If a European Directive is to be introduced, it will take over the same safety standards.

Significant progress in the harmonization of the legal framework for international inland waterway transport in Europe has been made in the field of liability rules. The so-called 'Budapest Convention', signed in October 2000, resulted from a diplomatic conference held by the CCNR, the Danube Commission and the UNECE. The Budapest Convention on the Contract for the Carriage of Goods by Inland Waterway (Convention de Budapest relative au contract de transport de marchandises en navigation intérieure, CMNI) was signed by 16 countries, among them all the countries along the most important European rivers, the Rhine and the Danube. There are still two exceptions: Poland and the Ukraine, which signed the CMNI, but did not ratify it, so it is not in force in these two countries (status: 13 March 2013). The CMNI covers all international inland waterways such as the Rhine and the Danube, as well as the interconnections between them. The state parties can also declare that the CMNI will also be applicable for national goods carriage on their inland waterway networks. CMNI specifies the following elements:

- the rights and obligations of the carriers;
- the rights and the obligations of the shippers;
- the content and the meaning of the transport documents (consignment note, bill of lading);
- the liability of the shipper concerning insufficient or inadequate relevant data and missing transport documents; and
- carrier liability for the loss or damage of goods and delay in delivery.

One of the central benefits of the CMNI for the inland shipping sector is that there is no longer the necessity to conduct cost-intensive research into foreign law and the avoidance of costly litigation (legal dispute).

Today, there are a few gaps in the harmonization of the inland waterway transport market, one of which deals with fiscal policy measures. Due to international conventions, inland shipping companies in the Netherlands, Germany, Belgium and Luxembourg are excluded from paying value-added tax on ship diesel for cross-border traffic. The European Commission has often criticized this.

Fiscal taxation of profits resulting from the selling of older vessels while reinvesting in newer ones used to be treated differently by the national governments in the Netherlands, Belgium and Germany, but this is now rather harmonized, after a change in the German income tax regulation. Further harmonization in this field will depend upon the fiscal policy and tax law of the states.

While the Netherlands guarantees the loans when inland shipping companies invest in new inland ships, German operators regard this very problematic, as no such guarantee exists in Germany. This would lead to an increased share of the (already dominant) Dutch fleet with regard to overall capacity, and a capacity surplus causing low freight rates. The Organisation for Economic Co-operation and Development (OECD) (1997, p. 17) stated:

> As transport on the busiest European waterways was not regulated, the main public interventions consisted of subsidisation and infrastructure provision.

Heavy subsidisation has taken the form of tax reductions or investment aids for new vessels and premiums for the demolition of old vessels. In particular, the Netherlands and Germany have been caught in a push-and-pull competition on direct and indirect subsidies for their shipping industry, enforced by pressure on governments from domestic navigation industries. The resulting subsidy-driven business cycles of capacity extensions temporarily lead to over capacities and price drops, indicating an unstable market. Beginning with the Directive 70/1107, the harmonisation of subsidisation policy in member countries' transport sectors has helped to calm the run on subsidisation and to stabilise the inland waterway shipping market.

Other gaps in the harmonization can still be observed in the social insurance system, and in the funding of inland ships.

The harmonization deficits in regulation that still exist are faced by the relevant national and supranational organizations. Most notably, they will have to address the qualification of the personnel working onboard, as the harmonization of the social insurance and tax systems as well as subsidies can neither be regulated by the commissions for European rivers of international importance, nor by the UNECE (and the European Commission also has limited authority in this field).

7.5 CHANGES IN THE INLAND WATERWAY TRANSPORT MARKET

The inland waterways transport sector was gradually deregulated and this has led to the emergence of new actors. In the 1970s, in the EEC, the diminishing demand for inland waterway carriage was confronted by an inelastic supply, stemming from market regulation combined with a generally higher productivity of the inland navigation industry. As a result, the capacity use of the ships became poor. This led to a crisis for the inland shipping companies, from which the whole sector suffered. In Germany, many of the small shipping companies such as the *Partikuliere* (owner-operators) gave up. In contrast to the larger inland shipping companies, they did not have a marketing organization on land, so it was more difficult for them to acquire transport orders from shippers. Further deregulation partly helped to clear the market.

In recent years, the owner-operators have gained in importance: 'Nearly 90 per cent of all enterprises consist of one-vessel-companies' (de Vries 2009, p. 46; figures are for the Dutch fleet, which is the largest in Europe). Through the establishment of owner-operator cooperatives, they can strengthen their position. In the Netherlands, the start-up of such cooperatives has been publicly financially supported to enable the owner-operators to combine their forces after the cessation of the system of chartering by rotation (see section 7.3), that is, to improve their acquisition and marketing, and to improve the quality of their services (e.g. guaranteed sailings, additional logistical capabilities). Some of them also operate as bound owner-operators, always sailing for the same client, which secures employment. Since the 1990s, owner-operators have been favoured in Rhine container shipping (a growth market). That is because of savings in personnel costs. Fixed long-term charter contracts are usually used to engage ships and their crews on certain routes (Eller, 1998, p. 74). The crews are said to be treated like employees of the inland waterway container operators. This means that the carriers do not bear the risk of low capacity usage.

Recently, in the context of the financial crisis in 2008–09, the demand for inland waterway transport decreased enormously. For example, turnover in the dry bulk and container segments went down by 50 per cent (Depuydt, 2009, p. 12). Again, structural overcapacity made the freight rates in the most important European navigation areas drop well below cost. More than 1300 vessels were added to the European fleet in the period 2000–2008, and the newer ships have been larger than the older ones that were withdrawn from the market. 'As a result, the total capacity of the inland shipping fleet has kept increasing (by over five million tonnes), while the number of units transported decreased' (de Vries 2009, p. 42). In addition to that, during a peak in demand in 2007–08 with high freight rates, following the pork cycle, many inland shipping companies invested heavily in new inland vessels, and these vessels had just come into service when demand slowed (CE Delft et al., 2011, pp. 44–45, 121). The increased supply caused the dramatic fall in rates. Many newly built inland vessels were financed by hypothec loans. The reduced market value of the vessels makes it unattractive for the banks to call in the loans, sell the ships and let the vessel operators suffer financially. But that would be a requirement for a clearance of the market by an exit of inefficient operators. Even if the operators go bankrupt, this does not inevitably mean that the ship capacity is withdrawn from the market: it may be the case that the ships are sold at a dumping price, and this would give the buyers of the used ships the chance to calculate even lower freight rates when this capacity is offered to the market.

A solution to this problem would be the temporary and organized withdrawal of vessel capacity from the market. On a national level, in the Netherlands, such a programme was demanded by the inland navigation sector (*Oplegregeling*) but was not allowed by the Dutch competition authority in 2010 (Schuttevaer, 2010).

As a consequence, some transport operators have wanted the EU to state a 'serious market disturbance'. According to Council Directive 96/75/EC Article 1 (d):

> 'serious market disturbance' shall mean the emergence, in the inland waterway transport market, of problems specific to that market likely to cause a serious and potentially persistent excess of supply over demand, thereby posing a serious threat to the financial stability and survival of a large number of inland waterway carriers, unless the short and medium-term forecasts for the market in question indicate substantial and lasting improvements.

This market disturbance statement can be made if one member state (e.g. the Dutch or German government) puts in a request. The initiative to make such a request came from the inland waterway transport sector, so there is still a demand for regulation. The market disturbance statement would allow the EU to take measures in order to prevent any increase in transport supply available on the IWT market. This is also covered by Council Directive 96/75/EC. In 2012, a market disturbance statement was requested by German inland shipping companies for the inland waterway transport of liquid bulk, but the prospects of this have been poor, because the requirements set by European regulation for this statement have not been fulfilled. Prior to this, in 2010, a request for the statement of a serious market disturbance by the Dutch government as defined by Council Regulation (EC) 718/1999 was rejected by the European Commission. Of course, shippers (and their clients) are not fond of such attempts, as this could make the freight rates recover, making transport and products more expensive. Thus, shippers' associations have been resisting such initiatives and, through lobbying, have influenced the political decision-making process.

Another development is the discussion on inland waterway infrastructure funding and user charges that has been brought up regularly for decades. This topic is linked with the discussion on harmonized infrastructure user charges across transport modes. The Convention of Mannheim still holds today, but is now under discussion once again, because some parties argue that the utilization of infrastructure that is maintained for specific users should be (partly) compensated for by these users. In November 2011 the German Minister of Transport announced that waterway user charges could be introduced for the rivers Rhine, Elbe and Oder. This may either result in a cancellation of the Convention of Mannheim (which states that for the Rhine all existing regulations on waterway user charges are completely removed) by Germany, or a joint revision of the Convention of Mannheim by all its signatories.

7.6 IMPACT OF (DE)REGULATION ON THE PROTECTION OF THE ENVIRONMENT

The impact of measures and subsidies that aimed to scrap the ageing fleet is not only an issue that relates to overcapacity in the market, but also has to do with the objective of making the inland navigation mode more environmentally friendly, both by making rules about using more environmentally friendly fuel, but also by the introduction of more environmentally friendly engines and other innovative technologies used in new or renewed ships.

Environmental studies on the production of sulphur dioxide (SO_2) and nitrogen oxides (NOx) per mode of transport (Den Boer et al., 2008) have shown that the ships used in inland navigation are a major source of pollution. See for instance Figure 7.5.

The European Union adopted Directive 98/70/EG dealing with reduction of emissions, especially where inland shipping exhaust gas emissions are concerned. This Directive together with EU Directive 1999/32/EC and 2005/33/EC amendments required reduction of the gas oil sulphur level to a maximum of 10 ppm as at 1 January 2010 for coastal waters, ports and inland navigation. EU Directive 2009/30/EC of 23 April 2009 however resulted in postponement of implementation of low-sulphur gas oil with a sulphur level of maximum of 10 ppm for inland navigation until 1 January 2011.

Originally the European Committee, in improving emissions of inland navigation, a few years ago intended to introduce one type of low-sulphur fuel specification in accordance with the EN590 standard. However, due to the fact that only the maximum fuel sulphur content is regulated by the EU Directive, it cannot be excluded that different qualities of gas oil will be supplied throughout Europe, which although most probably applying to the maximum allowed sulphur content, on different fuel specifications might be less up to standard than would be desirable.

It is a fact that quite a number of vessels (estimated for instance to include approximately 84 per cent of the Dutch inland vessels) are equipped with 'older' propulsion and auxiliary engines which are less equipped for low-sulphur fuel. These so-called 'older' engines are more susceptible to wear of their fuel system components, with all the consequences of this. Also, fuel system component seals of the 'older' engines might suffer leakage when using low-sulphur fuel (Amtz, 2010). So the regulation for clean fuel is a first step, and should be combined with a regulation on 'clean engines' in order to produce the maximum effect.

The conclusion is too easy that the policies aimed at protecting the environment ask for regulation instead of deregulation. Yes, the introduction of cleaner engines and cleaner fuel could probably not have been reached

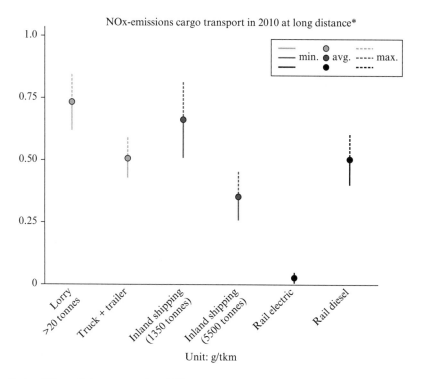

Note: * Long distance: more than 150km

Source: De Vries (2009, p. 58), referring to Den Boer et al. (2008).

Figure 7.5   Comparison of NOx emissions for standard situations for different modes of transport

without regulation, but at the same time deregulation has helped to create a more innovative and entrepreneurial environment, in which the introduction of larger and more environmental friendly ships has become more easy to realize.

7.7   CONCLUDING REMARKS

This chapter has shown that although the situation for a major part of international inland navigation is very different from other modes of transport, and from some parts of the national markets for inland navigation, discussion on the necessity and usefulness of regulation and deregulation has been a permanent source of debate within the EU for more than a century. Deregulated markets have existed next to regulated markets, and some carriers have switched frequently from deregulated to regulated environments and vice versa, as a result of changing market situations. The unification of Europe has given an impulse to further deregulation of markets that previously were regulated, and has also stimulated the further harmonization of rules that were felt necessary to guarantee the safety and environmental-friendliness of this specific mode of transport.

We also conclude that although, or maybe because, this sector has shifted in the past from being heavily regulated to being deregulated, there is potentially a need for more regulation, especially if the present over-capacity in the sector persists. This overcapacity is mainly caused by the economic crisis. The difference from earlier measures of the same sort is that earlier the overcapacity was due to the many old ships that were still present in the market, and they caused market distortion. Nowadays, it is not old ships, but the affluence of newly entered ships on the market that cause the overcapacity, and that is a completely different issue.

NOTES

1. Member states of the Danube Commission are the Republic of Austria, the Republic of Bulgaria, Hungary, the Federal Republic of Germany, the Republic of Moldova, the Russian Federation, Romania, the Republic of Serbia, the Slovak Republic, Ukraine and the Republic of Croatia.
2. Mandatory fixed rates for inland waterway transport were not only an issue concerning Germany, but were also applied in the Netherlands, Belgium and France.

REFERENCES

Aberle, Gerd (2009), *Transportwirtschaft: einzel- und gesamtwirtschaftliche Grundlagen*, München, DE and Wien, AT: Oldenbourg.

Amtz, H. (2010), 'IVR report on the impact of low sulphur fuel on the seagoing and inland navigation', Rotterdam, NL: IVR.

Bellack, M. (2006), 'Den gesamteuropäischen Charakter weiter ausprägen', *ZfB Binnenschifffahrt*, **61** (5), 24.

Buck Consultants International, ProgTrans, VBD European Development Centre for Inland and Coastal Navigation and via donau (2004), 'PINE prospects of inland navigation within the enlarged Europe', available at http://ec.europa.eu/transport/inland/studies/doc/2004_pine_report_summary_en.pdf, (accessed 31 July 2012).

CE Delft, Planco, MDS Transmodal, via donau and NEA (2011), 'Medium and long term perspectives of IWT in the European Union: final report – main report', Zoetermeer: NEA – Panteia.

Den Boer, L.C., F.P.E. Brouwer and H.P. van Essen (2008), *STREAM – Studie naar Transport Emissies van Alle Modaliteiten*, Delft: CE Delft.

Depuydt, P. (2009), 'Binnenvaart zit met financiële kater', *NH*, 27 October, 12.

De Vries, C.J. (2000), *Goederenvervoer over water: Achtergronden bij een bedrijfstak in beweging*, Assen: Van Gorcum.

De Vries, C.J. (2009), 'The power of inland navigation: the future of freight transport and inland shipping in Europe 2010–2011', Rotterdam: Dutch Inland Shipping Information Agency (BVB), available at http://www.bureauvoorlichtingbinnenvaart.nl/pageflip/UK/pageflip/ (accessed 15 September 2012).

Eller, D. (1998), 'Rhine masters', *Containerisation International*, **31** (12), 73–75.

European Commission (2006), 'Green light for Czech state aid to compensate inland waterway transport operators', EC press release IP/06/1260, available at http://europa.eu/rapid (accessed 31 July 2012).

European Conference of Ministers of Transport (ECMT) (2006), 'National measures to develop combined transport', European Conference of Ministers of Transport – Group on Intermodal Transport and Logistics, document CEMT/CS/TIL(2006)6, 27 September.

European Court (1985), 'Judgment of the Court 22 May 1985 in case 13/83', available at http://eur-lex.europa.eu/LexUriServ/LexUriServ.do?uri=CELEX:61983CJ0013:EN:PDF (accessed 31 July 2012).

Eurostat (2011), Database data query, available at http://epp.eurostat.ec.europa.eu/tgm/table.do?tab=table&init=1&plugin=0&language=de&pcode=ttr00007 (accessed 03 March 2011).

Kolkman, Joost (2009), *Binnenvaart en containerlogistiek*, Den Haag: KiM.

OECD (1997), *Liberalisation and Structural Reform in the Freight Transport Sector in Europe*, Paris: Organisation for Economic Co-operation and Development.

Platz, Tilman (2009), 'The efficient integration of inland navigation into continental intermodal transport chains – measures and decisive factors', TRAIL Thesis Series, T2009/7, Delft: The Netherlands TRAIL Research School.

Schuttevaer (2010), 'NMa staat oplegregeling binnenvaart niet toe', available at http://www.schuttevaer.nl/nieuws/actueel/nid13287-nma-staat-oplegregeling-binnenvaart-niet-toe-.html (accessed 31 July 2012).

Sengspiel, J. (1993), 'Grundlegende Probleme des Ostverkehrs – Desiderata und Realitäten', in DVWG (eds), *Die Zukunft der Binnenschiffahrt in der gesamteuropäischen Verkehrsteilung*, DVWG Schriftenreihe B 164, Bergisch Gladbach: Deutsche Verkehrswissenschaftliche Gesellschaft.

Via donau Österreichische Wasserstraßen-Gesellschaft (2006), *Nationaler Aktionsplan Donauschifffahrt*, Wien: bmvit Bundesministerium für Verkehr, Innovation und Technologie.

8. Short sea shipping in Europe: issues, policies and challenges

Adolf K.Y. Ng, Sergi Saurí and Mateu Turró

8.1 INTRODUCTION

In the past three decades, the European shipping industry has undergone rapid transformation, both globally and domestically. Increasing competition from other continents in terms of fleet registration and shipbuilding, changes in freight flow patterns due to global economic development, progress in the establishment of the internal market of the European Union (EU) and growing concern about the environment has fostered some policy initiatives in maritime transportation aimed at improving the sector's performance.

In Europe, at least three types of freight shipping can be identified (for both deep and short sea shipping), namely liner, tramp and own shipping. They serve different requirements depending on the type of freight, packaging, services to be provided, shipment size, frequency of sailings, to name but a few. Liner shipping maintains regular services between specified ports at publicized schedules. They are mainly designed to carry unitized cargoes, notably containers, trailers and pallets. Tramps, widely known as the 'maritime taxi', do not sail on publicized schedules and are usually used by a single shipper for full shiploads – either for a single voyage or for more frequent use. Tramps may carry specialized unit loads (in containers, trailers or pallets), but they are more frequently used for oil, gas and dry bulk (such as coal, iron ore and cereals). Finally, own shipping is defined as ships which are neither owned or long-term chartered by companies and are often used to transport companies' own supplies and products. Own shipping is very common for oil, gas and mineral extraction companies.

The maritime transport subsector that has received more attention from the EU in the past few years is short sea shipping (SSS). The first White Paper on transport policy published in 2001 (hereafter: the 'White

Paper') stated that a key goal of the EU's transport policy was to achieve a more sustainable transport system in Europe by fostering a modal shift towards the transport modes less harmful to the environment, namely maritime transport and railways. The updated version of the White Paper (European Commission, 2011) insists on the need to endorse these two modes of transport, paying particular attention to the need for the transport sector to reduce carbon dioxide (CO_2) and greenhouse gas (GHG) emissions. SSS is regarded as essential for the establishment of efficient multimodal logistic chains that could represent a viable alternative to (unimodal) road vehicles for some transport links.

Against this background, this chapter discusses the major issues affecting SSS development in Europe, focusing on the EU's regulations and initiatives. After this introductory section, a brief overview of SSS in Europe is given in section 8.2. Section 8.3 analyses the current EU SSS policies, including three aspects: a brief history of the interest of the EU in SSS; the relevant regulations and programmes; and the results. Sections 8.4 and 8.5 deal with two topics closely related with SSS, namely the role of ports and environmental issues. Finally, the conclusions are found in section 8.6.

8.2 AN OVERVIEW OF SHORT SEA SHIPPING

8.2.1 EU Definition

Defining SSS is not straightforward since there is no general agreement on the concept (Douet and Cappuccilli, 2011). Hence, it is quite difficult to carry out a universal analysis of SSS, to develop successful public policies and even to understand the conditions for setting such policies (Lombardo, 2004). In 1999, however, the EU adopted a definition for SSS:

> the movement of cargo and passengers by sea between ports situated in geographical Europe or between those ports and ports situated in the non-European countries having a coastline on the enclosed seas bordering Europe. SSS includes domestic and international maritime transport, including feeder services, along the coast and to and from the islands, rivers and lakes. The concept of SSS also extends to maritime transport between the member states of the Union and Norway and Iceland and other States on the Baltic Sea, the Black Sea and the Mediterranean. (European Commission, 1999)

This definition is clearly based on geographical criteria and indicates that SSS is indeed far from being a homogeneous concept. As it stands, SSS could be divided into various categories: freight (which can be containerized or non-containerized) versus passenger traffic; feeder (serving deep sea liners) versus intra-European traffic (where both the origin and destination are located within Europe); and so on. Due to its significance in terms of recent EU policies, the analysis in this section focuses on intra-European traffic for freight transport.

As mentioned above, the EU definition is not generally accepted. Different approaches have been used within the literature to refer to SSS. For example, Marlow et al. (1997) associated SSS with the type and size of ship, cargo handling methods, port terminals, networking and information systems. Other authors (Crilley and Dean, 1993) set a maximum ship size for SSS of 5000 gross tonnage whilst Stopford (1997), instead of using technical criteria, defined SSS in terms of its function as a feeder service in competition with unimodal road transportation.

As stated above, the main goal of EU SSS policy is to transfer the maximum number of ton-km from road to multimodal chains involving maritime transport, in order to reduce the environmental impact of freight transport. Although shipping constitutes the critical link in the multimodal chain, this will always require trucks and trains, and in some cases barges, to provide a door-to-door service.

To better reflect this approach and to enhance its competitiveness against road, a new concept was introduced at the beginning of the twenty-first century, the Motorways of the Sea (MoS). According to Paixao Casaca (2008), MoS can be understood as 'the floating infrastructures that move goods by sea from one EU member state to another which aim to substitute motorways of land to avoid congested land corridors, give access to countries separated from the EU mainland and enable a better integration of waterborne transport with surface modes'. Although there is no official definition from the EU of MoS, it can be understood as regular door-to-door links including ports with quality standards in travel time, financial costs and flexibility. In practice, MoS refer to a maritime service between at least two European ports (or an EU port and a port of a Mediterranean partner country) with road hauliers as customers and operated by roll-on, roll-off (ro-ro) ships. Current EU SSS policy mostly gravitates around the concept of MoS.

8.2.2　Some Data

SSS traffic has experienced a substantial increase in recent years. According to Eurostat (2003), almost 1.5 million tonnes of cargo were moved in the EU-15 in 2001 through SSS. Traffic increased by 250000 tonnes in 2008, before it dropped due to the global financial crisis. In 2010 SSS traffic was almost 1.7 million tonnes, meaning that it had grown by 12 per cent between 2001 and 2010.

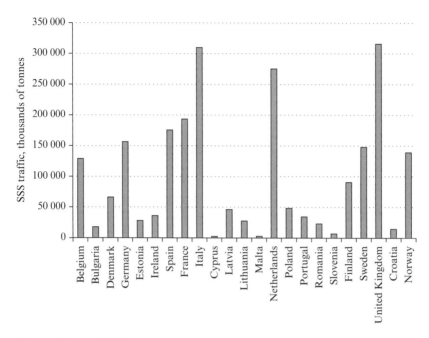

Source: Eurostat (2012).

Figure 8.1   SSS traffic of the EU in 2010 in '000 tonnes

Figure 8.1 illustrates the situation of SSS in the EU in 2010. Italy, the Netherlands and the United Kingdom (UK) generated 39 per cent of the total SSS traffic. A second group, consisting of France, Spain and Germany, generated 23 per cent. Even with the positive evolution of SSS, the modal split between road and SSS has remained similar over the past years. According to Eurostat (2012), it had not changed at all between 2004 and 2010: 90 per cent for road and 10 per cent for SSS. Some additional action must be taken if the much-sought-after modal shift is to be accomplished in the foreseeable future.

8.3   SHORT SEA SHIPPING POLICY OF THE EU

8.3.1   The Promotion of SSS as One of the Key EU Transport Policies

There are three major aspects in present EU policy initiatives on shipping. Competition issues regarding liner conferences and environmental issues have generated some actions by the European Commission (EC), but the

Regulating transport in Europe

most relevant initiatives refer, without doubt, to the promotion of SSS (and multimodal transport chains) and to port improvements to facilitate MoS development.

Although the development of SSS could be dated back to 1985 when the EC proposed the full liberalization of shipping services for intra-EU trade (including cabotage) (Pallis, 2002), it did not attract serious attention until 1995, when the EC published its first Communication on SSS (European Commission, 1995). Indeed, during the post-war period, SSS was largely a 'forgotten component' within European transport, as indicated by the salient fact that neither the Treaty of Rome (signed in 1957) nor the Common Transport Policy (CTP) mentioned anything about its development (Nijkamp et al., 1994). The discussions on intra-European freight transport were dominated by the discussion about harmonization and liberalization of road haulage. Hence, SSS was largely restricted to a few regions, often within a particular country and in relation to the links with their islands and archipelagos (notably Greece, Italy and Spain).

There were several reasons explaining such ignorance. Firstly, it was due to administrative complexity. Secondly, the existence of poor supporting infrastructure (in ports) had resulted in high costs of using SSS. Thirdly, the fragmented nature of the industry (European Commission, 1995) and the numerous regulations and restrictions on cabotage within the sector due to protectionism (Chlomoudis and Pallis, 2002) had further restricted its development. Finally, the views on maritime transport among EU member states were quite contrasting, with some countries favouring strong links between industry and government while others adopted a more laissez-faire approach. The adoption of a common understanding and generally accepted measures to develop shipping was thus very difficult (Urrutia, 2006). As a consequence, while SSS met a decent standard of quality in cargo safety requirements, other critical factors to ensure efficient transport system such as time, flexibility and frequency were of 'unacceptably low standard' (European Commission, 1999). In most cases, SSS was unable to match the flexibility that road transport could provide. For example, between Sweden and the rest of Europe, most general cargoes were carried by trucks with SSS often being confined to the movement of low-value bulk products (raw materials) or specialized cargoes (i.e. paper rolls).

Poor performance, besides tarnishing its reputation, made SSS unable to satisfy the needs of the just-in-time industrial concept, so European shippers often found better alternatives elsewhere. The situation was not helped by the completion of several public infrastructure projects, such as the Channel Tunnel and the bridge connection over Öresund, opened in 1994 and 2000, respectively, favouring alternative modes. While the former allowed transport to and from the UK by rail and road (on the shuttle trains), the latter had an even bigger impact. Except for the connection between Helsingor and Helsingborg, all ferry services (both freight and passenger) across the Öresund were closed, entailing a substantial modal shift.

Nevertheless, in the late 1990s SSS experienced a change in fortune. Attention to this mode had increased and it was regarded as essential for the development of an integrated transport system in the EU. The White Paper of 2001 identified SSS as a key alternative to unimodal road transport (EC, 2001). The main reasons for such a change of attitude are liberalization, the Trans-European Transport Network (TEN-T), externalities and geopolitical changes.

Firstly, liberalization. Despite some tough negotiations, the regulatory packages of 1986 (Council Regulations 4055/96) and 1989 (Official Journal C 073) which proposed to freely provide maritime services within the EU, enforced the liberalization of maritime cabotage between and within EU member states since the 1990s, except for a few island–mainland connection routes in the Mediterranean, for example Greece, Spain and France. Liberalization created a better platform for SSS to compete. By the mid-2000s, the opening up of national markets for shipping was largely completed.

Secondly, the TEN-T. The signing of the Maastricht Treaty in 1992 (and the establishment of the European Internal Market) triggered the need for a more comprehensive transport policy that would include the basic infrastructure required to facilitate the international trade flows that the European Internal Market was expected to generate. This led to the introduction of the TEN-T, with the objective of creating efficient infrastructure and management networks for all transport modes within the EU, characterized by 'interoperability', 'interconnectivity' and 'intermodality'. The development of the TEN-T requires important investments and enhanced operation in all transport modes. In the first TEN-T Guidelines of 1996 (Decision 1692/96/EC), SSS was only indirectly included, through a specific aim of port projects: 'supporting the principle of sustainable mobility by helping to relieve congested land corridors . . . and promoting coastal navigation'. The need for more concrete support to SSS was, however, clear because it was a potential contributor to 'the three objectives of competitiveness, sustainability and cohesion' (Turró, 1999). In the first revision of the Guidelines (Decision No 1346/2001/EC), the 'infrastructure necessary for the development of short-distance sea shipping' is already included as having common interest. In Decision No 884/2004/EC the network of MoS is finally included among the TEN-T networks in order to:

concentrate flows of freight on sea-based logistical routes in such a way as to improve existing maritime links or to establish new viable, regular and frequent maritime links for the transport of goods between member states so as to reduce road congestion and/or improve access to peripheral and island regions and States

The last revision of the Guidelines (Decision No 661/2010/EU) has given a higher profile to MoS and defined the condition for the incorporation of a maritime link in the network. The TEN-T policy and the financial resources from the EU budget accessible to MoS projects encouraged the improvement of facilities necessary for developing port infrastructure and hinterland connections adapted to SSS.

Thirdly, externalities. Despite some concerns about sulphur oxides (SOx) and nitrogen oxides (NOx) emissions, many studies on European transport suggested that maritime transport is a more sustainable and environmentally friendly mode than road haulage as it consumes less fossil fuel per tonne-km (see Nijkamp et al., 1994; European Commission, 1999; ECMT, 2001), and produces less noxious emissions and CO_2. On the other hand, trucks are a main cause of congestion and accidents across Europe, notably in the most important urban and industrial areas around the North Sea ports and in Central Europe. As noted by EC (2002): 'The development of short sea shipping is a central element of the strategy for achieving a clean, safe and efficient European transport system.' With air cargo largely out of the equation due to its high costs, and rail transport showing strong technical difficulties (operational difficulties, interoperability problems, lack of capacity in some nodes, etc.) and requiring high investments to expand capacity both in lines and terminals, SSS appeared as a reasonable option to reduce the environmental impacts of transport in Europe.

And fourthly, geopolitical changes. The incorporation of the East European countries to the market economy since 1989 signified a substantial increase in the number of ports that could be easily served by EU vessels. This market expansion was enhanced by the accession to the EU, in 2004, of a considerable number of states with maritime interests (notably Poland and the Baltic States). The EU coastline was extended by more than 98 000 km. As a consequence, SSS was increasingly seen as a catalyst in enhancing the unity and integration of the establishment of the EU-25 in the mid-2000s. In fact, shipping projects that could accelerate the integration of new EU member states had already been given priority in pre-accession support, notably through loans of the European Investment Bank (EIB) (EIB, 2003).

All these considerations were raised by the European Commission to convince member states that SSS could become a critical component of an integrated multimodal transport system in Europe. Three main objectives were identified to support SSS (European Commission, 1999):

● to promote the general sustainability of transport: SSS should be emphasized in this context as an environmentally friendly and safe alternative, in particular, to congested road transport;
● to strengthen the cohesion of the EU, to facilitate connections between member states and between regions in Europe, as well as to revitalize peripheral regions; and
● to increase the efficiency of transport in order to meet current and future demands arising from economic growth.

These objectives clearly illustrated that the promotion of SSS was not only economically motivated, but also environmentally, socially and, perhaps more importantly, politically driven. However, given its rather negative image and the competitiveness of other transport modes, a substantial modal shift from road to sea was by no means an easy task. As pointed out by the European Conference Ministers of Transport (ECMT, 2001): 'In Europe . . . automatic shift [from other transport modes] to short sea shipping is not possible and that it is necessary for [the] EC and other European transport ministries to promote actions and programmes to improve the competition of short sea shipping'.

8.3.2   EU Initiatives for the Promotion of SSS

The EU's policy aims at allowing a regulated market to establish an efficient equilibrium. In promoting SSS, the EC wants the support of the various industrial stakeholders. Hence, all the initiatives are addressed to support the private sector potentially involved in SSS in order for it to implement supply chains with maritime legs. The goal envisaged for the public sector is to create the appropriate framework for the expansion of SSS. Moreover, EU support is directly linked to general policy measures, to grants contributing to the construction of infrastructure and the execution of feasibility studies, and to assist in the establishment of new SSS routes. Whilst cohesion and structural funds could finance port and access infrastructure useful for SSS, specific grants are concentrated on the following programmes: TEN-T, Pilot Actions for Combined Transport (PACT) and the Marco Polo Programme.

As mentioned earlier, the EC finally included SSS in the TEN-T Guidelines revision of 2001 and developed the MoS concept in 2003 (European Commission, 2003), which was recognized as a TEN-T network in the 2004 revision. This document established the conditions that SSS projects should fulfil to obtain financial support from the TEN-T Budget Line. Also, among the 30 selected priority projects, MoS was incorporated as one of them (No. 21), and four maritime motorways have been identified (European Commission, 2004a):

- Motorway of the Baltic Sea, linking the Baltic Sea member states with those in Central and Western Europe (including the route through the Kiel Canal);
- MoS of Western Europe, leading from Portugal and Spain to the North Sea and the Irish Sea via the Atlantic Arc;
- MoS of Southeast Europe, connecting the Adriatic Sea to the Ionian Sea and the Eastern Mediterranean, including Cyprus; and
- MoS of Southwest Europe (Western Mediterranean), connecting Spain, France, Italy and Malta as well as linking with the Motorway of the Sea of Southeast Europe, including links to the Black Sea.

TEN-T Guidelines allow MoS funding for infrastructure, facilities and logistics management systems under the TEN-T Budget Line. The eligibility criteria include, besides those required to be considered as MoS, a requirement that the project is not distorting competition and is financially sustainable, without subsidies, after the public funding period.

Another EU initiative was PACT, the first programme in financing innovative projects with the objective to increase the use of multimodal transportation. It worked from 1992 to 2001 with a budget of €51 million. It financed 167 projects (feasibility studies and operating projects), only 51 per cent of which were finally implemented. As a follow-up of PACT, and based on its experience, various legislative, technical and operational actions had been introduced, including two further initiatives, the Communications on Short Sea Shipping (European Commission, 2004b) and the Proposal for Regulation to Establish the Marco Polo Programme (European Commission, 2004c). The Communication on SSS (European Commission, 2004b) stated that, even though SSS was growing, there were still some main obstacles that had to be addressed, including:

- full integration of the logistical supply chains (door-to-door services);
- improvement of the image of maritime transportation, which was seen as an 'old-fashioned' transport mode;
- simplification of the currently complex administrative processes; and
- enhancement of port efficiency so as to compete effectively with unimodal road vehicles.

In accordance with that, the Commission identified the main areas where all efforts should focus: (1) bottlenecks (door-to-door transport, administration and documentation, etc.); (2) customs procedures (simplified processes); (3) port services and security (increasing efficiency and lower costs in ports); and (4) loading units (standardization of loading units).

The Marco Polo Programme is divided into two periods: 2003–06 and 2007–13. It was originally designed to provide financial support to projects aiming at transferring cargo from road to alternative transport modes (sea, barge and rail) with the goal of shifting 12 billion tonne-km of freight per year. The budget of Marco Polo I was €102 million. In July 2004 the Commission proposed a second programme, Marco Polo II, with the goal of improving the environmental performance of the freight transport system (European Commission, 2004c). It was included in the EU's budgetary agenda (2007–13) and endowed with up to €450 million for the seven-year period. The programme expects to shift 54 billion tonne-km cargoes per year from the road. According to the EC, this would represent a benefit for society of €1400 million in avoiding environmental and social costs. Two types of actions were introduced in the new programme: traffic avoidance actions and MoS. For the latter, public funding is available for the development of modern transhipment facilities and/or start-up costs. The maximum subsidies assigned to a single project in Marco Polo II have reached €7.5 million.

Besides these programmes, SSS has been promoted through policy initiatives. Besides the White Papers, the Communication on SSS (COM (2004) 453) and the Communication on An Integrated Maritime Policy for the EU (COM (2007) 575 final) stated the need to keep supporting SSS, notably due to the better energy efficiency of shipping compared to road transport. The policy initiatives to boost the competitiveness of SSS included the preparation of guidelines for custom procedures, the identification and elimination of obstacles, and research and technological development (such as the application of electronic data interchange for customs procedures). To improve the image of maritime transport, Short Sea Focal Points (SSFP) in major European cities have been opened with the aim of providing concrete information on SSS to EU member states, promoting it as a valid alternative to road haulage and collecting useful statistical information.

Other EC initiatives addressed the harmonization of regulations at the Community level, such as the conditions for obtaining boatmaster certificates or the technical requirements for SSS vessels. Further updating and harmonization are currently being undertaken in accordance with the action programme outlined in the White Papers. Finally, there are actions in creating 'one-stop' offices for administrative and customs formalities so as to enhance interoperability and intermodality in Europe. Directive 2002/6/EC on reporting formalities for vessels arriving in and/ or departing from ports in the EU member states, for instance, simplified the administrative procedures involved by introducing five standard forms (rather than the initial 50). Finally, the EC introduced a practical guide on customs procedures applicable to SSS for ports located within the EU (European Commission, 2006). Nevertheless, the Communication on An Integrated Maritime Policy for the EU (European Commission, 2007) recognized that an internal market for maritime transport in Europe has yet to exist, and more simplification of administrative and customs formalities for intra-EU maritime services is necessary.

8.3.3 Results

Despite the aforementioned efforts, results have been rather mixed. Although, in terms of tonne-km, SSS has maintained a significant share of intra-European freight transport (around 37 per cent, but down from 43 per cent in 1990), the road share within the market increased slightly to 46.6 per cent in 2009 (European Commission, 2011). In 2010, in terms of tonnes, 82 per cent were moved by road, 9 per cent by SSS and 8 per cent by railway (Eurostat, 2012). These figures indicate that the preference for road vehicles is still very much prevalent. In a EC Communication (European Commission, 2006), even the EC admitted that the progress was much slower than it had hoped for. The situation, however, is not as bad as foreseen by the Commission, which argued (European Commission, 2004b) that, if the status quo were maintained, by 2013 road transport in Europe would grow by 60 per cent. The reality is that between 2003, the reference date for the document, and 2007, road transport grew by almost 18 per cent, but due to the financial crisis, this increase was reduced to only 4 per cent by 2009. Since then road transport has recovered a little, but has not reached pre-crisis levels. The forecast was thus not very fortunate. But, in any case, SSS is not improving its modal share as expected.

Such mediocre results have led to some criticisms of the initiatives undertaken. First, it is argued that the EU definition of SSS in terms of political boundaries does not fit in with potential SSS market areas (Douet and Cappuccilli, 2011). Currently, the SSS policy, based on MoS, refers to a maritime leg between two EU countries. There are many ro-ro services between Europe and North Africa, which are not eligible for the Marco Polo Programme, although there is EU Technical Assistance for the MEDA MoS project (http://www.meda-mos.eu/). A second weakness is related to the SSS potential for modal shift. Most ro-ro services are used to cross a strait or to connect an island; that is, the maritime transport leg is captive and few of these services remove trucks from roads (Gouvernal et al., 2010). Another important aspect is the market distortion created by the different competitive environment between SSS and land transport. Indeed, while EU transport policy is focused on sustainability and supports SSS, expecting a substantial transfer from road to maritime transport, national governments are directly or indirectly subsidizing road and rail transportation (Baird, 2007). For instance, an action supported in the Marco Polo Programme must be economically viable in the long term, and self-financing, which is not necessarily the case for rail and road infrastructure investments. However, the EU policy of internalizing the cost of externalities which is being implemented (the 'Eurovignette Directive' for heavy goods vehicles) could partially redress this distortion (European Commission, 2011).

8.4 THE ROLE OF PORTS

In 2004, the EC reviewed the progress of promoting SSS (European Commission, 2004b) and observed that four main obstacles to its development persisted, namely incomplete integration in the multimodal transport chain, the perception of its being an 'old-fashioned' industry, complicated administrative procedures and inefficient ports. These obstacles are, in many ways, closely linked to port inefficiency (EC, 2004b):

> The EU's seaports are vital to the competitiveness of its internal and international trade, and as links to its islands and outlying regions. . . . The development of SSS . . . as the EC White Paper (published in 2001) makes clear, will require an increase in the capacity and efficiency of ports and port services, as well as improved intermodal connections between ports and inland transport networks.

The significance of ports can be reflected by the fact that, in Europe, port handling costs represent more than 50 per cent of the total cost in a typical multimodal door-to-door service that includes SSS (de Monie, 2003). Such significance was further confirmed by Ng (2009) who found that port efficiency was pivotal in deciding the competitiveness of SSS connecting Western Europe and the Baltic States. However, as the EC White Paper concluded, effective connection links between different components within the multimodal supply chain were missing because most ports in Europe were simply too inefficient (European Commission, 2001). For example, according to a study undertaken by Napier University and Partners (2002) investigating the feasibility of introducing an intermodal ro-ro service between Southeast England and Scotland, while the sea leg was cheaper than the road leg, the overall competitiveness of the multi-modal door-to-door transport chain was severely penalized by an extra 40 per cent cost in cargo handling in ports and port access, so the overall cost figure was estimated to be 15–20 per cent higher than the pure road transport alternative. Such a cost difference highlights the importance of ports for the success of SSS-based multimodal transport in Europe.

This importance is present in EU's transport policy. The EC White Paper of 2011 insists on the need to abolish current barriers to SSS and argues that seaports have a major role as logistics centres and require efficient operation and hinterland connections to handle the increased volumes of freight both by short sea shipping within the EU and with the rest of the world. The proposed European Maritime Transport Space Without Barriers that would ensure free maritime movement in and around Europe, to allow waterborne transport to be used to its full potential, seems however a distant objective due to the vested interests of may stakeholders who abhor competition. On the other hand, the various administrations involved in port activities are reluctant to loosen their grip on a powerful sector.

The lack of progress in establishing a proper EU ports policy is, essentially, explained by the former comments. Port managers were mostly concerned about international and deep-sea services, as existing SSS was essentially captive. Competition to attract shipping lines was fierce although heavily distorted by the geographical and physical (extreme differences in protection and dredging costs) conditions and the intervention of the public sector through investments, subsidies, tariff regulations, and so on. The preparatory works for the definition of TEN-T confronted EU decision-makers for the first time with the need to approach port policy with a EU-wide perspective, incorporating the inspirations of TEN-T – that is, cohesion, integration and intermodality of the European transport system – into their considerations (Nijkamp et al., 1994). This was, however, insufficient to reach a consensus on a proper TEN-T network for ports, as EU support was seen as a potential competition distorter. The result is a list of ports classified according to traffic volumes that is useless in practice (Turró, 1999).

However, port policy was gradually getting into the mainstream of EU policy and, with the increasing importance of SSS on the EU agenda, ports experienced a change of fortune (Bekemans and Beckwith, 1996) that led to the EC Communication on SSS (European Commission, 1999). The Communication endorsed a fundamental transformation of ports so that they would operate commercially under free and fair competition based on the 'user-pays' principle. Also, under such a liberalized environment, ports should establish dedicated state-of-the-art facilities to serve SSS, so that they could be integrated into multimodal transport chains in Europe. In addition, efficiency improvements in port operations were necessary to ensure the success of SSS.

The EC thus proposed a framework of sound technical and operational solutions in ports, notably in relation to information exchange between ports and shipping lines, and the removal of unnecessary costs. To solve the problem of the poor presence of ports in the TEN-T Guidelines, the Communication redefined the port concept from being a simple sea–land interface to critical distribution centres along the logistics supply chains in Europe, which were rapidly changing due to geopolitical and economic developments. It recommended that priority in EU funding should be given to port projects dedicated to the promotion of SSS and multimodal transportation.

To enhance port efficiency and to promote fair port competition, the EC addressed the need of harmonization of the charging principles across European ports. The first step in this direction was taken with the Green Paper on Sea Ports and Maritime Infrastructure (European Commission, 1997) and the White Paper on Fair Payment for Infrastructure Use: a phased approach to a common transport infrastructure charging framework in the EU (European Commission, 1998). The EC proposed a pricing system based on short-term marginal social costs (including external costs). All users should pay for the costs they impose on using the infrastructure, including ports. Under such a system, the EC hopes that ports can recover the costs of new investments in addition to operating and external costs, thereby ensuring fair port competition and a more strategic pricing system (Strandenes and Marlow, 2000). Many experts argue, however, that this tariff system does not allow the financial coverage of upfront investments in infrastructure. In practice, it has not been implemented across the EU. Besides, the internal distribution of protection and dredging costs among users is extremely difficult to make fair.

Finally, a Directive on market access to port services of a commercial nature was proposed by the EC in 2001 with the aim to improve efficiency and reduce the cost of certain port services, and to ensure that future port planning would be undertaken in a more integrated (EU-wide) way. The Port Package included proposals related to port services encouraging port competition, such as transparency regulations for subsidies to ports and/ or their enterprises, state aid to ports, advertisement of the concessions for the usage of publicly owned port land, remuneration regulations, liberalization of port services by permitting shipping firms to appoint independent contractors to load and unload vessels, ending terminal operator monopolies on cargo handling, and so on. In 2003, the European Parliament and the Commission could not agree on a common position and the proposal for a Directive was withdrawn, so no common legislation is currently in force in the EU.

The degree of success of the EC initiatives on ports can be qualified as rather modest and it is safe to suggest that there is still a long way to go to achieve efficient ports and a good integration into multimodal logistics chains. Many ports in Europe, especially secondary and inland ones, still face considerable obstacles in terms of capacity constraints and administrative inefficiency. By May 2006, 12 of the 22 bottlenecks of European SSS identified by the EC (excluding country-specific ones) were directly linked to ports (European Commission, 2006), involving poor infrastructure, non-flexible working hours, lack of information technology and systems (IT and IS) adapted to SSS, terminal congestion, unnecessary costs and poor hinterland connections. For example, a typical Portuguese port was controlled by five different authorities, while Italian ports did not allow ship unloading until all paperwork was completed (European Commission, 2004b). In many ports this could not be done until customs officers attended the ship, even if they had no full-time customs officer in residence. Compulsory local pilotage, even if the shipmasters are certified to carry out the job themselves, has raised complaints by ferry service operators in many ports (for instance in Poland and Spain).

Obstacles to efficient performance are not just reserved to secondary ports. For example in Antwerp, until recently, Flemish regulations stated that ship operators should pay a whole loading gang from the pool of dockworkers even though only some of them were required to handle the cargo, while on the other hand, tariffs for SSS were not negotiable. These contradictory regulations pose serious problems affecting the competitiveness of SSS, as unlike deep sea general cargoes, substantial SSS cargoes are not containerized. As port calls represent a high percentage of ship usage (in the mid-1990s, they represented about 60 per cent of it; European Commission, 1995), it is not surprising that inefficient ports continue to haunt the competitiveness of SSS-based multimodal transportation. After the unsuccessful attempts to approve the first Port Package on liberalization measures in 2003 and 2006, the EC is preparing a new proposal that should be discussed in 2013 to improve the competitive environment, reduce red tape and improve the transparency in port financing. Hopefully, the EU representatives will not in this case, as in the past, bow to the pressure of dock labour unions, always belligerent in the defence of their privileges, nor to short-term national and regional interests.

Hopefully, the new regulations will represent a breakthrough and finally establish a European and multimodal approach in port planning.

Ports are often regarded as strategic assets which suit national or local vested interests. This is reflected in various measures such as state aid and protective labour regulations for strongly unionized dock workers. On the other hand, the fragmented nature of port administration and management entails difficulties in transforming the status quo. Until recently, state port control and the relation between the EU member states and the EU on port affairs were largely based on the Paris Memorandum of Understanding, signed in 1982 by 14 countries (including nine EU member states), which stated that intergovernmental cooperation was voluntary and port regulations were outside the remit of EC treaties (Urrutia, 2006). In other words, national and regional authorities were not obliged to abide with the common rules on port matters. This often distorted free and fair port competition and is directly at loggerheads with the objectives laid down by the Green Paper on Sea Ports and Maritime Infrastructure (European Commission, 1997). For example, state aid to ports, whether necessary or not, persisted although the European Parliament had made it clear that it considered such aid to be anticompetitive.

However, it must be stressed that there is some rationale behind public support to ports. Being a capital-intensive industry, it may be necessary to provide some seed funding to allow ports to reach the critical mass necessary to become efficient enough to be competitive, so as to allow SSS to be developed in Europe (Turró, 1999). However, from the EU's perspective, the paradox is that it is difficult to distinguish whether particular aid is encouraging or distorting competition. Ports mostly compete directly with each other rather than with other transport modes (Pallis, 2002) and tend to see any financial support as affecting their capacities to compete for deep sea markets (even though SSS is a just modest component of port business essentially devoted to competing with road transport). On the other hand, as the promotion of SSS is politically driven, it is sometimes difficult to distinguish whether a particular project is ultimately serving European, national or regional interests.

Thus, in proposing initiatives to promote SSS, the EC must face the dilemma of increasing financial support to SSS, which is clearly required if it has to reach the critical mass to compete with road transport, while at the same time not violating its own principle of fair and free competition. In practice, support through the Marco Polo programmes or the loans of the EIB have been very modest, as illustrated in Table 8.1.

The above analysis clearly indicates that there is still some way to go before the EC can achieve its objective of improving 'nodal efficiency' and the competitiveness of SSS. While technical improvements have been made, SSS-based multimodal chains are still a rarity in Europe, in part due to significant, artificially created obstacles. To realize TEN-T objectives,

Table 8.1   Port and maritime transport project funded by the European Investment Bank, 2000–2011*

Category	€ (millions)
Main EU ports (with the highest container traffic, down to Barcelona)	3036.1
All remaining (secondary) ports in the EU	2794.7
Mediterranean non-EU ports	304.0
Ro-ro ships dedicated to short sea shipping to and from the EU	1659.6

Note: * Only including projects for which contracts had been signed and not cancelled.

Source: European Investment Bank database, 2012 (unpublished).

the EC should treat ports as an important nodal component along the multimodal transport chain and not simply as a sea–land interface.

8.5   ENVIRONMENTAL ISSUES

Although it is generally accepted that shipping possesses environmental advantages compared with other transport modes (Ng and Song, 2010), an important drawback is vessels' rather high emissions of sulphur oxides (SOx) and nitrogen oxides (NOx). Sulphur emission is directly proportional to the sulphur content of the bunker oil, while nitrogen oxides are produced when nitrogen and air, due to high temperature and pressure, oxidize in the combustion chamber of the ship's engine.

Facing this problem, the EU initiated some regulatory measures. In 2005, a Directive was adopted by the European Parliament and the Council which would enforce the maximum sulphur limits at 1.5 per cent for marine fuels in the Baltic Sea (from August 2006), the North Sea and the English Channel (from autumn 2007) (European Commission, 2006). The Directive is also responsible for ensuring that vessels running inland waterway and coastal routes are in line with the EU's environmental policies and CO_2 targets.

The existence of regulations implies investments in vessels to meet such measures. The most direct way is to shift to low-sulphur bunker fuels, which can immediately decrease sulphur emissions while requiring no modifications in the engine. The problem is that low-sulphur bunker oil is significantly more expensive. NOx also has to be considered, and its reduction can be achieved by technical improvements to engines. Water emulsion in the fuel and the injection of fresh water into the combustion

chamber are two methods of reducing NOx emissions. The latter is technically complicated and requires engine rebuilding, but at a relatively low
cost can reduce NOx emissions by 20–40 per cent without any significant
increase in fuel consumption (Kågesson, 1999).

Other efficient methods of reducing NOx emissions are humid air motor
(HAM) and selective catalytic reduction (SCR) techniques. HAM can
prevent the production of NOx in the combustion chamber by adding
steam to the combustion air in the engine. As seawater can be used in the
system, there will be no additional operating costs for water. Furthermore,
the method is not sensitive to bunker oil quality and to the engine's work-
load. The reduction of NOx will be 50–80 per cent without any increase in
fuel consumption. The method will require investment in installations, but
the effect on operating costs is limited (Swedish Maritime Administration,
1998). On the other hand, using urea, the SCR technique can reduce NOx
emissions by 80–95 per cent. This is a system for after-treatment of exhaust
gases. The catalytic converter requires low-sulphur bunker oil of good
quality and an exhaust temperature above 300°C. By mixing water and
urea into the exhaust gas before passing it through the catalytic converter,
nitric oxide (NO) and nitrogen dioxide (NO_2) are reduced to N_2 and H_2O.
Although causing no increase in oil consumption, by using SCR, urea
consumption would amount to 2–3 per cent of fuel consumption. Also,
due to the need to instal catalytic converters, inevitably it is likely to create
an additional financial burden on operating costs (Swedish Maritime
Administration, 2001).

Nevertheless, recognizing that emission control within Europe by
enforcing regulations can be difficult in the short term – especially
given the potential difficulty in finding low-sulphur bunker fuels and
the question of whether investments in NOx abatement techniques are
cost-effective if ships have few years left in operation – the EU is also
considering environmentally differentiated fairway and port dues in sup-
plementing regulatory measures. Such systems have already been implemented in Scandinavian countries (notably Sweden and Norway), but
have yet to be implemented in any other EU member states. The Swedish
experience, effective since 1998, offered some encouragement to ship
owners shifting to low-sulphur bunker oil and invested in NOx abatement
techniques, thereby reducing SOx and NOx emissions by sea transport
(Kågesson, 1999). Apart from regulations and charging, the EU also
noted that active initiatives are needed to promote the 'green' image of
shipping, especially given the increasing cleanliness of road vehicles due
to technological improvements and innovation (European Commission,
2006).

8.6 CONCLUSIONS

This chapter discusses the main issues that SSS is facing in the EU today. In the past several decades, transport liberalization, the development of the trans-European networks concept and rising concerns about the externalities generated by transport have made possible an increasing interest of the EU in promoting SSS. The approach adopted for this promotion is to encourage the private sector to make higher use of SSS with the support of public funds where it is involved in logistics chains having a maritime leg. In accordance with that, several EU programmes, for example the TEN-T Budget Line, Marco Polo and PACT, have been developed in order to finance feasibility studies, trans-shipment facilities and other infrastructure and start-up costs. The TEN-T funding is focused on land infrastructure whilst the Marco Polo Programme mostly supports maritime operations.

In spite of public support for SSS across Europe, road transport is still overwhelmingly the most important freight transport mode in the EU. Modal shift has been less than expected. One of the reasons for this is the EU's SSS policy itself. Firstly, all the actions are focused on the concept of MoS and thus exclude non-EU ports. This means that some important connections which can be considered SSS, such as those linking North Africa and the EU, are not eligible to receive EU funding. Secondly, whereas SSS policy is driven by the private sector and, as a consequence, every SSS service should be financially sustainable in the long term, the rail and road sectors are directly or indirectly supported by public funds. This has created market distortions and makes it difficult to estimate the potential modal shift from road to sea under a free-market scenario. Port performance is also a key factor in SSS and should be substantially enhanced to foster the desired modal shift. So, in spite of the important efforts from the EU to establish a common EU maritime area and to improve port efficiency, there is still a long way to go to reach an optimal market presence of SSS in Europe.

ACKNOWLEDGEMENT

This study is supported by the University of Manitoba's VPRI and the I.H. Asper School of Business. The project code is 314942. The usual disclaimers apply.

REFERENCES

Baird, A. (2007), 'The economics of motorways of the sea', *Maritime Policy and Management*, **34** (4), 287–310.

Bekemans, L. and S. Beckwith (eds) (1996), *Ports for Europe: Europe's Maritime Future in a Changing Environment*, Brussels: European Interuniversity Press.

Chlomoudis, C.I. and A.A. Pallis (eds) (2002), *European Union Port Policy: The Movement Towards a Long-Term Strategy*, Cheltenham, UK and Northampton, MA, USA: Edward Elgar Publishing.

Crilley, J. and C.J. Dean (1993), 'Short sea shipping and the world cargo-carrying fleet – a statistical summary', in I.N. Windjnolst, C. Peeters and P. Liebman (eds), *European Short Sea Shipping, Proceedings from the First European Roundtable Conference on Short Sea Shipping*, London: LLP.

de Monie, G. (2003), 'Strategic vision of shortsea shipping in Europe', presentation to Shortsea Conference, Brugge, 16 October.

Douet, M. and J.F. Cappuccilli (2011), 'A review of short sea shipping policy in the European Union', *Journal of Transport Geography*, **19** (4), 968–976.

European Commission (1995), 'The development of short sea shipping in Europe: prospects and challenges', COM (95) 317 Brussels.

European Commission (1997), 'Green Paper on sea ports and maritime infrastructure', COM (97) 678 final, Brussels.

European Commission (1998), 'White Paper on fair payment for infrastructure use: a phased approach to a common transport infrastructure charging framework in the EU', COM (98) 466 final, Brussels.

European Commission (1999), 'The development of short sea shipping in Europe: a dynamic alternative in a sustainable transport chain – second two-yearly progress report', COM (99) 317 final, Brussels.

European Commission (2001), 'White Paper – European policy for 2010: time to decide', COM (2001) 370 final, Brussels: European Commission.

European Commission (2002), *Seaports: Gateways to Sea Transport Growth*, Brussels: European Commission Directorate-General for Energy and Transport, Brussels.

European Commission (2003), 'Programme for the promotion of short sea shipping: proposal for a Directive of the European Parliament and of the Council on Intermodal Loading Units', COM (2003) 155 final, Brussels.

European Commission (2004a), 'Amended proposal for a Directive of the European Parliament and of the Council on Intermodal Loading Units', COM (2004) 361 final, Brussels.

European Commission (2004b), 'Communication from the Commission on short sea shipping', COM (2004) 453 final, Brussels.

European Commission (2004c), 'Proposal for a regulation of the European Parliament and of the Council establishing the second 'Marco Polo' programme for the granting of Community financial assistance to improve the environmental performance of the freight transport system', COM (2004) 478 final, Brussels.

European Commission (2006), 'Mid-term review of the programme for the promotion of short sea shipping (COM (2003) 155 final)', COM (2006) 380 final, Brussels.

European Commission (2007), 'An integrated maritime policy for the European Union', COM (2007) 575 final, Brussels.

European Commission (2011), 'White Paper. Roadmap to a Single European Transport Area – towards a competitive and resource efficient transport system', COM (2011) 144 final, Brussels.

European Conference of Ministers of Transport (ECMT) (2001), *Short Sea Shipping in Europe*, Paris: European Conference of Ministers of Transport, Organisation for Economic Co-operation and Development (OECD).

European Investment Bank (EIB) (2003), 'EIB Group activity report 2003', Luxembourg: EIB.

Eurostat (2003), 'Panorama of transport: statistical overview of transport in the European Union', Luxembourg: Eurostat.

Eurostat (2012), 'Maritime transport statistics – short sea shipping of goods', accessible at: http://epp.eurostat.ec.europa.eu/statistics_explained/index.php/Maritime_transport_statistics_-_short_sea_shipping_of_goods.

Gouvernal, J., B. Slack and P. Franc (2010), 'Short sea and deep sea markets in France', *Journal of Transport Geography*, **18** (1), 97–103.

Kågesson, P. (1999), 'Economic instruments for reducing emissions from sea transport', Swedish NGO Secretariat on Acid Rain, European Federation for Transport and Environment (T&E) and the European Environmental Bureau (EEB).

Lombardo, G.A. (2004), 'Short sea shipping: practices, opportunities and challenges', available at http://www.insourceaudit.com/WhitePapers/Short_Sea_Shipping.asp.

Marlow, P.B., S.J. Pettit and A.D. Scorza (1997), 'Short sea shipping in Europe. Analysis of the UK, Italian markets', Occasional Papers No. 42, Department Of Maritime Studies and International Transport, Cardiff.

Napier University and Partners (2002), 'United Kingdom Marine Motorways Study', Future Integrated Transport (FIT) Link Programme, Department for Transport and Engineering and Physical Science Research Council (EPSRC), Edinburgh: Napier University.

Ng, A.K.Y. (2009), 'Competitiveness of short sea shipping and the role of port: the case of North Europe', *Maritime Policy & Management*, **36** (4), 337–352.

Ng, A.K.Y. and S. Song (2010), 'The environmental impacts of pollutants generated by routine shipping operations on ports', *Ocean and Coastal Management*, **53** (5–6), 301–311.

Nijkamp, P., J.M. Vleugel, R. Maggi and I. Masser (1994), *Missing Transport Networks in Europe*, Aldershot: Avebury.

Paixao Casaca, A.C. (2008), 'Motorways of the sea port requirements: the viewpoint of port authorities', *International Journal of Logistics: Research and Applications*, **11** (4), 279–294.

Pallis, A.A. (2002), *The Common EU Maritime Transport Policy: Policy Europeanisation in the 1990s*, Aldershot: Ashgate.

Stopford, M. (1997), *Maritime Economics*, London: Routledge.

Strandenes, S.P. and P.B. Marlow (2000), 'Port pricing and competitiveness in short sea shipping', *International Journal of Transport Economics*, **27** (3), 315–334.

Swedish Maritime Administration (1998), *Environmental Differentiated Fairway and Port Dues*, Norrköping: Sjöfartsverket.

Swedish Maritime Administration (2001), *Action Plan for Maritime Transport in the Baltic Sea Region*, Norrköping: Sjöfartsverket.

Turró, M. (1999), *Going Trans-European: Planning and Financing Transport Networks for Europe*, Oxford: Pergamon.

Urrutia, B. (2006), 'The EU regulatory action in the shipping sector: a historical perspective', *Maritime Economics and Logistics*, **8** (2), 202–221.

9. Intermodal transport

Walter Vassallo

9.1 INTRODUCTION

During the 1990s increased emphasis was put on the need to achieve inter-modality in order to shift the balance between modes, away from road-based passenger and freight transport towards other modes.

Intermodalism or intermodality imply the use of at least two different modes of transport in an integrated manner in a door-to-door transport chain. Intermodalism is not limited to the promotion of a modal shift from road to other modes. It also stands for the sustainable development of and improvements in the transport chain through the optimal usage of different modes in combination, without modal shift.

Intermodal transport, in the context of seamless movements of goods from origin to destination by two or more modes, is a growing component of the transport sector. With heightened emphasis on increased productivity and efficiency in the transportation industry, the importance placed by the manufacturing and service sectors on such concepts as just-in-time, the shift towards e-business, and the ever-increasing movement towards a global economy, mode-specific approaches are no longer able to meet the needs of shippers, manufacturers and consumers effectively. Industry is thinking in terms of management of the entire supply chain. In turn, governments are re-examining policies and regulatory frameworks to ensure that the provision and management of transportation networks and infrastructure are able to meet the needs of the future.

The chapter will examine the main regulatory concerns and challenges for this intermodal transport over the period: what was the background to reforms, what issues have been attempted to be addressed from a regulatory perspective, how these initiatives have been implemented and what the main effects are. As intermodal transport is the combination of several modes of transport which all contribute to the regulatory framework there are particular challenges for this sector and the regulation of it. This chapter is divided into five further sections:

- 9.2 Introduction to the intermodal sector, providing an overall comprehension of its complexity, including problems and challenges.
- 9.3 Analyses of the main features and actors involved in the intermodal market to better appreciate their impact on regulatory frameworks. The main domains governing intermodal transport management, its structure, and the implication in the functionality of the sector will be fully explained.
- 9.4 Overview of the main European policy initiatives with focus on legislative measures and other actions directly related to intermodality from 1990s to promote intermodal transport.
- 9.5 The impact of the reforms will be considered in terms of effects on the intermodal transport development (freight market share) and socio-economic impact.
- 9.6 Conclusions. One of the main problems of legislation is that intermodalism is seen as a combination of different transport modes and not as a single one. This part of the section will highlight the expected future scenario and draw some key considerations and recommendations for the sustainable development of the intermodal transport sector.

9.2   BACKGROUND

Increasingly congested motorways, rising oil prices, and concerns about the environment and climate change, demand the optimization of transport systems and transport processes. For all transport which needs to be carried out, a rational choice must be made of the most effective and efficient transport option. The framework conditions are in favour of intermodal transport operations, in which the most efficient transport options are used for the different transport legs. A characteristic feature of intermodal transport is its use of standard loading units, which are carried by road as well as by rail or waterborne transport (sea, inland waterways). This chapter will be focused on the regulatory framework, as there are particular concerns and challenges for this sector due to the fact that intermodal transport is the combination of several modes (as illustrated by Figure 9.1).

There can be little doubt that the primary barriers to sustainable transport are institutional and regulatory. Certainly, there are technical and operational barriers to the creation of infrastructure and the vehicles that use it, but most of these are well understood over the short and intermediate time horizon and involve fairly routine actions for implementation once institutional and regulatory impediments are overcome. This is

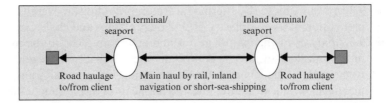

Figure 9.1   Schematic overview of continental intermodal transport chain

mainly due to the fact that the implementation of technological innovation is more rapid than the implementation of policy and regulatory
actions, especially within a domain – intermodalism – which involves
several transport modes and a complex variety of actors and issues. A
point of overall concern is the sustainability aspect of these institutional
changes and regulatory reforms. The lesson is that institutions can serve
both as barriers to solutions and as vehicles for facilitating solutions.
Institutional changes and regulatory reform have had a strong focus on
efficiency goals during the past several decades. Therefore, an important research question is how regulatory frameworks and institutional
actions can be brought forward for the sustainable implementation of
intermodalism.

9.2.1   Main Problems and Challenges

In day-to-day practice, intermodal solutions are in a minority, and prom-
ising innovative initiatives often fail. The main reasons, which can be
tackled by supportive regulatory measures, are:

- Integration of intermodal transport in logistics and supply chain
  solutions: the main challenge here is how shippers, freight integrators and intermodal operators can apply the opportunities offered
  by intermodal concepts.
- Agreement on roles, risks and responsibilities: successful intermodal
  initiatives are those that seek for collaborative solutions in which
  shippers and consignees, and logistics and transport service providers, work together on an equal level. However, due to market power
  constellations among the supply chain actors such collaborations
  are difficult to achieve in practice.
- Integrating funding in intermodal cost and financial models: intermodal solutions require considerable investments in the design and
  preparation of services and in physical resources. On European
  Union (EU) and national levels, various funding possibilities exist,

derived from legislative measures related to intermodal transport concepts.

- Providing service-level agreements: for intermodal transport to be as attractive as road transport, it should offer similar types of contracts and service-level agreements. From the shippers' point of view this is often seen as a major prerequisite for using this transport mode.
- Cooperation and coordination networks, capacities and timetables: it is often not possible to combine operators into a network, for commercial reasons. As a result it is difficult to present integral, transparent and reliable end-to-end solutions to shippers.
- There are often conflicts between international transport efficiency and environmental goals.
- Regulatory reform in one specific transport mode may affect the others, and hence intermodalism. Everything is connected. For example in the railway sector regulatory reform has not yet produced sufficiently fruitful results during the past decades, and that has a clear direct impact on the development of intermodality. The European share of rail in freight transport is much lower than in the United States (US). Efforts to stimulate the emergence of efficient operators at the EU level have had little effect thus far. One of the strategies to achieve greater efficiency was the separation of infrastructure ownership and operations. But this tended to have adverse effects on passenger transport, which has a predominantly national orientation. This leads to the question of whether or not complete separation of ownership and operations can achieve non-discriminatory access for freight.

As can be seen from the points above, the intermodal sector is complex. To better understand the regulatory framework it is important to first analyse the main characteristics and actors involved in the intermodal market, as well as the main problems and challenges to be addressed by regulatory actions.

9.3 STRUCTURE

The combination of different transport modes (e.g. a transport chain) is synonymous with increased complexity and a large number of players, which can sometimes involve as many as 25 different parties. This situation also has an impact on the key modal drivers and affects the modal choices of the operators.

The main domains governing intermodal transport management and the

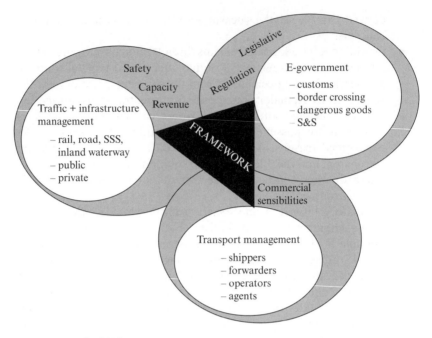

Source: Vassallo (2008).

Figure 9.2   Three domains governing intermodal transport management

implication in the functionality of the sector will be fully explained in this section.

Figure 9.2 is focused on illustrating the allocation of responsibilities in terms of both physical handling and information. Basically, each partner in the chain has two tasks: to carry out the transport itself, and information provision concerning the transport. The latter often builds on information provided by partners upstream in the chain. Partners are thus not only consumers, but also producers of information. They can improve the quality of available information by adding contextual cues (e.g., by informing on irregularities or by modifying estimates of arrival time). When considering the information needed to plan and manage intermodal transport in a wider context, it is necessary to include a third domain, in addition to predominantly commercial transport management and predominantly public traffic management: by introducing the institutional domain, we include the impact of legislation, regulation and standardization.

9.3.1 The Intermodal Market

The reason for using intermodal transport can simply be that there is no connection by one mode of transport between location A and location B, and the shipper therefore has to change to another mode of transport. For example, trucks which use ferries or the rail tunnel to cross the English Channel are, technically speaking, intermodal transport. On the continent of Europe, the main reason for using intermodal transport is the cost advantage which it brings on longer distances. The terminal and handling costs as well as trans-shipment have to be offset by the scale advantage of rail, barge and short sea shipping at a certain transport distance.

Intermodal traffic flow of cargo in maritime containers is the biggest market in intermodal transport. Continental flows have their origin and destination within Europe and are usually door-to-door flows. Although this market is dominated by road haulage, there are intermodal transport options. For example, roll-on, roll-off (ro-ro) services are often used in Continental transport chains or railway connections between inland terminals. For Continental cargo, the maritime container is less popular and the transport systems are usually based on the movement of semi-trailers, swap-bodies, or 45-foot, pallet-wide containers.

9.3.2 The Intermodal Actors

A typical trade process involves the shipment of goods between countries and the management of information and business processes required to complete the shipments. It also involves a complex network of trade participants, namely shippers and exporters, forwarders, carriers, consignees and buyers, banks, customs and regulatory agencies – sometimes as many as 25 different parties and 30–40 different trade documents, as illustrated in Figure 9.3. Various documents and types of information are exchanged at each step of the process. The information sharing is critical to ensure a smooth, secure and optimized transaction. From a government or regulator's point of view, the information exchanged at each step of the process ensures proper control and audit trails in the supply chain.

The key actors involved in the identification and choice of transport solutions are the shippers and freight forwarders. It is their decisions that will determine how modal market shares will move over the next decade or so and how they will respond to the development of intermodality. The research has been targeted on discovering how their decisions are made and how they may best be influenced. It is important to understand the modal shift drivers affecting the intermodal chain development for a better identification of regulatory options to be made.

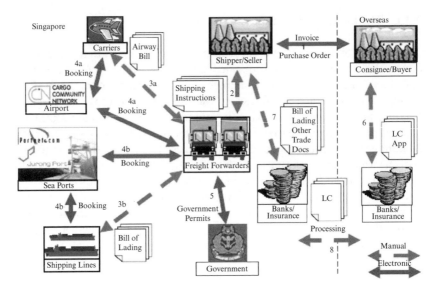

Source: Vassallo (2008).

Figure 9.3　Illustration of a typical trade transaction

There are national cultural differences to account for the tendency to select road-only transport chains. These cultural differences lie mainly in the structure of the infrastructure provision and morphology of the countries. For example, in Italy the density of the road network is very high compared to other transport modes and this is in line with the composition of the transport market, which is very much fragmented with a predominance of small and medium-sized transport operators.

Freight forwarders

The freight forwarding market has been a major beneficiary of an increasingly globalized world economy. The development of extended supply chains, integrating manufacturers, suppliers and retailers on a worldwide basis, has led to significant year-on-year growth in international trade volumes.

These changes have included an unprecedented level of mergers and acquisitions from which a small number of global players has emerged. Many long-standing brands have been subsumed: MSAS, AEI, Emery, Danzas, ASG, Wilson, Circle, to name but a few. In their place have evolved mega-carriers such as DHL Global Forwarding, Schenker, UPS Supply Chain Solutions and Kuehne + Nagel. As with the rest of the logistics market, private equity is also starting to play a major role in the development of the sector.

International freight forwarders play an integral part in the transportation process. A freight forwarder organizes the safe, efficient movement of goods on behalf of an exporter, importer or another company or person, sometimes including dealing with packaging and storage.

Over time freight forwarders' role has changed. Instead of only acting as an intermediary, many freight forwarders have became transport operators and have their own transportation assets. Furthermore, to achieve competitive rates most of them hold contracts or special arrangements with other transport operators. This makes them less neutral in their decision-making.

One example of this lack of transparency is in the IATA (International Air Transport Association) agent system. As they are getting a percentage of the prices the airline charge, these agents will try to sell their customers a transportation solution containing air transport. This might not always be in the interest of the customer, and even less in the interest of a sustainable environmental policy. Neither is the very common practice of filling up one's own assets, trucks for example, by consolidating shipments or using full load shipments, a method in which sustainability is achievable.

Freight forwarders, in these cases, are mostly not even considering other possibilities that might be cheaper, safer or better for the environment. There cannot be unprejudiced decision-making regarding the choice of mode of transport or the most efficient combination of varying transport modes, if this procedure prevails. So a more sustainable solution, as regards environmental issues, can sometimes, for the reason mentioned above, be the less attractive option for a forwarder.

Comparing this model with the newly evolving one of freight integrator, shows a lot of similarities but as yet too many differences. The similarities, especially when looking at the freight forwarder in the traditional meaning of a '*spediteur*', rest on the independence it has and therefore neutrality regarding the different modes of transportation. Also the handling of all of the documents concerning one shipment, the choice of transportation mode, the arrangements for pick-up, the filling in of necessary documents with authorities, the monitoring of the shipment and so on bear a certain resemblance to what would be desirable tasks for a freight integrator.

When it comes to differences there are quite a few to mention, particularly when the freight forwarder acts simultaneously as a transport operator with its own assets. In this situation, the required characteristic of a mostly neutral freight agent, considering all possible transport modes, is a somewhat utopian view. When organizing transport or accomplishing it, especially in the harsh business of freight forwarding, it very often all comes down to the price as the main decision parameter. Therefore, filling up own existing capacities is more important than trying to achieve the best solutions for customers and the society.

The freight forwarding market is highly fragmented with low barriers to market entry and exit. This has historically allowed very small enterprises to enter the market and compete effectively with the major players, depressing margins. However, this situation is changing as a small number of companies have achieved product differentiation through worldwide freight networks, underpinned by global technology.

The forwarding sector has also been helped by a significant increase in international trade volumes, driven by the economies in the Asia Pacific region, especially China. This is increasingly changing the way in which this sector is perceived. The global scenario changes rapidly; to stand out from the crowd it is necessary to position oneself in the market with value-added services. This means that the additional services today could become the basic requirements for customers when choosing a freight forwarder in the future. This clearly has an impact on regulations, as additional services means higher complexity.

The status and development of the most common value-added services are shown in Figure 9.4. It is clear that forwarding and haulage of shipments are and will be the key aspects for freight forwarders. They appear in about 80 per cent of all relevant cases and this will not change over time. The same basically applies for distribution and warehousing as physical, transport-related tasks play an important role in the transportation chain.

The difference between a freight forwarder and a broker: why it matters

A forwarder is a 'common carrier'[1] under the law and, as such, a forwarder must file evidence of cargo insurance. Brokers, on the other hand, do not have a statutory freight claims liability and can get by with contingent coverage (less than half the cost of primary coverage) because they are not liable in the event of a loss, unless due to negligence on the broker's part.

Indeed, a broker is not a carrier. Brokers arrange transportation with a carrier, either on behalf of the shipper or on behalf of the carrier. Under the law, brokers are not statutorily responsible for loss or damage and cannot issue their own bills of lading with their name in the carrier field. Brokers typically forward freight claims onto the carrier for handling. Some brokers carry contingent cargo insurance rather than the more comprehensive primary cargo coverage as required for forwarders.

It is important to appreciate the difference between contingent and primary cargo insurance coverage. Contingent cargo insurance is for the protection of the broker, not the shipper. If a carrier, through tariff

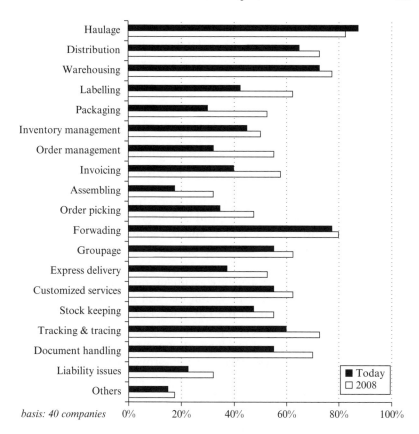

Haulage
Distribution
Warehousing
Labelling
Packaging
Inventory management
Order management
Invoicing
Assembling
Order picking
Forwading
Groupage
Express delivery
Customized services
Stock keeping
Tracking & tracing
Document handling
Liability issues
Others

■ Today
□ 2008

basis: 40 companies   0%   20%   40%   60%   80%   100%

Source: Vassallo (2008).

Figure 9.4   Added value services

or intransigence, determines an otherwise valid claim to be invalid, it is unlikely that any cargo insurance of the broker will cover the claim.

In most cases, contingent coverage steps in only if the carrier's insurance coverage is defunct. If a motor carrier simply refuses to accept the claim, often the shipper's only remedy is to hire counsel and attempt to prosecute the claim and the trucker in court. Prosecuting the broker would have no effect due to their lack of liability under statute.

The important part of the process here is responsibility and the approach to the application of that responsibility. A shipper using a broker is not the carrier's (trucker's) core customer. Whether a trucker responsibly proc-esses and pays a claim without being forced by a court of law is sometimes a matter of customer relations and, without a true customer relationship, the outcome is not assured. A forwarder, on the other hand, is not only more comprehensively covered by cargo insurance, but also its commercial focus is on the customer needs, including dealing with any issue related to the carrier.

The shippers
Shippers are primarily producers of goods and services which they market, sell and distribute to their customers. As such, shippers are users of freight transport services in all modes of freight transport: deep sea shipping, short sea shipping, air transport, road transport, rail, and inland waterways.

Globalization and the steady growth in world trade increasingly require from industry a rapid and time-sensitive delivery of goods (just-in-time solutions). To satisfy these demands and to remain competitive, companies are increasingly dependent on user-oriented, high-quality and reliable transport networks.

Europe's transport infrastructure is under pressure from increasing traffic levels both on road and on rail (as well as other modes). With surging levels of imports from the Far East, Europe's limited maritime infrastructure is also under severe pressure. As a result, journey times and the number of unanticipated incidents of congestion are also increasing, while reliability is decreasing. Pressure for improved delivery performance standards imposed by production requirements and customers is putting greater strains on existing logistics operations.

Products are competing for market share. Shippers see that products must compete on price and quality and there is a persistent drive to cut costs at every stage in the supply chain, including the logistics chain. In this context industry needs logistics solutions that can cope with the pressures put on them from the different stakeholders including governments, the public, competitors, customers and the supply chain itself. As part of this the shippers would prefer to have a range of logistics options to choose from.

The amount of road-based logistics services used varies, but the reliability of road freight is coming into question. This is due to the pressure on road freight, which stems from the attempt by the European Commission (EC) to raise the regulatory burden on road freight. This is seen as an attempt to compel transport users to consider other options. In addition to the point above, a significant part of the pressure comes from congestion and capacity constraints. It is commonly recognized that a level playing field will not be reached without internalization of external costs as put forward in the Commission's 1998 White Paper on fair and efficient pricing (European Commission, 1998a). The positive effects of rail freight liberalization will take years to be felt, but the pressures on road freight from new regulations such as the Working Time Directive, rules regarding drivers' hours[2] and road user charging are immediate.

Freight villages

A freight village is a defined area within which all activities relating to transport, logistics and the distribution of goods, for both national and international transit, are carried out by various operators. These operators can be either owners or tenants of buildings and facilities (warehouses, break-bulk centres, storage areas, offices, car parks, etc.).

According to the outcomes of the EU-funded project FV-2000,[3] freight villages can contribute to the solution of the problems deriving from the growing demand for transport of goods in Europe. This also explains why these areas have been developed widely in Europe and strategically located along the main traffic lines. An optimal distance between two intermodal terminals could be about 150 kilometres. In any case, these terminals should be located at the heart of the infrastructure, for example as a city delivery centre.

In order to comply with competition rules, a freight village must allow access to all companies involved in the activities. A freight village must also be equipped with all the public facilities (e.g. access to motorways, railway lines) to carry out the operations. If possible, it should also include public services for the staff and equipment of the users. A freight village should preferably be served by a range of transport modes (road, rail, deep sea, inland waterways and air) in order to encourage intermodal transport for the handling of goods.

The main target market of a freight village is represented by all the actors of transport because of the variety of services that could be provided in terms of infrastructure, superstructures and related services in the context of logistics. In particular, freight villages could support the role of freight integrators (see below) regarding: (1) specialization on full loads; (2) relevant market participation in the field of intermodal transport; (3) intermodal transport as a relevant business field within the company; (4) commitment to intermodality; (5) support towards environmental sustainability; and (6) a framework for intermodal cooperation and partnerships.

Freight integrators

Freight integrators organize door-to-door freight transport using different modes (intermodal transport), combining these modes of transport to build high-quality, efficient and sustainable intermodal transport solutions. They are seen by the European Commission as being the catalysts to facilitate full exploitation of the potential – sometimes hidden, sometimes still to be developed – intermodal solutions.

Some of the key operations involved in managing freight transport are:

- Organizing transport. This is facilitated by defining a transport chain by describing a set of services that must be undertaken in order for the transport to be performed smoothly. In practice this means handling contracts, quality indicators, timetables and so on. The services thus defined and linked may or may not be involved in the physical handling of cargo (a customs office is an example of an actor in the transport chain that is important to the success of smooth transport, but does not handle the cargo, only the documentation related to the transport). When the chain is defined, the services may be booked automatically through the exchange of electronic booking and confirmation messages. Bookings might be triggered via an enterprise resource planning (ERP) system or by a stock control system in a warehouse.
- Handling documents. The different service providers along the transport chain need different forms of documentation, to ensure that the transport occurs not only efficiently but also legally. These documents are distributed to the different actors when they are needed. Product documents may also be transmitted to the receiver of the cargo.
- Monitoring and controlling the transport. It is important that the transport chain manager has a complete understanding of the status of the transport and the cargo at all times. It is particularly important that information regarding deviations from the agreed schedule is made available as soon as possible. If the deviation from the schedule is unacceptable, the transport must be reorganized, by using the same functions that were used to organize the transport in the first place. If the deviation is acceptable, information about it must still be communicated to the actors in the remaining part of the chain, and to the receiver.
- Informing other parties of the status. As indicated in the previous paragraph, many persons may be interested in knowing the status of the transport. In order to make the intermodal transport chain more transparent, this status information should be made available to the authorized persons.

All of these functions come within the role of a freight integrator, but in addition, freight integrators need to integrate the differing interests of shippers and transport operators, and (in the aspiration of the European Commission) the wider needs of society at large.

Third- and fourth-party logistics providers

The fast development of logistics and its significance to industrial companies has led to the development of third-party logistics providers (3PL). The definition of 3PL is that a third party is involved in the relationship between a supplier and a customer, and handles not only the transport function, but also other logistical functions, such as warehousing. Close and long-term relationships are catchwords for 3PL. They led the way in logistics outsourcing. Drawing on their core business, whether it be forwarding, trucking or warehousing, they moved into providing other services for customers. This presented a way for a commodity-service logistics provider to move into higher-margin, bundled services.

By definition, 3PL are independent companies that design, implement and manage a client's supply chain logistics needs. While many of the logistics service capabilities required in a 3PL environment are shared by companies that perform their own logistics functions, there are unique multi-client capabilities that are often required if 3PL are to be successful. For example, providers must apply optimization to logistics functions across multiple clients, while maintaining key data elements for reporting and billing on an individual client basis.

As the third-party logistics markets have matured, a new type of logistics service provider has emerged, namely fourth-party logistics service providers (4PL). A fourth-party logistics service provider is defined as 'an integrator that assembles the resources, capabilities, and technology of its own organization and other organizations to design, build and run comprehensive supply chain solutions'. Instead of supplying traditional transport and warehousing services, a 4PL offers expanded services with higher added value.

Main hard and soft modal shift drivers

There are several factors affecting the modal choices of the operators. Some of the main selling points for large operators, that is, criteria for purchasing transport services, are: (1) trust (safety of delivery), reliability and predictability; (2) flexibility and responsiveness; (3) costs; (4) ability to purchase a complete and tailored service; (5) meeting key performance indicators (KPIs); and (6) reducing end-to-end network time (Van Landeghem and Persoons, 2001).

As an example we interviewed P&G[4] on its decision-making process used to evaluate whether a possible transport solution can be adopted, and found that its pre-screening requirements include:

- delivery time from production: distribution to final customers within 24 or 48 hours (depending on the goods);

- time windows to be met (e.g. delivery of the goods when the customer is open);
- reliability (e.g. tracking and tracing).

If these three requirements are ensured, the following other criteria are used to choose a transport logistics solution: technical specifications of the transport operator to be matched with the specifics of the company cost.

The example of P&G has been made intentionally as it represents a major actor in the international market. Furthermore, it should be noted that the changes in the location of production and distribution of major producers impact upon the overall transport network in Europe in terms of new transport solutions to be adopted.

It is therefore important to stress that the majority of the other operators might have different selection criteria to be used to identify and choose a possible transport solution. Usually, smaller shippers (in terms of geographical coverage, size and market share) appear to be more influenced by different variables, such as cultural behaviour and habits (e.g. they have used predominantly road-based transport so may find it difficult to consider a change to another mode or combination of modes).

It is clear that all the above-mentioned peculiarities, modal drivers and actors make the intermodal market very complex, with the consequence that regulatory actions are much more difficult to decide upon and implement.

9.4 OVERVIEW OF MAIN REGULATORY MEASURES TO PROMOTE INTERMODAL TRANSPORT

Intermodal transport in the context of the seamless movement of goods from origin to destination by two or more modes is a growing component of the transport sector, which has been tackled by regulatory measures for its sustainable development since the early 1990s. In turn, governments have been re-examining policies and legislative and regulatory frameworks to ensure that the provision and management of transportation networks and infrastructure are able to meet the needs of the future.

The main reasons for government involvement in intermodal transport policy and regulation are to promote the efficient use of infrastructure, improve the efficiency and effectiveness with which the entire transport network is used, support the economic growth, improve transport costs, facilitate improved services to users, and address environmental and social concerns associated with the usage of individual transport modes. It must

Table 9.1   Legislation and regulations favouring intermodal transport

	G	A	CH	NL	S	F	UK	I	B	US	CZ
Max. gross weight of road vehicles (tonnes)	40	40[1]	28	50	40	40	38	44	44	40	48
Exemption for 44-tonne vehicles, provided they are used for intermodal transport	yes	yes	yes	–	yes	yes	yes	–	–	no	–
Driving ban for lorries on certain days or at certain times	yes	yes	yes	no	yes	yes	no[2]	yes	no	no	yes
Exemption for vehicles used for intermodal transport	yes	yes	no	–	no	no	–	no	–	–	yes

Notes:
1. The maximum gross weight of road vehicles in Austria is generally 38 tonnes; however, for vehicles registered in the EU, it is 40 tonnes.
2. Only in London at night.
G = Germany, A = Austria, CH = Switzerland, NL = the Netherlands, S = Spain,
F = France, UK = United Kingdom, I = Italy, B = Belgium, US = United States,
CZ = Czech Republic.

Source: OECD (2001, p. 26).

be noted that the text which follows focuses on the European policies and actions on regulatory issues related mainly to intermodality.

Varying levels of legislative and regulatory instruments are in place across member states to encourage and implement intermodal activity. In the 1990s these initiatives were already encouraging intermodal transport by allowing increased loads and driving time, as illustrated in Table 9.1 for selected countries in Europe. However, the table also demonstrates variation regarding these aspects, such that international transport may not necessarily be significantly assisted due to non-harmonization.

Users of combined transport were exempted from bilateral contingents and similar restrictions for foreign transport operators. In some countries (e.g. Austria) an extensive system of political and legislative measures is in place to promote combined transport, ranging from financial aid for construction of terminals to the purchase of specialized rolling stock required for intermodal transport. In Eastern Europe, many countries signed bilateral agreements that encourage the use of combined transport. Other countries, such as the Netherlands and Germany, defined specific objectives during that period in order to stimulate the growth of this form of goods transportation (OECD, 2001, p. 24). In the case of the Netherlands the objective was to 'achieve a modal shift of 50 million tonnes (20 to rail, 20 to inland shipping and 10 to short sea) over the period 1994–2010'. The objective for Germany was to 'triple 1994 volume of intermodal freight (30 million tonnes) to 90 million tonnes in 2010'.

The European Commission has developed clear goals to promote competition within and between modes of transport by harmonizing transport regulations, thereby dealing with earlier non-harmonized frameworks for intermodal transport. In particular, the EC is seeking to create a European transport network by improving the interoperability of different systems and making better use of existing infrastructure. The latter is proposed to be achieved through, among other measures, internalization of external transport costs.

The initial competencies of the EC referred to the internal market and to the need to ensure the free provision of transport services across the borders between EU member states. For many years, the EC's transport policy was modal oriented. When the EC obtained competencies over both infrastructure and environment, the limitations of a modal approach became more apparent than ever. In 1986, the Single Market Act gave the Community direct competencies in the field of environment, requesting that environmental protection requirements become a component of other policies. Following the Single Market Act, the Trans-European Networks (TENs) concept was launched and incorporated into the Treaty of the European Union in order to support and strengthen the internal market. This initiative upgraded the legal status upon which Community infrastructure support measures had been developed during the 1980s. Thus, the core part of the Common Transport Policy, which sought to develop a level playing field between the transport modes, was joined by the TEN policy layer, which already included combined transport, and made the development of an intermodal approach necessary. The need to integrate environmental considerations into transport policy could only reinforce this process. As such this process was triggered by evidence of capacity problems on the existing networks particularly in the road and air transport networks. The implementation of the Internal Market and the run-up to the European Monetary Union have, among other elements, contributed to the rapid growth of freight transport and to an increase in the length of the trips made. The intermodal vision of the Commission has been consistently expressed in various policy documents, starting with the White Paper on the Future Development of the Common Transport Policy from 1992 where the development of integrated transport systems was a priority (European Commission, 1992).

In this White Paper it was pointed out the different regimes applied to the liability of intermodal operators not only between member states but also for the different modal stages of an intermodal journey. As a United Nations Convention on multimodal international transport of goods had been adopted in 1980 but had not yet come into force, the European Commission called for an investigation into the extent to which a more uniform approach would increase the attractiveness of multimodal services. As part of the 1992 White Paper the need for technical harmonization to facilitate and encourage intermodal transport was highlighted. The policy document also contained proposals for the harmonization of rules regarding classification, labelling and packaging of dangerous substances across the transport modes, put forward in order to enhance the efficiency of intermodal transport (European Commission, 1992, p. 47).

The EC considered other measures to stimulate intermodal transport, including favourable tax treatment for road vehicles respecting high safety and environment standards used in intermodal operations; assistance regarding investment dedicated to intermodal transport, and facilitation of cooperation between transport enterprises engaged in intermodal operations. The latter would in particular build on the provisions in Directive 91/440/EEC (Development of the Community's railways including limited rights of network access) which introduced access rights for operators in different member states wishing to provide international combined services. Further details on railway reform in Europe are given in Chapter 3 in this volume.

Intermodality was also considered as part of the Common Transport Policy Action Programme (1995–2000), where it was emphasized that better integration of transport modes is essential, though without providing specific regulatory EC action (European Commission, 1995). In 1996 the EC demonstrated its commitment to the promotion of intermodalism in transport through the legislation concerning the development of the Trans-European Networks,[5] mainly addressing a general reference framework for the implementation of the networks, which includes the interconnection and interoperability of national networks (key elements for developing intermodal transport).

Further specifics on the EC's policy objectives regarding intermodality were put forward in 1997 (European Commission, 1997). The key aim for European action was expressed as follows: 'to develop a framework for an optimal integration of different modes so as to enable an efficient and cost-effective use of the transport system through seamless, customer-oriented door-to-door services, whilst favouring competition between transport operators'.

Accordingly, the integration of modes was considered at three levels: infrastructure and transport means; operations and use of infrastructure; and services and regulations. As part of this EC policy document an overview of existing friction costs with regard to intermodal transport was set out and an action programme was put forward. The most important areas of action related to:

- the establishment of a uniform intermodal liability regime;
- standardization of loading units;
- the creation of an electronic commerce market for intermodal transport.

In 1998 the EC gave emphasis to identifying common charging principles for the development of intermodality, with the White Paper 'Fair payment for infrastructure use: a phased approach to a common transport infrastructure charging framework in the EU' (European Commission, 1998a). A framework for common charging principles was proposed in order to create a level playing field and correct intra- and intermodal imbalances. A common charging framework would also facilitate intermodal transportation. The need to promote intermodalism was also highlighted, and progress assessed, in the updated version of the EC's Common Transport Policy (CTP) rolling programme from 1998 (European Commission, 1998b) building on the core CTP goals with emphasis on integration of national networks and integration of transport modes.

An important step forward for intermodality was reached in 2001 with the Transport White Paper 'European transport policy for 2010: time to decide' (European Commission, 2001). In contrast to previous initiatives, the EC put as its first priority the need to bring a real change in the Common Transport Policy. For the first time, significant emphasis was given to intermodality, with particular reference to sustainable development of economic growth. There was strong consensus across Europe about setting new objectives for achieving a real change with respect to restoring the balance between modes of transport and developing intermodality, combating congestion and putting safety and the quality of services at the forefront of the EC initiatives while maintaining the right to mobility. One of the main challenges was to define common principles for fair charging for the different modes of transport.

On intermodality, the 2001 White Paper recognized that previous policy initiatives had not brought tangible results. Therefore, a series of proposals were put forward. The particular priorities on intermodality were decided to be technical harmonization and interoperability between systems, particularly for containers. In addition, the new Community support programme Marco Polo[6] targeted innovative initiatives, particularly to promote Motorways of the Sea (see Chapter 8 in this volume), with the target of making intermodality a competitive, economic and viable reality. For the development of intermodality, much attention was mainly given to linking up the modes, through a rapid introduction of a series of technical measures, particularly on containers, loading units and the profession of freight integrator (as described above, section 9.3.2).

Gradually, more and more operators have taken responsibility for the whole transport chain under one single contract. The problem is that, in the event of loss or damage to goods involved in multimodal transport, shippers and consignees prefer to pursue a single operator responsible for the overall transport, rather than dealing with several unimodal carriers. At this stage, despite various attempts to establish a uniform legal framework governing multimodal transport, no such international regime is in force. In the absence of a uniform international regime of liability in multimodal transport, it is covered by a jigsaw of international rules and conventions. The Hague, Hague-Visby and Hamburg Rules cover maritime transport; the Convention on the Contract for the International Carriage of Goods by Road and the Convention concerning International Carriage by Rail, in some countries, cover international road and rail transport, respectively; while the Warsaw Convention covers global air transport. Apart from possible confusion concerning the applicability of Conventions, when a loss cannot be localized and blame attributed, liability often depends on national laws or contractual agreements

The present legal framework consists of a complex array of international Conventions designed to regulate unimodal carriage, diverse regional and subregional agreements, national laws and standard term contracts. As a consequence, the applicable liability rules and the degree and extent of a carrier's liability vary greatly from case to case and are unpredictable. The shippers may often find it cumbersome and only achievable through extensive administrative effort to determine the scope of the liability and its limits.

The liability of the intermodal transport operator for loss of or damage to goods can differ depending on which stage of transport the loss has occurred. The question becomes even more complicated if the loss or damage cannot be localized, or the loss occurs gradually during the entire transport. Where goods are carried in sealed containers, it is often difficult, if not impossible, to identify the stage and mode of transport where a loss, damage or delay occurs.

The problems of a lack of uniform carrier liability arrangements have already been recognized by the European Commission in 1997 (European Commission, 1997) as well as in other more recent EC policy documents. Indeed, this situation tends to lead to additional (i.e. friction) costs surrounding the associated insurance system and is an impediment for further development of freight intermodalism in the European Union. In particular, this creates uncertainty, which in turn results in transaction costs as it gives rise to legal enquiries, costly litigation and rising insurance costs. This is of particular importance for small and medium-sized transport users. Without a predictable legal framework, equitable access to markets and participation in international trade is much harder for these stakeholders by restricting their competitiveness.

As part of the European-funded project Integrated Services in the Intermodal Chain (ISIC), a task was carried out in 2005 by an independent panel of legal experts, aimed at drafting a set of uniform intermodal liability rules which 'concentrate the transit risk on one party and which provide for strict and full liability of the contracting carrier (the intermodal operator) for all types of losses (damage, loss, delay) irrespective of the modal stage where a loss occurs and of the causes of such a loss' (Clarke et al., 2005). Under the proposed voluntary regime the transport integrator is strictly liable for loss of or damage to the goods occurring between the time he takes over the goods and the time of delivery, unless and to the extent that the transport integrator proves that it was caused by circumstances beyond its control.

According to the mid-term review of the EC White Paper 'Time to Decide', the goal set in 2001 to increase the share of intermodal transport as a mean to make better use of existing transport capacities was not reached (European Commission, 2006).

This outcome is a reflection of the complexity of intermodal transport. There are many commercial, technical and organizational obstacles to overcome in the process of combining a number of transport services to form an efficient transport chain. Rapidly changing business and administrative requirements demand a high degree of flexibility from the transport industry in terms of the services offered and the related management systems. Integrated transport management also requires a certain level of business integration, which demands the trust and close interaction of a variety of actors involved in managing the chain, and a commitment to a potential perspective of long-term cooperation. Information access and communication possibilities are key elements in this context. Business partners must have the opportunity to communicate with each other and with the concerned authorities. This highlights regulatory challenges for intermodal transport in terms of facilitating the cooperation and integration of different industry stakeholders within a competitive environment.

After the mid-term review of the 2001 Transport White Paper, in 2007 the EC issued as a follow-up the Freight Transport Logistics Action Plan based on extensive consultations with stakeholders (European Commission, 2007). In the Action Plan the EC puts forward specific measures to develop intermodality. These measures include:

- Advanced information and communication technologies. The concept of e-freight was coined with the objective of creating the 'Internet for cargo' where information would be made available online in a secure way, as is the case with the 'Internet for people'. One characteristic of this is the capability to view and compare online information on the services provided by freight transport operators and administrative simplification. In the context of intelligent transport systems (ITS) attention was given to the set-up of a framework for the development of ITS applications addressing also freight transport logistics, including monitoring of dangerous goods and live animals transport, tracking and tracing, and digital maps.
- Freight transport logistics personnel and training. The target set up was to draw up a list of minimum qualifications and training requirements at different levels of specialization to be incorporated into a framework that could ensure the mutual recognition of training certificates, thereby facilitating intermodal transport between EU countries.
- Simplification of administrative compliance, through the establishment of a single window (single access point) and one-stop administrative shop for addressing administrative procedures in all modes.
- Single transport document. The EC recognized the fact that multimodal transport documents existed, but they were not sufficiently widely used in electronic format nor harmonized. The Commission included a measure to work towards establishing a single European transport document that can be used in all transport modes, thereby facilitating multimodal freight transport and enhancing the framework offered by multimodal waybills or multimodal manifests.
- Liability. The EC recognized that multimodal transport was suffering from friction costs induced by the absence of a uniform, cross-modal liability regime. Work towards creating a multimodal regulatory structure for liability was taking place at global level (UNCITRAL[7]); but
- failing rapid progress the European Commission would start exploring other options for Europe such as:
  - a legal Act could be envisaged with a standard liability clause for all transport operations; it could be a fall-back clause, meaning that if

nothing else is agreed between parties to a transport contract, this standard clause would automatically apply; the contracting parties could also explicitly mention it in their transport contract;
   – gaps between existing international liability regimes could be addressed in such a way that coverage is provided for those parts of the logistics chain that currently fall between the modal-based liability regimes.
● Security. The EC recognized the need to start developing European standards, in line with existing legislation, international conventions and international standards, in order to facilitate the secure integration of transport modes in the logistic chain.
● Loading unit. The EC put in its agenda the update of the 2003 proposal on European Intermodal Loading Units[8] (European Commission, 2003).

Among these initiatives there were also measures to be developed in consultation with the relevant stakeholders, and for that reason the European Commission anticipated to report on progress made regarding their implementation by 2010–11. With some delay, the EC published its long-awaited Transport Policy White Paper in March 2011, called 'Roadmap to a Single European Transport Arena – Towards a competitive and resource-efficient transport system' (European Commission, 2011). It consists of a roadmap of 40 practical initiatives for the next decade, to build a competitive transport system that will increase mobility, remove major barriers and stimulate economic growth and employment. The aim is to deliver a fully functional and EU-wide core network of transport corridors, ensuring facilities for efficient transfer between modes by 2030, with a high-quality, high-capacity network by 2050 and a corresponding set of information services. These elements are clearly relevant in relation to the development of intermodal freight transport, showing the importance given to this sector in EC policy documents.

9.5   IMPACT OF THE ACTIONS UNDERTAKEN FOR PROMOTING INTERMODAL TRANSPORT

At the outset it is important to highlight that consideration of the possible impacts of the regulatory and other measures on the performance of intermodal transport requires the development of a suitable evaluation methodology, including the necessary indicators that will define the situation before and after the implementation. Our research on possible quantitative data and information that could indicate performance impacts of laws and regulatory frameworks related to intermodality show that it is difficult to establish the possible linkages. The parameters that may affect the performance of intermodal transport are numerous, and data such as freight flows in intermodal transport, share of shippers in the market or the development of intermodal nodes could certainly be an indication but not a proof of any relationship. In particular, this is also affected by the fact that the measures concerned in many cases are directed towards individual modes rather than intermodal transport. Furthermore, quantitative analyses are limited by data availability, where it is very difficult to get reliable quantitative data on intermodal transport and data sources are few (Beuthe, 2007).

The limited data available (e.g. on combined transport, road–rail solutions) indicates that intermodal transport is increasing. For example, the EU Statistical Pocketbook on Transport (Eurostat, 2011) shows that for almost all combined transport companies where data is available in both 2000 and 2010, the number of consignments in international transport is significantly higher in 2010 compared to the 2000 level. It is clear that all the various European initiatives and policy actions which have been undertaken during 10–15 years to promote intermodality and to strengthen the development and adoption of appropriate legal and regulatory framework have produced some tangible results. Furthermore, initiatives such as Marco Polo and other programmes to finance intermodal initiatives have allowed the introduction of specific services in this sector. Notwithstanding, it is important to take into account the danger of competition distortion with respect to existing services that may occur as the result of this form of initiatives (with state funding).

On the other hand, many of the objectives for intermodal transport set by the European Commission have not yet been reached. The situation shows that many of the issues which the EC has tried to address for more than a decade have not been resolved yet. For example, the European Intermodal Loading Unit and the uniform liability regime are still under discussion. As such, obstacles to intermodal transport are still numerous, limiting the usage of intermodal transport. Beuthe (2007) shows that despite the recent growth in intermodal transport the relative share of this type of transportation is still small compared to total transport. Recent quantitative modelling regarding the generalized transport costs of intermodal solutions point towards key elements to be considered in promoting intermodal transport in comparison with road-based solutions (Sandberg Hansen et al., 2012, p. 10):

- promote cross-border standardization of intermodal equipment to increase the efficiency of terminal operations;

- reduce transport costs for vehicles used for pre- and post-haulage in urban areas;
- give higher priority for freight trains in the rail network;
- implement additional charges for road transport (to increase the marginal generalized costs for truck based transportation relative to that of multimodal transportation);
- stricter enforcement of resting periods for road-based transportation.

9.6 CONCLUSIONS

One of the main problems relating to the development of appropriate regulatory frameworks for intermodal transport is that it is seen as a combination of different transport modes and not as a single sector of its own. This creates the risk of a lack of sufficient focus on intermodal transport specifically, rather than derived through other transport sectors. The promotion of intermodality requires significant coordination and cooperation between multiple types of stakeholders across modes and industries as well as authorities at local, regional, national and European levels.

However, over the past decade there has clearly been increased focus on this form of transportation at both the industry and the authority level. Despite this increased attention, important obstacles to the development of intermodal transport within Europe remain.

Looking to the future, intermodality has a greater role to play in achieving sustainable mobility. Notably, in the latest White Paper (European Commission, 2011), several specific references are made to intermodal transport (apart from the general direction towards enhanced integration of transport systems across and within the EU), such as possible adaptation of the legislation on weight and dimensions to new circumstances, technologies and needs (for instance the weight of batteries), and better aerodynamic performance.

It will be particularly important to ensure that liability regimes promote intermodal transport. Special attention will have to be given to streamlining the rules for the intermodal transport of dangerous goods to ensure interoperability between the different modes.

It will also be important in a core network of strategic European infrastructure that European action focuses on the components of the TEN-T network with the highest European added value, such as developing missing cross-border links, intermodal hubs and key bottlenecks that today limit multimodal transportation.

The attention towards intermodal transport has increased at national and European levels. In the coming years there will be important policy and regulatory challenges to deal with in order to ensure that the intermodal transport market is functioning appropriately and achieving its full potential.

NOTES

1. A 'common carrier' is a person or company that transports goods or people for any person or company and that is responsible for any possible loss of the goods during transport.
2. Directive 2002/15/EC lays down minimum requirements with regard to the organization of the working time for all persons performing mobile road transport activities, including self-employed drivers, in order to improve road safety, health and safety of drivers, and prevent distortion of competition. It also supplements the provisions of Regulation (EC) 561/2006 which lays down common rules on drivers' driving time and rest periods.
3. The Freight Village-2000 (FV-2000) project aimed at the development of user-oriented guidelines and simulation tools for the evaluation of the FV structure and organization, in order to increase the attractiveness of intermodal transport for industrial and transport operators.
4. P&G: Procter & Gamble, a US-based multinational consumer goods company.
5. Decision No. 692/96 on the Community Guidelines for the development of the trans-European transport network, Official Journal L228 of 9 September 1996.
6. The proposal of the 2001 White Paper was to launch a large-scale programme (Marco Polo) to support intermodal initiatives and alternatives to road transport in the early stages until they become commercially viable.
7. UNCITRAL: United Nations Commission on International Trade Law, http://www.uncitral.org/
8. The 2003 proposal suggested European Intermodal Loading Unit (EILU) had to combine the benefits of containers (their solidity and stackability) with those of swap bodies (in particular their greater capacity). Such an EILU could be used in four modes of transport (rail, road, sea and inland waterways) and its trans-shipment between these different modes would be simplified. In order to meet the necessary requirements for maximum intermodality, it should be stackable, suitable for top lifting, and seaworthy. The unit should offer the maximum allowable space for transporting ISO pallets, and it should also offer fast loading and unloading of pallets in order to reduce costs and delays.

REFERENCES

Beuthe, M. (2007), 'Intermodal freight transport in Europe', in T.R. Leinbach and C. Capineri (eds), *Globalized Freight Transport, Intermodality, E-Commerce, Logistics and Sustainability*, Cheltenham, UK and Northampton, MA, USA: Edward Elgar Publishing.

Clarke, M.A., R. Herber, F. Lorenzon and J. Ramberg (2005), 'Intermodal liability and documentation', ISIC Final Report Task B to European Commission.

European Commission (1992), 'The future development of the Common Transport Policy', White Paper from the Commission to the European Council, COM(92) 494, December, Brussels.

European Commission (1995), 'The Common Transport Policy Action Programme 1995–2000', COM(95) 302, 12 December.

European Commission (1997), 'Intermodality and international freight transport', COM(97) 243, Brussels.

European Commission (1998a), 'Fair payment for infrastructure use: a phased approach to a common transport infrastructure charging framework in the EU', White Paper, COM(1998) 466 final, Brussels.

European Commission (1998b), 'The Common Transport Policy. Sustainable mobility: perspectives for the future', COM(98) 716, 21 December, Brussels.

European Commission (2001), 'European transport policy for 2010: time to decide', White Paper, COM(2001) 370, Brussels.

European Commission (2003), 'Proposal for Directive on Intermodal Loading Units', COM(2003) 155 final, 7 April, Brussels.

European Commission (2006), 'Keep Europe moving: sustainable mobility for our continent, mid-term review of the 2001 Transport White Paper', COM(2006) 314 final, Brussels.

European Commission (2007), 'Freight transport logistics action plan', DG MOVE, COM(2007) 607 final, Brussels.

European Commission (2011), 'Roadmap to a Single European Transport Area – towards a competitive and resource-efficient transport system', White Paper, COM(2011) 144 final, Brussels.

Eurostat (2011), 'EU Statistical Pocketbook on Transport'.

OECD (2001), *Intermodal Freight Transport – Institutional Aspects*, Paris: OECD Publishing.

Sandberg Hansen, T-E., T.A. Mathisen and F. Jørgensen (2012), 'Generalized transport costs in intermodal freight transport', 15th edition of the EURO Working Group on Transportation, Paris.

Van Landeghem, R. and K. Persoons (2001), 'Benchmarking of logistical operations based on a causal model', *International Journal of Operations and Productions*, **21** (1–2), 254.

Vassallo, W. (2008), 'Freight market structure and requirements for intermodal shifts', European Project Freightwise (TREN/06/FP6TR/S07.60148), Deliverable D.11-1.

Index